Maria Calleja's Gozo

Maria Calleja in 1990.

Maria Calleja's Gozo

A Life History

Edited and Introduced by
Micheline Galley

Utah State University Press • UNESCO Publishing
Logan   Paris
1994

UNESCO COLLECTION OF REPRESENTATIVE WORKS
European Series

Cover photograph: Lunzjata, in Kerċem, Maria's village.
(*Photograph by Joseph Sammut, Department of Information, Malta.*)

Cover design by Mary Donahue

UTAH STATE UNIVERSITY PRESS
Logan, Utah 84322-7800

Calleja, Maria, 1915-
    Maria Calleja's Gozo : a life history / edited and introduced by Micheline Galley, with notes and commentaries.
        p.   cm. -- (UNESCO collection of representative works. European Series)
    Includes bibliographical references and index.
    ISBN 0-87421-169-7
    1. Calleja, Maria, 1915-   . 2. Gozo Island (Malta)--Social life and customs.
3. Women educators--Malta--Gozo Island--Biography. I. Galley, Micheline.
II. Title. III. Series.
DG992.77.C35A3   1994
945.8'5--dc20   93-45582
                                                                CIP

Contents

 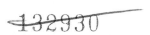

Foreword

The island of Gozo forms part of the Maltese archipelago. Famed as the legendary home of Calypso, it has a long history, going back beyond classical times to the prehistoric period represented by the famous megalithic temple at Ġgantija. Its scenery and physical features, and its domestic and church architecture, together with its traditional way of life, have drawn visitors to its shores and inspired poets as well as scholars, travelers and writers of many nationalities to study and describe its antiquities and art, its customs and legendary lore.

Maria Calleja's Gozo may be described as another account of Gozo—but an account with a difference. Here for the first time, we have an educated Gozitan lady, a retired headmistress now in her seventies, recording her recollections of everyday life in Gozo as she has known it from her childhood days, and the changes that have taken place before her very eyes in the wake of economic and social development over the last half century or so. To quote her own words: ". . . in my mind I have a whole documentary of Gozitan life: the simple, quiet, peasant life which farmers led . . . a Gozitan life changing in these latter years, changing into the fast, modern way of life."

The society among which she grew up, and which persisted practically up to the last war, was made up of various strata ranging from the depressed group of fishing folk to the upper echelon of Gozitan professionals. Maria recalls the hard time which hit these islands at the onset of the First World War and which drove hundreds of Maltese and Gozitans to emigrate to Australia. Some of them, her father among them, returned to their families after a few years.

Times were hard. By and large, however, "we were relatively well fed, we had clothes, and most people had, somehow or other, their own house." And again, says Maria, "everybody had a bit of land and that provided for food and something to sell"—whether that something was fruit, chickens, eggs or lambs.

The island's people had certain rules, tacitly accepted and observed, concerning status symbols. Thus, only the best families had a loom in their house; and families which fed on white bread were considered to have a higher status than those eating brown bread. The notion of paying for goods by installments was unheard of, for it was a source of family pride not to incur debts of any kind. Even expectant mothers sought to avoid having their babies delivered in the hospital, for those doing so were looked down upon.

Into this humdrum existence, the church brought a note of elevated thought and hope, regulated and colored by its functions and periodic religious activities. Particularly important in this respect was the local *festa* in honor of the patron saint, for this was also an occasion for social intercourse, to make new friends or perhaps meet one's future wife or husband. As Maria puts it, ". . . you see, on *festa* days, many hearts are mended, many hearts are broken sometimes, and friendships start."

Against this island setting, Maria Calleja tells her own story. Her life history is inextricably linked with that of Gozo. Her experience and education make her particularly well fitted to observe and describe her island and its now-vanishing mode of life, for she herself has lived it and seen it change. Throughout the interview with Micheline Galley, the narrative runs easily in a plain, straightforward style—in unrehearsed English with a Gozitan flavor, and aiming at no literary effect. She explains frankly why she chose a teaching career rather than marriage; at the same time, we note how her unstinted devotion and attention to her brother Anton throughout his sickness and the funeral that followed show that she is essentially human and capable of touching affection and self-sacrifice.

Micheline Galley knows Malta and Gozo well, having visited both islands frequently since 1968. Her "interview" with Maria Calleja was the culmination of a friendship forged over a period of more than twenty years by a high degree of mutual respect and understanding. She herself makes no comment on the characters mentioned and the events narrated, allowing Maria free rein to tell her story naturally. In so doing, Maria provides an insight into the variety and complexities of human life on a small Mediterranean island.

In presenting this book, Micheline Galley has had the benefit of previous experience in the publication of material based on field and other research. During her four years' stay in Algeria (1963-66), she gained the confidence of Aouda, a storyteller from the mountainous region of the Ouarsenis, who narrated to her a large repertoire of Algerian tales, of which she later edited seven, with a French translation and commentaries, under the title *Badr az-Zîn et six contes algériens*. A jealous guardian of her country's cultural heritage, Aouda was persuaded to allow Micheline Galley to record her traditional tales on tape, provided, however, that Micheline would *not* write her life history. Unlike Aouda, Maria Calleja made no conditions and wholeheartedly agreed to collaborate with her interviewer in writing a book jointly about her life and experiences in her native Gozo.

In addition to conducting the present inquiry, Dr. Galley has rearranged the whole narrative under major topics, organizing them into the individual chapters of this useful book. She has supplemented Maria Calleja's story with footnotes on Maltese vocabulary to help the non-Maltese reader, and with rich commentaries embodying the results of recent research. Especially useful are the analytical index and the name and place index. Together with the comprehensive bibliography, maps and other illustrations, these enhance the value of the volume for scholarly purpose.

The "marriage of minds" between Maria Calleja and Micheline Galley should help readers to understand Gozo and suggest new and meaningful ways of interpreting its life and mind.

Ġ. Cassar Pullicino
Former editor of the *Maltese Folklore Review*
Balzan, Malta
September 1992

Note on Maltese Pronunciation

In order to help the reader pronounce the Maltese names and sentences that appear in the text, here are some clues indicating approximate pronunciation:

Of the 24 consonants, the following are pronounced as indicated: *ċ* (tʃ) is like English "cherry"; *ġ* (dʒ) is like "joy"; *g* (g) is like "gold"; *j* (y) is like "yacht"; *h* is silent; *ħ* is aspirate; *għ*, or *għajn*, is usually silent; *q* is usually unvoiced (glottal stop); *x* (ʃ) is pronounced like "sherry"; *ż* (z) is like "zinnia"; z (ts) is like "cats."

The vowels, *a*, *e*, *i*, *o*, *u*, have roughly the same sound as they have in Italian. Note the digraph *ie* (iə) as, approximately, "fear"; and diphthongal combinations with *w* and *j*, such as *aw* (au) like "cow," and *ej* (ei) like "may."

For a more elaborate guide to Maltese letters and sounds, please consult J. Aquilina, *Teach Yourself Maltese* (London: The English Universities Press Ltd, 1965), 11-34.

Introduction

"Let's make a book!" One fine day in 1987 at Maria's house in Kerċem, she and I felt—simultaneously, so to speak—a strong impulse to "make a book" together, as if it was the natural, almost predestined outcome of the long conversations we had had for the previous two years during my stays in Gozo. Our predominant subject had been Maria's life experiences: born at the time of the First World War, she has lived during a period of great economic, social and cultural change on her island, Gozo.

Obviously, we had reached the point where Maria had become conscious of her desire to tell her "life history," as it is described these days, whilst I knew from what I had already heard that her narration would make a very personal contribution to our collective memory in general, and more particularly, to the memory of her fellow countrymen. I was convinced that Maria, when telling about her life, like other informants observed by Linda Degh, would not limit herself "to the succession of bare facts but frame these with subjective evaluative commentaries that reveal personal and societal elements of ideology and worldview" (1989, 43).

Therefore the decision was reached jointly: "we'll make a book!" On my part, I had in mind one primary objective: to preserve the natural, spontaneous character of the conversations we usually had, and allow Maria maximum liberty to express herself. It was decided that our working sessions would take the form of an interview recorded on tape, with no questionnaire prepared beforehand, yet conducted, to a certain (flexible) extent, by the interviewer. We chose English as the language of the interview because English was our usual means of communication, but of course this would not exclude the use of Maltese by Maria whenever she felt like changing to her mother tongue, either for the sake of accuracy in the choice of a word or a saying, or—as I realized only later—as an outlet for her emotions. The important factor was that there would not be any linguistic barrier between us; that would help ensure complete understanding. These were, undoubtedly, favorable circumstances: the mediation of an interpreter considerably changes the nature of a relationship (Jelmini 1987, 67-112).

Our relationship was based on trust and esteem, which constituted the starting point of the joint enterprise, an absolute prerequisite, as realized by pioneer authors of similar works: "I believe that it was because we were friends that he agreed . . . ," Sidney Mintz said about Taso, whose life story has appeared in book form under the title of *Worker in the Cane* (1960). In the same way, Oscar Lewis emphasized the determining factor which enabled him to compile *The Children of Sanchez* (1961): his friendly relations with the Sanchez family. As far as my own relationship with Maria's family is concerned, it dates back to my first visit to the Maltese islands in December 1968,[*] when I had the privilege of meeting, in their home, Maria, her mother and her brother, Anton. I still remember the exquisite local food prepared by Maria's mother for her French guest who, somehow, reminded her of her stay in French Algeria when she was still a young unmarried woman.[†] From that visit to her relatives who had emigrated (or whose ancestors had emigrated, as shown later in the book), she had kept in her memory a few French phrases which she, rather unexpectedly but very appropriately, uttered: "*ça suffit!*" she said to put an end to the recording she had let me do of some of her prayers, as well as a group of Maltese proverbs. I also remember on this very first occasion Anton's special attention to his foreign guest, whom he showed round the wild, impressive area of Wardija Point, which he preferred to

---

[*] At that time I was in Paris attending Professor David Cohen's lectures on Arabic dialects. At the end of the term which had been devoted to the Maltese language, David Cohen kindly suggested that I should start research in Malta, for which he provided facilities from the Centre National de la Recherche Scientifique. When I arrived on Maltese soil, I was encouraged and helped by Professor Ġuże (Joseph) Aquilina; I am also grateful to Miss Mary Rose Gatt for her efficient and friendly cooperation.

[†] I myself lived in Algiers from 1962 to 1966. It was during my stay there (as a teacher at the university) that I started collecting Arabic folktales.

other beauty spots on his island. Maria herself helped me in many ways during this memorable first trip: she took me to the village of Munxar to see Mari Ta' Nini, a very gifted popular folksinger who, on the occasion of our visit, one afternoon improvised more than sixty quatrains.

Since then, "time has flown with the wind" (*il-ħin tar mar-riħ*), as the song goes. But throughout this period, I have remained in contact with Maria, even though there was a time when, on account of professional commitments, I was held up on Malta itself without being able to cross over to its sister island as often as I wished.* In the meantime, Maria went through periods of great sorrow and bereavement: she lost her mother, then Anton himself (see Chapter 6). More recently, I have been visiting her practically every summer, and as she now has more spare time (she is a retired headmistress), we have been in a position to enjoy each other's company.

If being together has proved to be a real pleasure, I think on both sides, it has been due to the fact that we have learnt from each other, have shared and appreciated, although from different angles, periods of work and periods of recreation. For example, while I was busy taking photographs of some of the ex-voto items of Ta' Pinu sanctuary, Maria concentrated on writing down the corresponding notes for me, acting—she used to say jokingly—as my "technical assistant." But later in the day, we would assume different roles with equal ease and enjoyment, the ethnographer converting herself into a cook, and the "technical assistant" exercising her talent and humor as a poet-singer:

> Għandi koka minn Parigi
> X'qed issajjar kemm ifuħ?
> Dalgħodu telgħet ir-Rabat
> U xtratli ħuta minn gos-suq.
>
> (I have a cook from Paris . . . .
> What is she cooking which smells so sweet?

---

*As secretary-general of the International Association of Studies on Mediterranean Civilizations, I was in charge of the organization of the first two congresses which were held in Malta (1972, 1976), as well as of the editing of their proceedings (in both cases, printed in Malta).

This morning she went to Rabat
And bought me a fish from the market.)
   [Summer 1988]

Well, the day finally came when the interview began. Hardly had I switched on the tape recorder when, without waiting for any signal or question from me, Maria started in a very natural way: she presented the setting—her flat in Marsalforn—and made her own introduction. Her participation was total indeed, always a positive aspect of the interactional situation (Pollack 1986).

As the narration progressed, what were the degree and nature of my personal interventions? As I said before, the principle I had adopted was that of flexibility in order to keep the tone of a natural, straightforward dialogue, and at the same time facilitate associations of ideas on the part of the interviewee, at the risk sometimes of generating either short or long, yet always interesting, digressions. Perhaps the most interesting "digression" was during the very first session, the quite unexpected, direct and sincere address Maria made—she then glided automatically into Maltese—to her late mother at the moment when she caught sight of a photograph (reproduced later in the book), which was placed in a bookshelf just facing us. Needless to say, I gladly let the speaker pour out her gratitude to the contemplated portrait without any interruption (see beginning and end of Chapter 1). As a rule, however, whenever I intervened, either as the interviewer or as a listener to whom Maria's life history was being personally told, it depended always upon the particular context. The function of my interventions was, by asking questions, to elicit elaboration in the conversation, or to introduce new subjects within the stream of more or less interconnected themes, mostly at the beginning of a recorded session; eventually it was to maintain contact, as is normally done in ordinary dialogue.

However, later on when the stage of transcribing was reached, I found that I had to insert into the script interventions of a new type in order to provide the reader with a clear account of at least some, if not all, of the implicit information (see, for example, my first intervention in Chapter 1). As a matter of fact, because Maria knew that I was to some extent familiar with her background, she made no mention of certain items which an outsider would need to know in order to comprehend her story. This is particularly true of information related to her own family (hence my rather long intervention at the beginning of Chapter 4).

Transcribing has raised another problem, well known among folklorists with fieldwork experience. When one comes to give a written form to an orally performed narrative, the question of how to avoid the loss of all the nonlinguistic elements of communication has to be faced and answered some way or another (as illustrated later), because these elements are obviously a fundamental part of oral "performance." Maria herself, very naturally, resorts to all possible means of dramatization, such as imitating people's gait or their variations of speech and accent; she uses onomatopeia (e.g., cries of street vendors, sounds of gobbling turkeys, etc.), lengthens suggestive exclamations like "humm!" (written purposely with a double final consonant), etc. Sometimes, by combining rhythms of speech and modulation of voice and gesture, she conveys the psychological evolution of the protagonists in the scene described, or suggests the underlying features of their relationship. For example, an apparently simple sentence (in its written form) like, "My mother was not a spendthrift like me, and she spent her money wisely," was originally an extremely meaningful statement, based on the interplay between the different audiovisual elements. Maria said the first words—"my mother was not a spendthrift"—in a neutral voice; then she paused after "spendthrift," and uttered "like me" in a whisper, with a slight inward movement of her shoulders as of protection, and an expression of embarrassment on her face, as if to express shyness, fear maybe, and almost repentance on the young daughter's part. The two words, "her money," were said in a clear, assertive voice symbolic of the mother's authority, eventually reckoned as salutary, perhaps, to a child's education, as reflected, so it seems, in the tone of accepted submission attached to the last word, "wisely."

Sometimes an almost imperceptible sign of humor—a wink, a smile, a vocal inflexion—is addressed by the speaker to her listener (a mark of their mutual understanding). But there are also times when Maria, completely engrossed in conjuring up her past, temporarily loses contact with that listener. On one occasion, it seemed that the very taste of what she remembered as a magic beverage—the lemonade of feast days in her childhood—was brought back to her. The process has something in common—yet works in a different manner—with that experienced by Proust, when he recovered his past through the power of sensation (e.g., the episode of the "madeleine"); in Maria's case, it was the sound of the word *luminôta*, when pronounced with a strong local accent and repeated like an incantation, which called up the savory taste of the lemonade and radiated the mingled sensations of happiness connected with it.

Maria was amazed, and pleased, when she realized that whole sections of her life could be rescued from oblivion: "I had a feeling of elation," she said, "for being able to fish up, from the marvelous computer of my mind, the petty, sometimes pathetic, sometimes meritorious experiences of a lifetime" (Chapter 12). But the whole psychological phenomenon may have, as a counterpart, highly emotional implications (Perret-Clermont and Rovero 1987), in the sense that all of a sudden "forgotten" feelings are disclosed and emotions emerge uncontrolled. That happened once while Maria was in France, and perhaps because she was far from home, she was more vulnerable and felt more affected. We had to interrupt our work, which was resumed in Gozo during the following year, at Maria's request, during the final session (Chapter 12). We both agreed then that only the previous sequence, which had been too painful, would be deleted.

Once the almost fourteen hours of recordings had been transcribed, the question became, in view of its intended publication in book form, whether to leave the raw material untouched or to change it, and if so, to what extent. The choice depends, of course, on the aim of the publication, whether scientific or literary. It is commonly acknowledged that leaving the material as it is gives an impression of profusion, if not disorder, whereas the second alternative implies some degree of written composition and reorganization (Gonseth and Maillard 1987). In the present case, it is rather an intermediate position which was sought, so that the book might be available, and hopefully perhaps even attractive, to the general reader, whilst keeping as close and as faithful as feasible to the orally told original.

With that perspective in mind, I was determined not to alter the form of Maria's story, even more so because her style has aesthetic qualities of its own: it is fluent, lively, and rich in strong, accurate, sometimes humorous images. At the same time, it was clear that some reshaping of the narrative was advisable. Therefore I adopted a principle of "montage," which consisted in shifting either big or small units which seemed to fit other parts of the organic whole more appropriately. Meanwhile, a few repetitive sections were eliminated, unless they appeared to be significant in Maria's life (e.g., the episode of uprooting the potatoes by Uncle Daniel). Eventually the internal divisions in the story led to the formation of chapters (from 1 to 12). No other alteration was made except, here and there, the discretionary substitution of fictitious nicknames or first names for real ones.

However, additions of a complementary nature were needed to supplement Maria's narration, both inside (1) and outside (2) her text:

(1) An illustration of the vocal and/or visual, inevitably ephemeral, elements of oral expression has been made earlier. In order to provide the reader with an insight into the most significant among them, the following approximate notation devices have been used:

* short notes, inserted between brackets, such as "[laughter]," "[psalmody tune]," or "[gesture of turning whiskers upward]";

* capitals, indicating that emphasis was laid by the speaker on words and phrases, for instance: ". . . VERY CLEAN . . . ," or "CHURCH-GOING WAS PART AND PARCEL OF YOUR LIFE . . . ";

* hyphens, showing a broken, yet continuous, articulation (another way of laying emphasis), for example: "THIS-IS-NONSENSE!"

* ellipsis marks, marking pauses (other punctuation signs follow, as much as possible, the speaker's rhythm of speech).

(2) Since, as will be exemplified later in Maria's narration, life stories "never lose sight of the two poles of human reality, the individual and the social" (Burgos 1989, 31), they need to be supported by explanatory notes, as well as other items of information such as letters and photographs, which are likely to throw light on both the personal and social aspects. This is why, besides the linguistic footnotes which are provided whenever Maltese is used in Maria's text, the reader will find:

* "commentaries" placed after the twelve chapters (a total of 130 notes, including comparisons with other Mediterranean cultures);

* appendices, including a letter by Mr. Joe Gatt from Australia reproduced because it reflects, beyond dates and facts, the emotional implications of emigration; Mr. Gatt's father left Gozo in 1916 with a group of young men which included Maria's father.

Now that the "story" has been established, let us briefly examine the "life." During the last few decades, an increasing interest has been taken in life histories, not only by several publishing houses (and their readers), but also by researchers from various disciplines. One tendency among researchers has been to denounce the "biographic illusion" and to insist on more reliable, "objective" methods (Bourdieu 1986). However, most anthropologists have favored such "subjective" data, since they provide "a point of view from within the culture" (Langness 1965), or *"par l'intérieur,"* as Levi-Strauss himself said about "Sun Hopi": ". . . il réussit du premier coup l'entreprise sur laquelle s'acharne, le plus souvent vainement, le travailleur sur le terrain: celle qui consiste à restituer une culture indigène, si l'on peut dire, 'par l'intérieur,' comme un ensemble vivant et gouverné par une harmonie interne, et non comme un empilage arbitraire de coutumes et d'institutions dont la présence est simplement constatée . . ."(1949, 330).* As for the poststructuralist anthropologists, their position is very clear; as one of them puts it, "they want to ground their studies in the concrete reality of living, breathing, feeling, copulating and fighting human beings" (Gilmore 1987, 4).

Naturally one must be aware that an individual history is an ambiguous record of someone's life in the sense that it is deeply personal, sensitive and sincere, but at the same time, fragmentary, more or less staged, and distorted. I am aware that Maria may have somehow built up, even unconsciously, a picture of herself with which she would like to impress others. Yet in personal sequences, she ignores the supposedly unflattering image she might convey and discloses her feelings and views about herself in a sincere, lucid and courageous manner to enlighten the reader (in particular, see the first half of Chapter 11).

Perhaps her lifelong profession as a teacher has trained her to explain things. It is, indeed, in a clear, rational way—not devoid of humor—that she expresses herself on education, and analyzes the reasons, economic as well as personal, why it would have been "a sin," as she puts it, for her to get married instead of practicing a profession which she enjoyed thoroughly (chapters 8 and 9). However, acquiring economic independence,

---

*". . . he succeeds right away in the attempt upon which, vainly most of the time, the field-worker persistently slaves: the attempt which consists in restituting an indigenous culture, if one may say so, 'from the inside,' as a living organ governed by an internal harmony, and not as an arbitrary piling up of customs and institutions, the presence of which is simply established."

as well as social consideration, through professional achievement did not mean that a young Maltese woman at that time was free from social constraints. On the contrary, having a job and therefore earning money made her assume a different role within the family, that of a breadwinner. Personally Maria was delighted to be "useful," and "proud" to contribute to the education of her bright young brother, Anton. But it seems, on a wider scale, to have been taken for granted that a young daughter or sister would help the family with her salary, sometimes for life. Speaking of her colleagues and herself, Maria says: "We always had somebody to help—nieces or nephews or brothers. That is why most of the female teachers didn't get married. Not because they were not good looking; not because there was not somebody who fancied them!" (Chapter 8).

As already pointed out, this situation illustrates one of the main features of a life history—the connection between the two poles, the individual and the social—by the simple fact that attention is diverted from the person to his or her relationships with others. A glimpse at the index at the end of this book under the heading "Social relations" gives an idea of the importance of family ties.

As far as Maria's relations with her parents are concerned, both of them, in different ways, opened the child's mind to the world around. On the one hand, her father told her about his experiences on his way to Australia, or during his stay in Australia, and that, she says, broadened her horizon "quite beyond the village." On the other hand, learning the ways of day-to-day living through her very worldly wise mother made her familiar with the practical side of human existence. However, an individual exists within a network of much wider family relationships (Bertaux and Bertaux-Wiame 1988). Maria spent her childhood on the family farming complex, Ta' Ġanton, where her mother's brothers and sisters—at least those who had not emigrated and settled elsewhere—were living near one another with wives and husbands and children, a whole community whose members were linked by bonds of friendliness and solidarity, but who, now and then, might show "slight signs of [internal] jealousy," liable either to flare up (for a matter of inheritance), or to lurk underneath, but never to end in a feud (Chapter 4).

The relationships outside the family had their ambivalence, too: you might have very reliable friends in your neighborhood, like the nice group of lace-makers whom Maria's mother joined on certain days of the week; otherwise you were exposed to comment and criticism, and had better be cautious as the proverb recommends: "You eat according to your heart [but] go according to the eye of the people" (*Tiekol għall qalbek u timxi għall għajn in-nies*). Maria could be tempted to adopt a totally opposite attitude: "the best thing is not to pay attention . . . otherwise it will kill you!" But like everybody else, she was sensitive to the opinions of others, and very hurt one day when, from the next garden, her neighbor sang insidious allusions aimed at her: *l-għana*, or folksinging, served—Maria explains—as a means of "insulting" people (Chapter 9).

Inversely, "respect"—a recurring word in Maria's narration—is the sign of social recognition and therefore a source of family pride. In this case, people "paid respect" to Maria's family (that is the "nuclear" family, made up of parents, brother and Maria herself), perhaps less for the flourishing trade of the father than for their moral qualities and for the intellectual attainment of the children, as well as, later, for the prestige and political influence of Anton.

To be "proud" (another recurrent term), or to "keep one's head up," was one of the strong principles of Maria's mother, as reflected physically by her stately bearing (see photograph). She inculcated in her children's minds the idea that they were not people to be "cheated" or "outwitted," "downtrodden" or "trampled on." It was with "that frame of mind" that Maria went to Malta, the main island, and sat for the exam to become a head teacher. At that time, the Gozitans had a feeling of uneasiness in the presence of the Maltese according to Maria: "We were still feeling a bit . . . shy of people from Malta, not because we were stupid or not clever enough, or not prepared enough . . . . There was always that feeling that you were watched by the people from Malta." Therefore one can imagine what strenuous efforts a young woman from a small village in Gozo had to make when finding herself, at the exam, with two hundred or so Maltese candidates who were, for the most part, the children (mostly sons) of professional people, doctors or lawyers, and already had, in certain cases, a degree from London. In such a highly emotional situation, Maria seemed to convert her shyness into irritation, in order, perhaps, to reassure herself and give an emphatic expression to her energy: "Asses! I will pass you all!" she grumbled to herself at the others, or "said in her heart," as she puts it, adding: "I felt the challenge in me that I was not to be downtrodden by those . . . ." And she passed first in the women's section (Chapter 8).

Because the "challenge" Maria felt involved her whole person, as an individual as well as a Gozitan, it endowed her with boundless energy.

Such competitiveness is not a unique feature: rather it "seems to pervade all levels of Gozitan life," and still plays today a remarkably dynamic role within social groups, particularly in the field of culture (Chapter 10). Maria herself has, all through her teaching career (and in fact afterward), displayed considerable willpower and vigor. Her personal trajectory is a vivid example of the evolution of the whole society: in that sense, she is symbolic of her island.

Naturally, as witnessed by Maria's family, emigration has wrought great changes, sometimes in the space of one generation. Maria often refers to a present member of parliament and well-off gentleman in Australia, who comes from a Gozitan village where his mother worked as a family helper when a baby was born. However exceptional this case may be, the transformation of the Gozitan society is universal. One basic determining characteristic has been the indomitable courage of the Gozitan people—a small, rural, insular, Christian community in the Mediterranean.

We owe this oral history, now in printed form, to the "marvelous computer" of a woman's mind. As suggested by the title, *Maria Calleja's Gozo*, this book was conceived not as an attempt at an anthropological analysis of the Gozitan society, but as a means to convey Maria's view of *her* Gozo, placed in its wide sociocultural context. Well recorded in the "archives" of the memory and nurtured by feeling and thought, as is the present case, a life history creates a document for further research.

"Let's make a book!" Maria and I decided one day. We "made" it and hope that it will be, for the reader, a source of knowledge and pleasure.

The basil plant is associated with fertility and marriage.

A typical Gozitan farmhouse.

Chapter 1

Childhood Days

From her "summer residence," Maria looks back upon the farming estate of her childhood, a place which tells a tale of emigration, since in the last century several of her mother's ancestors went to Algeria (the house was inherited from them) and, in 1916, another wave of emigrants took Maria's father and one of her mother's brothers to Australia in search of employment: Maria was then a one-year-old baby.

Seventy years or so have passed. A certain way of life which, in the course of years, was to change profoundly is here revived. In Maria's memory, the central position is occupied by mother and house, inextricably linked together: a farmhouse in which space was shared in a functional manner between human beings and animals, and the mother who used to take part in the farming work, in addition to her everyday tasks as a housewife and mother at a time when a child was born practically every year. Such a hardworking life did not preclude the attention paid to social recognition, which was based on a certain number of status symbols, such as being clean and orderly, producing self-sufficient food, having babies born at home, owning a loom (when growing cotton), and so on. The pealing of bells and call to prayers punctuated the long, toilsome days. The whole year was lived to the rhythm of religious feasts associated with social gatherings and, for a child, with wearing one's best clothes and sharing games with other children.

While Maria was speaking, she cast a look on a nearby photograph of her mother and was obviously moved by the sight of someone who remains, in her memory, the symbol of courage, determination and dignity. All the sufferings endured by the mother were the price paid for providing the children with education, and with freedom.

Maria: Today we are sitting in the small back room in Marsalforn,[1] very near to a hill in Xagħra: English people call it "the smoking mountain" because refuse is all the time burning up there. Who knows how many beautiful, useful documents finally find their way up there! Sometimes people do not realize what treasures they have got and they do not know what they are throwing away.

Micheline: Maria, you have in mind the conversation we had yesterday with Joe,[2] when he told us that he had found, almost by accident, precious letters in the backyard of his neighbor, the baker, who was using all sorts of garbage for fuel.

Maria: Well, personally I do not own documents stored in my drawers, but I have the feeling that in my mind I have a whole documentary of Gozitan life: the simple, quiet, peasant life which farmers led . . . a Gozitan life changing in these latter years, changing into the fast, modern way of life. Some say that progress has brought well-being into the country. Those of us like me who remember the old simple way of life in Gozo—very few people had engines or mechanical equipment—sometimes we say that Gozo was a much better place where we could live in peace like human beings!

Look, Micheline, in front of me there is a small library and, between the books, some photos. I see the picture of a woman [emotional tone] looking out at me, *tittawwal*,* a woman very dear to me: *ommi, li kien jisimha* Ġanna Roża Buhagiar *u bil-laqam* Ta' Pantu.† That nickname, "Ta' Pantu," for me was always a dilemma because I could not understand what it meant. Now a distant relative, Michael Grima, who is a university student and who is writing a project on his family genealogy, found out that Pantu—wonder of wonders!—originated in Pantaleone, which is a nickname, and it came from the island of Corsica.[3] So I, Maria Calleja, on this small island of Għawdex,‡ I can say that one of my forefathers came from Corsica!

Now this woman, Ġanna Roża, was of a family of farmers and when I was a child, we lived at Ta' Ġanton[4] in a farmhouse, the typical peasants' house, which has a cubic outline with no ornamentation except for

---

*Literally, "she is lengthening," or stretching (her neck) as if to peep out.
† "My mother, whose name was Ġanna Roża Buhagiar, with the nickname Ta' Pantu."
‡ Gozo.

Front of a traditional Gozitan house with a
finely decorated balcony.

A Gozitan farmhouse, similar to the one where Maria lived as a
child.

waterspouts and a *ħarrieġa** or two. A *ħarrieġa* was a projection of the windowsill which had two very different uses: first, some of these *ħarrie-ġas* supported a loose slab of stone which could be easily pushed down on the head of housebreakers, most probably Arabs;[5] the second use of the *ħarrieġa* was more romantic: when a daughter was ready for marriage, her father would put out, on this *ħarrieġa*, a pot of basil so that young men might come forward as suitors.[6]

Micheline: Maria, when you reached marriageable age, did your father put a pot of basil on the windowsill?

Maria: No [smile]. At that time, we had moved to a new house in the village itself.

Micheline: All right. Let's go back to Ta' Ġanton. Do you have some vivid memories attached to that house?

Maria: Yes. Well, you see, the ground floor of these farmhouses was for animals: there was the *maqjel*;[†] another room served as a garage where the carts were kept and the harness which you put on your horse, or mule, or donkey, whichever you had. In larger farmhouses of course, as they had in Għarb, there was a room used as a *mitħna tal-miexi*,[‡] a mill moved by a mule going 'round and 'round and 'round two large grinding stones. Mind you, Micheline, nowadays Gozitan farmhouses fetch a lot of money. Foreigners buy them and convert them into beautiful houses: the *mitħna* is generally converted into a sitting room.

Micheline: Therefore, Maria, human beings had their dwelling area upstairs, hadn't they?

Maria: Yes, on the first floor. We had little furniture, apart from beds, tables and chairs, but we had a lot of rooms. We had, first and foremost, a "straw room," actually a storage room for straw and also for corn and clover. We had up there a huge sack of corn, and I am remembering the dog . . . *għamlithielna*, Ġann[§] [addressing her mother in the picture], I'm remembering the dog which played a trick on us. Because that dog used

---

*From *ĦRĠ*, which means "to go out." A *ħarrieġa* is "a stone projecting from a wall; a stone jutting out about a span from the wall of a country house beside a window looking on the yard, used mainly to keep provisions out of children's, dogs', etc., reach and to keep them fresh in the open air" (*Maltese-English Dictionary*, s.v. *ħarrieġa*).

† A sty for cattle, sheep or goats.

‡ Literally. "mill of the walking one," a mill rotated by a beast of burden for grinding corn.

§ Literally, "she did it for us," i.e., she played a trick on us.

to look for eggs in the chicken nests scattered about the house garden, then go up noiselessly, stealthily, there behind the huge corn sacks, out of sight, pierce somehow the shell and suck the contents, leaving the empty shells out of sight. One day, when the corn sack got lower and lower, to our surprise . . . we said: "*Oj, oj! hawn x'għandna!*" That is: "Hoy, hoy! What do we have here!" And we found a big heap of empty eggshells behind the corn sacks.

So, you see, we had in that straw room storage for animal fodder as well as corn for human beings. Some time before, it must have been a large room, and as my father was a carpenter, he put up a wooden partition: one part was kept for storage, and the other was beautifully done and decorated; it served as our best bedroom: a nice bed, and a canopy with bird drapery [tone of admiration], a shining wardrobe which one of my uncles had bought from Sliema,[7] the chest of drawers or credenza, which my mother had bought for one pound for her dowry;[8] on it, a clock *tal-kampnari,** bought secondhand for half a crown; in this *arloġġ tal-kampnari,*[†] there was an inscription saying, "Made in Connecticut" . . . I do not know how it traveled from the U.S.A. and found its way in Ta' Ġanton [sounding vivid and amused]. In any case, when we had a baptism in the family or a feast day, my mother used to take out of her drawers nicely starched linen with fine crochet lace made by herself and decorated with red initials, Ġ C, Ġiovanna Calleja, SIX INCHES HIGH, about fifteen centimeters . . . . Of course, in this room we had a washstand with jug and basin and towel.

Now the funny thing about this room was . . . I used to go into this room very often. Why? Not to sleep, because that was reserved for special occasions, but because overlooking the washstand, there was a small door leading to a smaller room, a *raff.*[‡] This *raff* was the ideal place to keep foodstuffs in the right condition, stop them from rotting; it had two small apertures, *rewwieħa,*[§] so that there was constant ventilation; in the middle, my mother hung a reed tray, a *qanniċ,* for soft cheeses to dry gradually; sometimes I brought down some semisoft cheeses; sometimes I fetched onions from a huge pile. You see, although we were not really

---

*A steeple clock. In Maria's mind, that clock looked like a church with a steeple on each side.

†Ibid.

‡A small wooden loft.

§A square opening in a wall, through which the air can pass to ventilate the room.

farmers, my mother's family was a farming one, so she could not bear not to have a huge stock of onions, beans and potatoes.

Well, further on, I discovered in that room a huge traveling case full of letters. I tried to read, but I was the age of just beginning to read. So I started to put letters together and somehow I understood that those letters came from my father in Australia.[9] My mother stored them in the attic, a sort of archives up there. Once I read: "If you do not want to come to Australia . . . ." This happened about in 1920. So: "If you do not want to come to Australia, would you like to join me in America?" I'm sure that my father, who was well known for his intelligence, saw that life offered better chances in Australia or America, where one could raise a family with a good standard of living.

Micheline: But your mother was, like the majority of young women in Gozo, reluctant—wasn't she?—to leave her native island and join her husband in so distant a country; and it is eventually your father, you said to me, who came back home after a period of five years?

Maria: Quite.

Micheline: Maria, when your father emigrated toward Australia in 1916, and before he was in a position to help his family by perhaps sending money, do you have an idea of the resources your mother had to live on, with you then a newborn child?

Maria: As far as I know, there was practically nothing to live on, except one sheep, a few hens, and my mother's lace . . . .

Micheline: But you had a house of yourselves, hadn't you?

Maria: Thank God, we had the house that my mother had inherited from one of her uncles settled in Algiers. That house was part of a large farmhouse complex built on each side of an alley in Ta' Ġanton and inhabited by my mother's relatives. As far as our house was concerned, it must have been divided in two, when, by contract—written in French in Algiers!—one part was given to us.[10] I remember one could easily see inside the house the doorways that had been stopped up, and on the other side lived three bachelor brothers, distant relatives of ours, with whom, from the terrace, my mother would occasionally exchange some conversation.

Micheline: Maria, from your description of the house indoors, one gathers that a lot of space was occupied by the storing of food for both animals and men. Was there a room for cooking? Did you have water available nearby?

Maria: At that time, you see, the modern oak kitchens were undreamt of [laughter]. You only had a small room all covered with soot, maybe a shelf and a fireplace with four or five pots, all black outside. Wells, we had "as many as you want," *bjar kemm trid*, as we say in Maltese. We had a large one in the interior yard. This well served many purposes: first, it was used for domestic purposes: cooking, washing, and so on; it was so well made: it was dug out of rock, and it kept very cool; it served as a fridge. When mother had a baby . . . well, in those days, a wife had a baby every year, and one didn't go to hospital or a clinic; she stayed at home, was assisted by a midwife, a *majjistra*. I still remember the *majjistra* coming from Victoria, walking slowly, dragging one foot after the other with fatigue, dressed in dark clothes, carrying a small black valise, and we children used to say: "Somebody is going to buy a baby!" We were so used to seeing a *majjistra* walking up and down the street—for us children it did not mean what exactly was happening—that we connected her with childbirth, because we would eventually see her at church for the baptism of a day-old screaming baby. Anyway, when mother had a new baby, she had a help, a lady called Ġużeppa tar-Rossina; she now lives in a small farmhouse not very far from Karmni Grima.[11] She used to wash the clothes, look after the children, maybe kill and prepare a chicken . . . although in those days, one didn't cook a chicken every day! Chickens and eggs were kept as means of livelihood: first, you would barter your eggs and later sell the hen itself . . . .

Micheline: People were thrifty, weren't they, living a particularly frugal life as compared to our modern standards? Now can you explain how, in your immediate surroundings in Ta' Ganton, they somehow or other supported themselves?

Maria: Well, as far as I know, everybody had a bit of land and that provided for food and something to sell, because generally the fruit one had, or the chickens and eggs as I said, or a young lamb were sold, and that provided the money with which to buy your necessities, such as clothing and other things you would need. The houses were adequately heated in the winter and cold in the summer because they were built in a way . . . you know, the outer walls were very, very thick—we used to call 'em *ta' l-imramma**—and that would be about, well, five feet thick.

---

*The phrase (literally, "of the wall") suggests the typical construction of the *mramma*, a very thick double wall, the cavity of which is filled with rubble and mortar.

SO . . . and of course, we had no large bay windows; we only had very small windows: the largest would be about three feet wide. No large windows, and that kept the houses relatively warm in winter and cool in summer. As for fuel—if you're a farmer, you always bring back some kind of wood which you store for eventual use.

So, as I said before, the fields themselves provided your corn. And as we had ourselves at home, every farmer had some sacks of corn stored in his house. Then every three months or so, you would put out a sack of corn and take it to the miller. We used to go to a miller in Għarb, and the mill was not so primitive: there was a sort of engine about it with wheels, and you would get your corn ground. When the ground corn was brought home, it was processed through three different sieves. The first one with rather big holes separated the husk from the rest of the meal; this husk, or *qxura*, was given to rabbits. Sieve number two with slightly smaller holes was used to separate the bran—*in-nuħħala*—which was mixed with water: an excellent meal for hens. Sieve number three, which had no holes but was made of fine hair, separated the *granza*, a mixture of fine bran and flour, used to feed young chickens. The result of this triple sieving? It was FINE-WHOLE-MEAL-FLOUR! So as for food,[12] that was all. Of course, we bought some groceries, and the groceries were sometimes paid with cash, sometimes paid with another sort of thing which you produced. With this barter system, I remember clearly, you would take some dozen-or-two eggs to the grocer; he would tot it up and say: "I owe you . . . five shillings," for example; then you would have a shopping list; maybe you would have some money back.

Micheline: And how were you provided with clothes?

Maria: For clothing, it's another story . . . . Not all people had a loom in the house.[13] Only the best families. It was a status symbol to have a loom because you'd have fields, and you'd grow cotton in your fields, and there would be weaving at home.[14] There was a special room for the loom, *in-newl*, and for many other implements to go with it. The weaving was mostly done by the women, but sometimes in very cold rainy days, the men would give a helping hand because they could do nothing in the house and they wouldn't be kept idle by the women. So weaving provided very strong, fine material for sheeting, which lasted for more than one generation: I still have some of Nana's* sheets and pillowcases. You

---

*Grandma's.

might have white sheets or white-and red-striped sheets because we had that "red cotton," *qoton aḥmar,* or rather fawn one. But the material might be plain, and it would serve for the men's trousers.

For women, we never had that strong type of material; we always bought our material from a shop in Victoria, and I still remember it was measured by *il-qasba.** For a chemise, for example, you would have two. For a dress . . . the older you are—if you are a woman—the longer it must be! Your feet must be covered. So you would have a doublet, a skirt with six panels which reach up to your ankles. And mentioning dress . . . women also had—especially those who were in charge of the household economy . . . how shall I say? . . . they also had a kind of pocket, huge pocket which they wore with a band 'round their waist, and this pocket had an access to it through the outer skirt. Sometimes there was no access to it, so the woman would first have a look around to see that nobody was looking, and then she would take up the skirt and get at her big, huge, deep pocket and get some money out of that, or keys. And that would be kept by the mother or the elder sister, or somebody who ran the house [laughter], the Minister of the Budget!

So you see, we were relatively well fed, we had clothes, and most people had, somehow or other, their own house: some were rather big, some had only two or three rooms above the ground floor which—you must remember—was for animals only.

Micheline: Maria, you mentioned that your father, a carpenter, had decorated a room in your house, the best room to be used on special occasions for visitors. Tell me about those family or social gatherings at home.

Maria: Of course, we had now and then social . . . actually very few social activities. The only social activities were in connection with the church, like *festas,*† like Eastertime, like Christmastime. We would have a nice dress on that occasion and we would go to church and have a little something out of the usual—you know. If there was a wedding in the family, or an engagement, or a baptism, there would be some *biskuttini tar-raḥal,*‡ as we call them. There used to be drinks, not heavy, strong

---

*Qasba (plural, *qasab, qasbiet*) is about eighty inches long.

† A *festa* is a feast, in particular the yearly celebration of the parish patron saint.

‡ Literally, "village biscuits," i.e., sugar cakes decorated with colored icing.

alcohol; we used to have something colored red like *rożolin*.* I always remember the rich, beautiful green and nice ruby which tasted like mint; there was a touch of mint in them . . . .

Well, this sort of social activities we enjoyed, but one special occasion for us children was at l-Għid il-Ħamsin,† when the church would be celebrating Pentecost and we would put up a *bandla*.‡ A *bandla* would mean a strong rope, which we got from the farming room, and we had special hooks in the wall. You could tie the rope in there. Sometimes we had two ropes so that, in the middle, there was a sort of seat . . . AND . . . we would SWING to our hearts' content [mimicking repeated swinging movement backward and forward], because somebody would push you as hard as . . . WOO . . . [mingled expression of fright and delight]. So that was the sort of play we had. I also remember summertime, when in the hot summer months, the farmers were threshing the corn and we children had lots of fun rolling on the straw or climbing up the top of a heap of wheat and jumping down . . . .

Micheline: I presume that for the grown-ups it was hard work. Can you give an idea of what was going on all around the threshing floor?

Maria: First, they had to make a threshing floor: they would find a field which was centrally placed; they would dig it up and then water it, throw some thin old straw on it, and with a very heavy stone roller, they would pass several times, so by the time it was ready, it was as hard as concrete . . . . I remember the threshing floor—in Maltese, *il-qiegħa*, we call it. Now the farmers would carry their wheat, and build it up in the shape of a circular wall 'round the threshing floor. Then they would have a stand for a *mingla*;§ they would cut the wheat in two parts, leaving the smaller part where the corn is, toward the middle of the threshing floor, and the straw would be in another part of the field. The farmers would bring the animals they had, whether it was a mule or a horse or a donkey. Sometimes they had two together. And this had to be in the melting sun . . . it was so hot you felt your skin or your body being melted . . . and the poor donkey would be blindfolded and somebody

---

*Soft liqueur or cordial made with many different flavorings (see *Maltese-English Dictionary*, s.v. *rożolin*).

†Literally, "the fiftieth day" (after the Resurrection), hence Whitsunday.

‡A swing (from *bandal*, which means "to rock").

§A sort of sickle-shaped tool attached to a wall, whereon *sulla* (clover), etc., is cut for animal fodder (*Maltese-English Dictionary*, s.v. *mingla*).

would drive it round 'nd round 'nd round 'nd round 'nd round 'nd round 'nd round until the corn would drop . . . and they would clear the corn from the straw.

I remember the well-to-do families would have many, many sacks, and this went down and down with your position of richness or poverty. Yet, on the whole, I believe everybody had his amount of corn all the year 'round, was provided with whole-meal bread all the year 'round. But in years of scarcity, years when the farmers would know in the wintertime that they were not going to have a good corn harvest, there would be prayers said . . . . Later on, we used to buy imported enriched flour—which I'd rather say "impoverished" flour, because they were taking the most important part of the corn in it—anyway we would mix the white imported flour with our fine whole meal-flour. It was a sort of status symbol which was very silly: the whiter the bread, the richer you were! Eating black bread, *ħobż iswed*—today we would say "brown bread," *ħobż ismar*—would mean that you were lowering your status. Now nowadays, some of the people of Gozo who are diet conscious, and of course the English people we have, who are living with us, and even government dieticians teach us that brown bread and whole-meal brown bread is the best, but that's beside the point we are speaking about.

Micheline: Not really. Now, going back to the time when you were living in Ta' Ġanton, one realizes the importance of corn: you have shown how it was threshed, how it was stored and ground; in other words, you made it clear that bread was the staple element of your food. What else, would you say, was essential?

Maria: As I said before, we had eggs . . . . Although we did not use the eggs frequently, we were provided with eggs. We had cheese and I never tasted any lovelier cheese than the ones we used to make in the farmhouse and we had several types: you could eat it as *baqta* or yoghurt, as we call it nowadays; you could eat it soft, or salted, and that makes lovely *torta** [laughter]; you could eat it a bit semihard, *ġobon moxx*,† and of course, we could always have it salted, marinated with vinegar—*ġobon maħsul‡*—covered with salt and pepper and stored in an earthenware jar,

---

*A sort of pie.

†Dry or partly dried cheese (ready for grating).

‡Literally, "washed" cheese, that is, marinated in vinegar, salt and pepper, and stored in earthenware jars.

and the more you leave it there, the better it is. And at the bottom of the jar, there would be left a certain kind of juice . . . . I remember my mother using a spoonful of that special juice from the bottom of the jar to have it with our vegetable soup.

Micheline: Did you grow your own vegetables?

Maria: Of course. We grew what we needed for the family consumption, not for sale or anything. You see, as everybody else in that Ta' Ganton complex, we had a bit of land where to grow our own vegetables, such as turnips, such as onions, such as pumpkins . . . . My mother would never have gone to a greengrocer; at that time, it was looked down, frowned upon . . . as beneath you [laughter] for a farmer to go to a greengrocer. Nowadays that's completely different!

Micheline: So you did not only live in a farmhouse, surrounded by farmers—I mean your mother's relatives—but you practically had a farming life, although your father was a carpenter.

Maria: It is true and my mother was very demanding in a way; sometimes she was complaining that our fields, in her opinion, were not well kept. I remember her saying: *"L-għalqa taqħna dejjem żdongota!"**

Micheline: You must have been all the time seeing the farmers 'round about you at work, in Ta' Ganton.

Maria: Yes, I was seeing them digging, watering, weeding, and later on, I very gladly, very gladly took part in that.

Micheline: Would you describe a day's work, for both men and women?

Maria: First, the day for them began at Paternoster; at 4:00 A.M., there was a peal of church bells to remind people to get up and pray,[15] and maybe go for the first mass—*quddiesa ta' l-ewwel*, we say—because it's a wonder how people who had such hard and long working hours used to begin the day with the Holy Mass. After, when everybody, including the womenfolk was up and about, the men would prepare the seeds, the implements, and whatever was needed according to the season and the state of the field, such as the plough, *il-moħriet*. Some of them had many animals—cows, sheep, goats, a donkey or two—so before leaving for the fields, they had to feed them, which was quite a job! You must cut the fodder on a *mingla*, or prepare a basket with cut-up leaves of prickly pears, or *bajtar tax-xewk*. Most of the time, the men would prepare the

---

*"Our field is always neglected."

right amount and leave the fodder ready for the women to feed the animals afterward.

But the women had first to prepare breakfast, not really an English breakfast . . . the very name was still unheard of! Our breakfast, that meant coffee, a big bowl of it with bits of bread soaked, *mxarrab,** in that coffee and milk. After that, they had to prepare their husband's cold lunch in a bundle, or *sorra,†* with bread, cheese—*ġobon maḥsul*—some handful of dried figs or whatever the Lord would provide because the farmers had to go to fields on the distant outskirts of the village, near l-Għadira ta' San Raflu,‡ and, you know, with that small donkey or mule of theirs, they could not afford to come home for lunch. That's why, even up to now, one can see those small rooms or huts in the countryside, to protect workers from the noonday sun, at the time when only mad dogs and Englishmen go out [smile], and in winter when they might be caught in a downpour. So . . . .

Micheline: You have mentioned the distance which separated the farmhouse from the fields. Could you explain the situation at that time, and say whether there has been perhaps some regrouping of lands since then?

Maria: The Gozitan farmer, you see, had and still has great difficulty because the fields are small and scattered on different estates. We, for example, have a very small one . . . *daqs il-mejda:*§ I could sit in the middle and start a meditation like a Mohammedan sitting on his carpet [laughter]! So you might have one field in the area of Tat-Tengħud,# the other near San Dimitri,[16] the other in Wardija, because through inheritance an estate would be divided and subdivided. Think of a family of seven children, all wanting their share of the cake!

In springtime, when these small fields look like a patchwork quilt, some brownish, some green, the scenery is marvelous, but the farmer, poor one, has a hard job to cope with scattered fields. And the means of transport was a donkey, a little one. Anyway these farmers were hard-working and they produced good crops. The crops were either corn, clover, summer fruit such as those exquisite melons—I am remembering

---

* Wetted, past participle of *xarrab* from *xorob*, which means "to drink."
† The food is wrapped up in a square piece of cloth.
‡ Saint Raphael Lake.
§ The size of a small round table.
# The area is named after a weed, *tengħud*, a species of *Euphorbia*.

the smell of them, *bettieħ ifuħ!**—or cotton, or cumin. I remember one year my father had a good crop of cumin seed, *zerriegħa tal-kemmun*, which fetched the GRAND PRICE OF TWENTY-SEVEN POUNDS!

Micheline: As far as cotton is concerned, was it still grown in Gozo when you were a child?

Maria: Yes, and you can be sure its cultivation involved a lot of work. For example, when the cotton plants were about four inches high, we had to go through all the small "holes"—*bejta*, we say—and leave only one out of four. You see, the farmer would generally put four seedpods in one *bejta*. Then if four plants came out, three had to be pulled up, *issaffi il-bjad*.† I felt pity for the strong plants I had to pull up, but one had to do it "as trade wants it," we say—*għax hekk titlob is-sengħa*. Later when the cotton plants grew up, the bindweed or *liblieba* would appear, and women had to pull it up. Then the plant would reach a height of about eighteen inches, and roundish pods, or *fosdoq*, would develop. These opened up and cotton—some red, some white—was nearly ready for picking. When I see pictures of American Indians cotton picking, I say to myself: "In Gozo, we used to do that on a small scale."

After cotton picking, there was more work at home for the women: in the evening, the farmers used to pile cotton pods in the entrance room of their houses. The ladies, who never went to a movie or disco, or a social, had to pull the cotton out of the pod. Then you would have to separate the seeds from the cotton wool, using the *reddiena tal-ħalġ*.‡ That *reddiena tal-ħalġ* was a source of fun for us children; sometimes we were allowed to turn it. But you see how hardworking those people were.

Micheline: Including women, who shared with men, as you have shown, a great part of the farming work, at least when needed at certain periods of the year. Now let's come back to the housewife we left at home, after she prepared breakfast, packed a cold lunch for her husband, perhaps helped in the harnessing of the mule or horse ready for going out in the fields, etc., so, apart from what has been mentioned already, what would you say she had to do as a housewife at home?

---

* "Melons are sweet smelling."

† "To clear the cotton pods." The process consists in pulling up some plants in order to keep the stronger ones.

‡ A wooden instrument used to separate cotton from its seed (*Maltese-English Dictionary*, s.v. *reddiena*).

Maria: More or less what the modern housewife does, with the exception that the modern one has many electrical gadgets which make housework much easier. In those days, they used to cook on a wood fire, or maybe on a small kerosene stove, a *kučiniera*. And EVERY DAY THEY HAD TO WASH! Because the farmers would generally wear thick woven or woolen clothes, and when they came back in the evening, they had to change after a day's work. Eh, eh! You are not sending your husband to work with yesterday's clothes full of dust, perspiration, and a foul smell— *ntiena*, we say in Maltese! Besides washing, sometimes you had to patch . . . to mend the flannel gussets. Oh! I hated that, but you are not going to say no when it is your own father's flannels.[17]

So you see how busy a woman had to be, and just imagine a bunch of kids, five or six, running about the house . . . . You had to clean them, to feed them, to cure those small ailments. Sometimes when a baby was seriously ill, the mother would take him to Qala sanctuary of the Immaculate Conception in San Kerrew crypt,[18] as you did, Mother . . . . [turns toward the photograph of her mother and addresses her in Maltese:] Ma, Ġanna tagħna, kemm ħdimt u batejt biex rabbejtna u ħallejtna l-iskola! Kont tqum mill ħamsa ta' filgħodu u wara dejjem sejra taħsel, issajjar, tiṭħen il-kafe, tagħlef it-tiġieġ, tinnegozja u tiġġebbed fuq il-bajd, jew tiġieġa, u kull tant titlob lil Madonna. Grazzi ħafna, Ma!*

---

* "Mummy, Ġanna of ours, how you worked and suffered to bring us up and let us have an education. You would get up at five in the morning and always be on the go: washing, cooking, grinding the coffee, feeding the hens, haggling to sell eggs or some poultry, and every now and then, you would pray to the Madonna! Thank you, Mummy."

The houses of emigrants in Gozo often display
where their residents have gone to settle.

Chapter 2

A Peasant Environment

S tarvation was nonexistent in Maria's peasant environment. Yet she remembers women coming, almost daily, from a fishing area to beg. As a child, she perceived nothing but the external signs of poverty (the beggars' dress) and the remedy (her mother's charity). She can now describe the well-known sequence of causes and effects: inadequate means of subsistence, early marriages, constant childbearing, infant mortality.

Contrasting with this image of stagnation was the vigor of young Gozitan men, including Maria's father, who started emigrating as far as Australia to find work. Gradually money coming from them contributed to the development of the island, thus reducing dependency on agriculture. Emigration also had a cultural impact. On his return home in 1921, Maria's father decided that his daughter had to go to school and, by a variety of ways, he aroused her taste for learning. Her mother reconciled herself to her husband's idea, although she would traditionally have expected her daughter to help at home. Nevertheless, she saw that Maria learnt and did "what should be done in any household." From both sides, the child was given exceptional, complementary training.

At home, tacit rules of decency were observed. Children were taken to relatives when the expectant mother was on the point of delivery. Within the extended family, Maria's father and mother are remembered as having behaved in a conciliatory, yet dignified, manner. And if she chose, the mother could have regular access to neighbors and friends in talking and lace-making sessions.

Family, neighbors, farming and religion were the constituents of what is presented as a quiet, simple, sometimes-cheerful, always-pious way of

life. Maria is concerned by the rapid growth in her society, a threat to the harmonious existence of the old days.

Micheline: Maria, it was undoubtedly a hard life. But the impression I get from what you have said is that at least you were relatively well fed, and I wonder whether it was the case with everybody on this island. Do you remember whether there were really poor people?

Maria: Yes. As a child, I did not realize that there were other families who did lack some of the necessities of life, but I remember that women, mostly from Xewkija, women poorly dressed, maybe with an old *faldetta*[*][19] drooping 'round their shoulders, would come into the village, knock on each door and ask for some kind of charity, and they would say: "*Għall-erwieħ! Għall-erwieħ!*"[20] That means, literally means: "For the sake of the souls (of purgatory, please give us some charity)." And my mother would give them either a piece of bread or some fruit, generally a small melon, or money—it might be a penny or even a halfpenny—and they would be very happy; and this happened many times. I think there must be a dozen of them coming nearly every day, and we took those *tallaba*,[†] as we called them, for granted.

In fact, I remember . . . you know, children like playacting, they imitate what they see, and I and my cousins used to put something on our heads looking like the old *faldetta*, and we would knock on the doors in our own street and say: "*Għall-erwieħ! Għall-erwieħ!*" Somebody even in fun would give us something to go on with our playacting and everybody would laugh, but that's beside the point. So, although we took that for granted, now I realize that in the village of Xewkija, the state of things was not as happy as the one in my immediate surroundings, that is, a small farming village of Kerċem. In Xewkija, they were mostly fishermen, with very small boats and fishing nets, and I realize their catch was small and poor, in those days without any mechanized fishing tackle.

And the families in Xewkija, for some reason, were larger and more numerous than those in other villages, and now, that reminds me,

---

[*] The diminutive of *falda* (Italian), which means the brim of a hat or train of a dress. The Maltese *faldetta*, or equivalent *għonella*, is a "rustic headgear of a village woman now out of use" (*Maltese-English Dictionary*, s.v. *għonella*).

[†] Beggars, people who live by begging (from *TLB*, which means "to request").

because I've read somewhere by somebody who studies anthropology, that in India in the poorer districts the families are more numerous [smile], and there was a breeder of pigs, an English breeder of pigs, who wanted to go deeper in this, and he organized something for his sexing of pigs so that it would bring about a state of things where the female pigs were not so well fed, and that meant he would have more pigs; they would breed better. The poorer they were, whether it is humanity, whether it is pigs . . . the poorer, the more they breed . . . . Now in Xewkija, they would marry very young—I do not know why—they would marry at sixteen, seventeen. So by the time the wife cannot have any more babies, you can imagine: the family would be thirteen, fourteen, and that means the poverty could not be alleviated easily. Of course in those days, there was no social service, there was none, and we had few charitable organizations, and what we'd call really rich people were nonexistent. There were only what we would call *is-sinjuri** in it-Tiġrija,[†] which was the main road in Victoria, but I think even those people just couldn't afford to alleviate that state of things over Gozo.

Incidentally, with these *tallaba* . . . it reminds me of a very happy event, because when a woman was going to give birth to a child, she wouldn't go to a clinic or to hospital. If you go to hospital for your childbirth, that would be considered . . . huum . . . as if you couldn't afford the basis and the equipment to have your baby born at home. So it's really the very poor people who went for their childbirth at *l-isptar*.[‡] *Tal-isptar* was looked down upon as something below your standard of living. It was only for the very low people [laughter]. Nowadays this idea of a hospital is totally eradicated and we have people from well-to-do families coming over from Malta in our Craig Hospital, because it is crowded in Malta and here they can have more personal and individual attention.

We come back to these *tallaba* and the time when my mother was going to give birth to one of my sisters, those baby sisters I hadn't the pleasure of living with, because they would die young: there was a certain

---

*Sinjur (feminine: *sinjura*; plural: *sinjuri*), an old-fashioned title of respect (*Maltese-English Dictionary*, s.v. *sinjur*), indicates wealthy people, usually represented by doctors, lawyers, or rich businessmen.

†Literally, "the racecourse" (from *ĠRJ*, "to run"); it refers here to the main street in Victoria, where horse and mule races still take place on feast days.

‡The hospital.

disease in connection with the intestines and, of course, there were no antibiotics in those days, and the women—I mean the mothers—had a bad, unhygienic custom of masticating the child's food in their own mouths, and they passed it on to the child by hand. I think that gave . . . that's why we had so many children dying young; it's a certain kind of fever in connection with the intestines.[21] And I remember my father was a carpenter, as I said before. He used to make coffins. I watched him doing the small white baby coffins. He did, on an average, two a week, and the church bells would ring, as we call it, a *frajha*; *frajha* really means "glory," because that's special when a baby dies; the church rings something beautiful, not something sad.[22] The *frajha*, we heard it twice a week, and for us children . . . it was always a delight to go to the house where the baby lay dead, and to follow this small procession [smile] . . . to church.

Micheline: But what was the happy event connected with the *tallaba*?

Maria: I'm coming to that. Now when my mother was giving birth to one of my baby sisters, she asked the *tallaba* of Xewkija, who would later be going to my aunt in Munxar, to take me, because I was still a child, to take me over to my aunt, and I would be staying with my aunt so that, as a child, I wouldn't see or hear anything unusual going on. Well, my aunt in Munxar, Aunt Lucia, was extremely well-off: she had fields, she had farms, she used to grow tobacco, and she had a terrace with lines and lines of tobacco, and I have seen that in Greece.

Micheline: How in Greece? Have you been on a tour there?

Maria: Yes, a few years ago. So in Greece, they have whole fields with lines like washing lines, with those big, big tobacco leaves drying up. My friends from Malta never realized what it was, and I had to explain . . . I felt so important because I could explain . . . [laughter] . . . in Greece!

Well, I stayed with my aunt and in the evening, we went on a sort of *bejt*. *Il-bejt* would be a flat roof and it was not dangerously high; in fact, we could reach the semiripe almonds, which we would eat! And I remember it was my first experience of listening to a GRAMOPHONE, because in the next street, there were people who had some business in Malta—in fact, we called them *tal-Ġermaniz**—who had happened to have a gramophone . . . and in the q-u-i-e-t summer evening . . . for me, as a child,

---

*Literally, "of the Germans," a family nickname. The reference to the Germans, Maria says, symbolizes certain features which were at that time attributed to them.

to hear that music from the gramophone was a totally new experience! So in connection with the childbirth . . . maybe my mother might be going through a difficult time as she was over thirty, and *I* was having the TIME OF MY LIFE [smile], living with this aunt, hearing music at night, eating on the roof, helping yourself to almonds because there was an especially tall almond tree.

So the *tallaba* for me had also that connection of taking care of me and transporting me . . . they were my guardian angels transporting me from the village of Kerċem across the valley, *il-Wied tax-Xlendi,** going up to a place where Professor Aquilina's[23] aunt used to keep turkeys, and I had to be careful not to put on a red dress because the turkeys would come up doing "KWA-KWA-KWA-KWA-KWA-KWA-KWA-KWA" all around me and on to my Aunt Lucia's farmhouse.

Micheline: Therefore, Maria, apart from the happy memories associated in your mind with the *tallaba*, these people were at that time synonymous with extreme poverty, weren't they?

Maria: Well, you could say that. Later on, when I grew up, I realized that in Victoria,[24] in the town, that is, the standard of living was a bit better than that in the country, because in the village the people had a hard time: you know, they had to get up at four o'clock in the morning, work out-of-doors, whether it was hot sun, whether it was cold; but in Victoria they had soft jobs, government jobs, poorly paid of course, but they used to have—the men used to have—coats on, and shoes, and stockings, and the women were better dressed than those in the villages. In fact, we had a saying: if you had a dress of an especially harsh color, you'd say: *Dik il-libsa raħlija!*"†

Micheline: And that was pejorative, wasn't it?

Maria: Of course. But my mother never wanted me to be dressed in a *libsa raħlija*. She always had the best clothes for me; she had my clothes from her French aunt in Algiers,[25] and even for my brother: he would have a sailor's dress, a sailor's suit rather, a *baħrija*.‡ When I grew up, we had the English catalogue, which was common in Victoria, and we ordered especially the school pinafore because that was the uniform—we didn't have a uniform at school, but we had a white pinafore—and my

---

*The valley of Xlendi.

† "That dress is countrified (with too showy colors)."

‡ Relating to the sea, hence a sailor's suit.

mother used to work lovely crochet with cotton thread, and she would put a piece of lace on the sleeves; she was always proud of her crochet lace. Those pinafores were specially made for maids; you know in England they have . . . generally the maids wore dark blue or black, and they used to have an apron with embroidery very stiffly starched, and a cap to go with that.

Micheline: I'm sure you were as neat and smart as a young schoolgirl from the city. Now, Maria, can you explain what you meant when you said the city people had, in comparison with the country people, a better standard of living?

Maria: Well, they were poor, but outwardly they had better houses—no sanitation at all in those days—but they had better houses, a better way of living, because with their little pay, they would go and get their green vegetables from the market, their fish from the market, so that people in Victoria were, to my eyes, *sinjuri,* or well-off. But actually there were very few people whom you could call well-off. The teachers . . . a teacher's salary was sixpence a day—you can imagine on sixpence a day . . . my father was a carpenter and he used to earn two shillings a day,[26] and I remember my mother sending me as a child—I wasn't self-conscious at all—she would say: "Go to that family So-and-So." She called that family by nickname—in the village, we were all known by nickname [laughter] and she'd say: "Please remind them that they owe your father some money." Because they were so poor . . . . Otherwise they would have paid as fast as they could: it was your family pride not to have any debt whatever. So they had ordered those small coffins we were speaking about, or they would order a small table or a window, and they wouldn't have the money ready to pay.

Nowadays it's the other way about: everybody is proud to pay by installments. Now they want to keep up with the Joneses, and they order all sorts of costly MAHOGANY kitchens. One thousand pounds for a mahogany kitchen which they don't use! It's just there for show, and they have a functional kitchen in a garage, or a room in the backyard, but that's in 1987, and so on. I'm speaking of 1925, 1927 . . . when people would pay as fast as they can to keep their heads up.

Micheline: In the twenties, your father had already returned from Australia. Do you know the circumstances in which he, like other young Gozitans, had decided in the previous decade to go and work in Australia?

Maria: In 1916, you know, there was a war on; it was the First World War, 1914-18, and that meant misery and hardships for the Gozitans especially. In Malta, it wasn't so bad because warships were coming in and out, and that created a kind of affluence in the country for the villages and the towns encircling the main harbor. But in Gozo, when people heard that you could go to Australia, some of the men decided to emigrate. Now to go to Australia in those days was like going to the moon [laughter]! They had no schooling, no atlas, no idea of geography whatever, and the means of transportation being literally nonexistent. Well, they finally decided to emigrate, because they heard that in Australia they were earning as much as TWELVE SHILLINGS A DAY . . . . At least for my village and for the next, which we would call hamlet, Santa Lucia, we had many men who decided to emigrate. There was a man called Wistin Gatt who knew a little English.[27] So that encouraged them to accompany him.

And of course there was no sanitary inspection, no proper passport; they just . . . I think it was the Cook's Agency, a man from Cook's Agency—I'm referring to Thomas Cook—who came over from Malta and he arranged the haphazard way of transporting the emigrants—"convicts," as my friends say more or less—of transporting these Gozo men over to Australia or some way around it, and there was a boat, a French boat, really a cargo boat with only enough accommodation for about forty passengers, and they had to carry live animals—because there was no freezing system in those days; we are speaking of 1916—and they had to carry their fuel—the fuel again was coal or wood, whatever they used—and their fodder . . . .

Anyway people had started to emigrate in Australia, and there they had a very hard time. They didn't find the Utopia they were looking for, and some of them came back, but most of them finally settled there, and bit by bit, things got better for the new emigrés, and I know people who buy . . . now the Maltese community is very well-off, and they have very good standard houses.[28] You'll come across people coming from Australia for holidays and they speak about their children going to college, to university, doing a soft job like computer, clerks and so on. In this very room where I'm sitting at Marsalforn, my SUMMER RESIDENCE [laughter], and there came about two years ago a very good-looking man, a well-educated man called Charlie Apap. In fact, the person, another chap who brought him, gave me a curriculum vitae of this man—he said: "So that you know the man"—and that showed that he was a councillor, a millionaire. He was a millionaire, although he didn't say that. He was Somebody in Australia. And we have doctors in Australia, we have legal men in Australia, we have three or four members of Parliament!

So, you see, the Maltese community in Australia . . . and they've kept their traditions, mostly their Christian traditions; they still adhere to their Catholic prayers. I'm not speaking 100 percent, but most of them still keep up their beliefs, the Catholic beliefs and their religious customs, and they like to baptize their children and have weddings in church. Well, it's not 100 percent because I'm ashamed to say that in Australia, some of them are called the *qulla** men; *qulla* men means they swear by Alla. Alla is God. "*Qulla! qulla! qulla!*"—it's a swearword bringing the holy name of God in vain. I remember one Australian man had a vacancy at his shop or in his restaurant, wherever it was, and he said, "Wanted . . . ," a man, a bartender or dishwasher or something like that. And he said: "NO MALTESE WANTED." And the priest, a friend of mine—priests, every now and then, go down to Australia nowadays to visit their relatives and to visit the community of their own village, because it seems there is a second village in Australia which is very similar to the village from which they originally came—so the priest said [tone of confidence]: "Mr So-and-So, why you don't want Maltese?" The Maltese are known for their . . . they are hardworking. But he said: "Because they SWEAR so much. I don't want a qullaman here!" But then, a Gozitan man came along—he wanted that job: "I'm not Maltese; I'm a Gozitan." So the other said: "You can have the job!"

Micheline: Maria, would you say that in Gozo the economic situation of the people 'round about you was gradually improving through emigration? Not at the beginning—in the twenties or thirties—naturally, but later in the fifties?

Maria: Yes, things started to brighten up, let us say after the war. We had new schools everywhere, and, you know, education helps a lot. The people were being educated. We still had, and we still have, illiterate people, especially the very old ones, but on the whole things started . . . . We had money coming from Australia, money coming from America,

---

*Qulla! is an "exclamation expressing impatience, irritation or anger, a euphemism for (*ħa)qq* Alla, the use of which would make an objectionable swearword" (*Maltese-English Dictionary*, s.v. *qulla*). The softened word *qulla* is coined after *ħaqq* Alla (literally, "justice of God"): it is composed of the last consonant, *q*, of *ħaqq* plus *ulla*, "a phonetic distortion of Alla" (*Maltese-English Dictionary*).

money coming . . . especially in the eastern part of Gozo. Now in Malta, they started the dockyards, and from Nadur and Qala and Għajn Sielem, people would get a job on merchant ships, and that was always a very well-paid job. So one thing links to another: we had good houses being built, and building means a job for the builders, for the stonecutters, for the stone dressers, for the carpenters, for the floor tile-making—we have some lovely patterned tiles, *madum bid-disinn**—and in most of the houses, you can see these beautifully tiled upper rooms, and English people who come to settle here and buy these old houses, they generally like to keep it as it is, to keep the tiles with the patterns; and it's very easy to wash, very easy to clean and all that . . . .

Micheline: Maria, you have underlined the beneficient role of schooling in general. Now I would like to know your own experience: I mean how—it was in the early twenties—you entered school yourself.

Maria: When I started going to my village school—not my village school, because when I was young there was no village school in Ker-ċem—I remember my father used to put me astride his shoulders, and carry me up the hill behind Saint Augustine across the Saint Augustine Square, and take me to my teacher, Miss Dolores Camenzuli; she died recently . . . . The primary school was in Vajringa Street—it's still there. So my father, who understood how useful it is, how useful education is for anybody, said: "Maria has to go to school . . . . We'll take her to Victoria." My mother was more practical. She said: "I have twins"— because my brother Anton was twin with Sylvia—"I have twins. I have to do all this housework, and Maria walks up and down . . . . Why doesn't she stay here, and help with the housework?" But my father was of the opinion that education was a must, and I'm grateful to my father, Salvu [tone of tenderness], who decided that I should be educated, because I'm of the opinion that parents who give their children a good education are giving them something that will last throughout their life, and it's better than thousands of money, of houses or land . . . .

Micheline: Quite. Now besides the education that you received at school, would you say that your own family environment contributed to your personal further development, and if so, in what way?

Maria: It's true I lived in a farmhouse at the end of the village, at Ta' Ganton, not the center of the village at all, but I think it provided for

---

*Literally, floor tiles with "designs."

me a rich environment which helped me to get on, and to get on with
my schooling later on, to understand people. First of all, I had my
family: my father had been in Australia, and when he came back, he was
always speaking of his experience of Australia, of how he lived, first in
New Caledonia[29] and later on, how he had to work so hard in the bush,
pulling up stumps of trees to level the land, so that they would lay down
sleepers for the new railway lines; very often he would get out an atlas
and show us the route from Australia to Malta, which took about three
months, and he would point out to several cities, especially in East
Africa; and he said they came across a tribe who understood; they could
dialogue with them because their language was very much like Maltese.
It must be where Addis Ababa is because there the language is . . . not
similar, of course, but perhaps the roots are also Semitic in origin.

Well, he used to tell us about these people; he used to tell us about
the people in Singapore who would come swimming along the boat, and
the people of the boat would throw pennies, coins, and they would dive
for them, and stories of that sort . . . . And that formed me, opened up
and BROADENED my horizon quite beyond Ta' Ġanton, quite beyond
the village, quite beyond Malta. And it started my understanding the
outer world through my father's stories, my father's small lessons, and it
also started my liking for books. I understood that books were one's
friends, with a storehouse of interesting facts. My father also taught me
to handle things like putting up a picture on the wall, although we had
not the right frame for it, like making an exercise book out of the papers
you had. He taught me, when I was very young, the alphabet by writing
it on the back of the door, of the door of the room, and you can be sure
the children at school were very jealous of me and they would say:
"Eh . . . she gets good marks because her father helps her, because her
father teaches her!" In the village, you couldn't imagine a father doing
the part of the teacher at all; that was only the part of the teacher,
because most of parents were at that time illiterate, more or less.

For my mother, who had always a NEAT drawer—my mother was A-
one for neatness in her drawer, besides her white folded handkerchiefs,
besides her neatly folded aprons—I never can do that; my drawers are all
in a muddle; she had those black-covered prayer-books, and sometimes
I used to go through them and read a little. They were books mostly
written by Monsignor Luigi Vella; besides being a good priest, he also
was a writer. So with my father's geographical, social learning, my

mother's religious books, my mother teaching me how to be PRACTI-
CAL and how to work about the house, although I was supposed to be
playing like other children, but she saw to it that I was learning and
doing what should be done in any household. I remember once, during
the midday break—because the midday break was two hours long, so we
would go home for lunch and return at about ten minutes to two for the
afternoon session—once I left home at about one o'clock . . . hum . . . and
I went to play beads; we used to have a small hole in the playground and
a sort of . . . we played beads with one finger throwing the beads at the
hole, and I was playing with my friends. She—I mean my mother— left
her home, and for a woman, to leave her home at one o'clock was . . . she
came quietly to the schoolyard, she took me by the hand, and she said:
"Did you forget that you should have ground the coffee before coming to
school?" So then we went back . . . I didn't object [said in a low voice,
then rhythm becoming quicker]. She shut me up in the big kitchen, I
ground all the coffee, and there was a big *rotolo** of it—all the coffee that
had to be ground—and I said: "I have finished the coffee, Mother" [shyly],
and she said: "Now you can go to school" [calmly]. THAT was a lesson
I never forgot. She saw that I was getting the best at the school, but she
also saw that the little things that a woman should be doing in her
home, I was learning to do them when they should be done.

So I think I got the best of both worlds. My father, although a carpenter, gave me the scholarly side, and my mother gave me the practical
side. I think I got along, I managed to do . . . [laughter] to do very well
in both aspects. I tried them both, because during your life you can be
philosophical, you can be—how shall I say?—a scholar, but you have to be
very functional, especially in Gozo where we say: *"Għal kull għadma, hemm
mitt kelb."* That is: "For every bone, we have a hundred dogs." We have
to be very functional, and very practical, and very worldly wise, but I'm
speaking about the environment in the home . . . and there was no
quarreling in the home, there were no rude words, there was no bad
language, there was no indecency . . . the children never saw what they
were not expected to see. In fact, at childbirth, I was taken to my aunt's,
as I said before, or a nearer . . . I remember when Anton was born, Anton
was a twin, and I remember one winter night I was put out of bed,

---

*Or *ratal*, a weight of about eight hundred grams.

wrapped up in a navy coat with gold buttons, and taken to my Uncle Daniele's house; of course I slept on. Then, in the early morning, they took me back again to my house, and they said: "You have a new brother and a new sister." And that was Anton and Sylvia, and I quite remember the long procession of godfathers—we must have two godfathers and two godmothers—the midwife, a woman in charge of function at church, and my uncles, and somebody else from the family, and we went in a long procession to the church of Saint Gregory because the babies were expected to be baptized either on the same day when they were born, or the day after, and of course the mother would be too weak; she would stay in the home. When they came back, we would have a small reception, I think . . . with *biskuttini** and drinks.

I remember also very vividly it was wintertime, and if you had babies, you had to wash not only their napkins next to their lower part of the body, but they were wrapped up, completely wrapped up: it was only their hands which were showing and their face. So when it was the time to bathe and change the baby, the bed would be literally covered with white—they were all white; there was no color—with white squares of some locally woven cotton and some imported, but you had to wash the WHOLE . . . some eight big squares of clothing besides the actual soiled napkins, and these were put in a place 'round that poor baby. They had what you'd call a bandage, but the bandage would be six inches wide and very strong—it was finely woven and it was called *fisqija*†—and it would go 'round and 'round this baby. In my garden, I come across a snail which looks like a miniature baby wrapped up in a *fisqija*, and that reminds me of my sister and brother babies.

So that was the immediate environment. Outside, of course, I had my other cousins with whom I played at shopkeeping: the groceries would be broken stone, broken pieces of glass and things like that, but we played at keeping shop; also we played at being mothers—we would have babies, homemade babies made of pieces of cloth, so that they would be our babies. And I remember once we had a neighbor . . . she was rather stupid, and I couldn't stand her stupidity—you wouldn't think as a child I did something. I took her baby doll and threw it down the well! At the back of my mind, I think I was drowning that stupid girl whom I

---

* Biscuits.
† Swaddling bands.

couldn't stand [smile]. I remember this very well. Then, of course, they had to bring a special *rampil*. A *rampil* was made of iron; it had three iron hooks with which you would bring up the pail, if the pail just lost control of the rope. So they had to clean the well, because we wouldn't leave that piece of ugly rags down there.

Another way of playing was, maybe, with beads, as I said, and at Christmastime we had hazelnuts, plenty of hazelnuts, and we played with that . . . *gestelli*, we called it; we never thought what we were speaking of: *gestelli* were castles, because you build three, and then on top of 'em, you put another small castle, and you throw a small piece of stone, and if you manage to pull the castle, you would be winning those hazelnuts. That's for the environment.

Of course I was living among farmers, and I would be happy when it was time for digging up potatoes because it was like a TREASURE HUNT: you had the plants and you never knew, when you pulled up the plant, what you would be finding. Sometimes you had FOUR lovely potatoes, sometimes you had a small one . . . . For me, that was a treasure hunt.

Now speaking of potatoes brings me to some very . . . [hesitant] you can say . . . Ha! [smile] . . . to something which our Uncle Daniele did once because he was jealous of my mother . . . . I remember this quite vividly: at the back of the house, we had a field: *nofs-siegh*.* *Nofs-siegh* is a measure for fields, but for me, *nofs-siegh* was the name of the field; it never meant any measure at all.[30] And we had a lovely crop of potatoes. Of course, in the evening, the crop was there. The morning after, I remember that it was all muddy, and the plants were not there any longer . . . . Daniele had pulled up all the water of the well so that the plants would be easy to pull up. He pulled 'em all up, walked further up, and planted them in his field which hadn't any green before. And there was HIS(!) CROP OF POTATOES which had been grown in the autumn . . . [laughter]. It was a spiteful thing, but at the same time, it was very clever to get plants pulled up and planted in a new place. Of course [slowly said], my father was intelligent and wise enough, he didn't make any objection about it because you would get into trouble and a

---

*Literally, "half one *siegh*"; this is equivalent to 18.74 square meters (see *Maltese-English Dictionary*, s.v. *kejl*).

fight would be the result. So we took care that we would be on the lookout for further trouble, but that one, my Uncle Daniele, everybody knew him: Daniele Ta' Pantu was somebody you had better . . . [laughter] avoid.

Micheline: Weren't you, as a child, frightened by him?

Maria: Yes. I remember very vividly one day—perhaps my father was in Malta or somewhere else, I don't know. Well, my father's carpenter shop was always down the village in another part of the village. So my mother, maybe she felt a bit by herself when he was away . . . . I remember once she said: "Let's put the *stanga** in the door." The *stanga* was a thick piece of iron, with which we fastened the door at night. Now during the day, that would be off, but she said: "Let's put the *stanga* against the door, and let's put the sacks of animal fodder against the door." It was like a barricade. We barricaded because . . . I don't know what was the cause, but I have the feeling she was afraid that Daniele was angry for something: Daniele was very jealous of us, seeing us get on in life.

But my mother used her intelligence, and she knew that you must have friends, and you must have people to help you. So she had friends a little beyond our house whom we reached through the back. I said that we had fields extending quite a long distance, so we would pass through the backyard, cross the fields, and I remember we had a fig tree. Every time I passed that fig tree I thought of Jesus, looking for the figs, but the tree wouldn't have any, and he would be disappointed. Anyway . . . she used to cross over our fields and some did not belong to us, but had a narrow path because we always were careful not to tread on other people's crops. And my mother used to go and gossip a little, and work the lace.

You never spent any time idle in those days. A woman was always doing something, either cooking or washing or weaving or sewing, stitching by hand, since they had no sewing machine, but they certainly had to make patches. I remember making a patch; for a girl, to know how to patch was a must, and it was not looked down on you if you had a clean dress but patched. You would be looked down if you didn't do your hair nicely, or if you were dirty or had dirty dress. But if you kept yourself tidy and CLEAN and even patched all over, nobody minded you.

---

*Crossbar.

And this reminds me of something beautiful, later, very later on in life. I once met—believe it or not—a Polish general at Nina Fitzgerald's party. Nina, you know, she comes from Poland, and she often gives dinner parties and her house is full of distinguished guests. Somehow I made friends with that Polish general who sent me a big box of chocolates from London, and I remember he was neatly dressed, but on his shirt, he had a little square of darning: his shirt was darned because this Polish general couldn't have a good pension . . . . The government in Poland looked down upon him—that's why he lived in London; he couldn't go and live in his own place; he would be sent to prison the moment he would land in Poland, and that's why Nina Fitzgerald had always a crowd of Polish poor . . . Polish gentry, and she fed them, she did her best, and I think that's an A-one, maybe for charity.

Now BACK TO OUR TALE OF LONG AGO . . . [laughter]. So my mother would spend a bit of time with her friends across the fields on the other side. In fact, yesterday—and we are in 1987—I was invited by my very nice friend, Micheline, for a bit of dinner down on the beach, and we went to the Victoria, and next to our table, there was a nice family, some coming from Australia, some living on Gozo. There was one whom I didn't recognize, I'm sorry, and she said: "Maria, I am Kelina's daughter," and for me Kelina was somebody whose house I used to go to, and she was one of my mother's best friends . . . they would be in a row; sometimes the lady of the house wouldn't have enough chairs for everybody, but that didn't matter; they would sit akimbo on the floor like that [gesture], like the Arab people, I think . . . with the lace, you know, the lace as a sort of longish cushion—*trajbu*,* we call it—and you had to support it on something, support it against a wall; and they had those lovely bobbins, and they would WORK THE LACE; their hands would be busy AND their tongues would be also busy! Somebody later would bring a pitcher of cold water, and they would have a drink. That was a kind of social life.[31]

Micheline: So, Maria, the women would be working the lace, the men would be somewhere in the fields or at their trade. Now what about you children?

Maria: We children played; we had to invent, sort of, our own kind

---

* A lace pillow.

of play, maybe *il-passju:** we would draw a rectangle with chalk either in the yard or on the street, because in those days the streets were safe . . . no cars, no buses, no traffic!

Micheline: Then everybody would go home and prepare the evening meal, I guess.

Maria: Yes. Maybe they would exchange the little amount of green vegetables they had; they would give you a *kromba.*† *Kromba* is a funny name; in agriculture, it's called *ġidra.* Well, it was a must to have a *ġidra* and a piece of *qargħa*—gourd, red gourd—and some potatoes, of course, and some dried beans, and I assure you that *minestra*, or soup—call it what you will!—especially with a local cheese in it . . . humm! I still do it and my friends, who now are international, I'm proud to say, like it very much. I have all sorts of friends coming in and out. Well, I offer them a bit of *minestra*, and they all like it. So those not-poor people, but relatively not well-off, I think were a nice community, and they were happy, and when you come across some of them—just some of them are still alive—they all say the same thing: "We were not rich, we hadn't any fridges, we hadn't any car, we hadn't any television, we hadn't any THOUSAND-pounds English oak kitchens [laughter]. We had only one *kuċiniera*, or a very primitive sort of fireplace, but we were MUCH HAPPIER than we are" [each syllable being stressed].

And we used to laugh. We used to tell clean jokes. Now nobody seems to care for jokes any longer. They only watch TV and they're like . . . I don't know what to say. Their minds seem to have stopped completely except if the subject regards politics, or [laughter] the means to fill your pocket the easiest way out or . . . [laughter] well, in that direction, their minds didn't stop. But as for dialoguing and making life more meaningful, there are very few people to come across . . . but I'm lucky I have one or two friends whose mind is active, and who still make life meaningful with the small beautiful things of life, and I still can have a good laugh at myself, and I can share a joke with the people who can UNDERSTAND the joke.

Now it was my environment as a child [in a melodious tone] . . . and

---

*A children's game roughly similar to a pavement game known as hopscotch (*Maltese-English Dictionary* s.v. *passju*).

†"A kind of esculent colewort, vegetables of the nature of turnips . . ." (*Maltese-English Dictionary*, s.v. *kromba*).

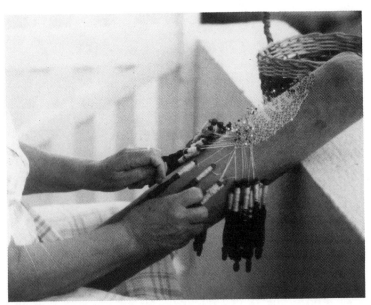

A woman making lace in the traditional way.

it was a rich environment, and predominating all, your family life, your neighbors' life, your farming life, AND your religious life, because religion—CHURCHGOING WAS PART AND PARCEL OF YOUR LIFE. Since the first day, at least the next day you are born up to the day you are buried—and you didn't resent it—it was part and parcel of your life, and we were churchgoers nearly every day, as I said before; people get up—hardworking people—at five o'clock—the men used to get up a bit earlier but the women . . . by five o'clock, everybody would be out of bed, and first they would go to church to hear mass. Then they would start the work of the day. There were stated times for prayers: the Angelus at eight o'clock, at twelve o'clock, and the Ave Maria. And that reminds me of Millet's beautiful picture where there are those people . . . I think they are picking up potatoes, but they have a special wheelbarrow we don't have in our country, and they put the sack on it; and I said these people were more . . . [laughter] intelligent, or they were softer than our local people. Well, Millet's *Angelus* for me reminds me of our people all stopping—mind you—stopping, and the men would put off their caps or hats, or whatever it was, and they would recite the Angelus.

Chapter 3

The Social Scene in Gozo

According to Maria, a clear demarcation separated the various strata of the Gozitan society of her childhood, from the poorer to the better-off: farm laborers (hardly above the beggars) in a state of dependency with no property of their own; farmers paying rent in kind; craftsmen more independent (but some had to emigrate); civil servants and business people in town, wearing shoes and good clothes; *sinjuri* in their beautiful dwellings in Victoria, the capital of the island.

Social structure was not a source of conflict. The poor were supported by those who could afford it, and modern jealousy was unknown. It was perhaps between town, where nepotism was practised, and village, with no opportunities, that rivalry could exist.

The clergy, a class of its own, well educated, unobtrusively charitable, living in a state of poverty sometimes, were dedicated to their work among the people.

With the visit of peddlers, including the colorful, slightly frightening "Turks," excitement came occasionally into the relatively enclosed space of the village. Health inspectors also visited to deal with undulant fever and tuberculosis. The fear, almost a phobia, of tuberculosis was general. Precautions were taken in particular before concluding marriages. Nowadays, Maria regrets, people get married without knowing each other and soon separate.

Among the *sinjuri*, language, more than housing and dress, was the sign of distinction: looking down upon the Maltese dialect, they spoke Italian and regarded it as the official cultural language. The fact that a village girl could pass a difficult Italian matriculation was, in their eyes, a promising event at the beginning of the thirties. Maria did not then

46

fully understand what political forces were at work. She does now, and proceeds, in defense of her native language, to show the flexibility of spoken Maltese in different sociolinguistic contexts.

Micheline: Maria, now that you have made me familiar with the kind of life you had as a child, surrounded with farmers, I would like to know more about the Gozitan society in general, as far as you can somehow visualize it as it was at that time. You already spoke about the *tallaba***** who would come from a fishing area and beg in your village. You have shown that the city dwellers had a softer life than the peasants. You also mentioned the existence of a few well-off families in Victoria. Now can you give me a sort of comprehensive picture of the whole population, with its various strata?

Maria: At that time, the line of demarcation was very clear with regards to social status. At that time, we had—apart from the *tallaba*—a small percentage of poor people, *il-foqra*;[†] they were farm laborers without any property of their own; they were, as we'd call them, "farmhands" working for the real farmer. They were people who, for some reason or other, had never inherited land, or who were not intelligent enough to somehow better their style of living and their standard of living, but as I said before, that was a very small percentage. They went about barefoot, not very well clothed, but you can be sure everybody had a house, whatever shape, whatever conveniences it had; everybody had a roof, where to go. Nobody was homeless, and it was an understood act of charity and obligation that those who had MORE than they actually needed would help these poor people. People—rather well-off families—would give them, for example, food or clothes; they might help them with the upbringing of a child; they might help them even with the education of a child, because, somehow, if there was a bright boy in a poor family, they couldn't afford just to send their boy to a secondary school; they just had no money for shoes and books. At that time, there were no social services so the middle-class people somehow helped, and you always come across a kindhearted family who would help in the education of the child.

---

*Beggars (see Chapter 2).
†Plural of *fqir*, which means "poor."

Next to that, we would have laborers, farmers, maybe servants—not civil servants, but servants working for the real upper class—we called 'em *sinjuri*, the rich ones. The farmers, even those who worked their own fields, were lower class because the fields were leased. And whether it was a good year or not, near the time of Santa Maria, these farmers had to go either to the *baruni** in Malta—because we had many landowners from Malta—one had to go to the *baruni*, or to somebody else from Malta,[32] or to a priest—the priest wouldn't be administrating his own property; he would be the administrator for a church or a congregation, because we had religious communities like the Carmelites, who had extensive tracts of land—and the farmers here, every year, had to go to pay rent; or they would pay in kind, that is, take animals or poultry, according to their contract. So we had that type of laborer—farmers who, especially when it was a bad year—for farmers, it seems always it was not so good, because if the products or the crops are good and in large quantities, then the price of their crops would fall; if it was a bad year, then they would have nothing to sell. So that was a class by itself . . . .

Then there were the tradesmen, like carpenters, like plasterers, like tile-workers. These should have been well paid, at least a bit better than the farmers—the small farmers—but because, over all the country, there was no affluence, they were paid on low scales; for example, my father, who was a carpenter by trade, and who was a very good one, and he was known not only in the village, but even outside the village such as in Nadur. In fact, my father made the school windows at Nadur: those are on the louver system . . . I always look at them because they were special windows then, but he would only earn a few shillings a day, and that was a good pay.

Next to that, we had the teachers, the postmen, the civil servants and the businessmen. These were found mostly in the town . . . and sometimes I wondered why in the town—because there were brains, there were brains in the villages, but because in the villages farming was the main source of livelihood, those who had children thought it was a waste of time sending your child WALKING, walking, walking to Victoria— that is, to school—twice a day, not keeping him or her at home to care for the sheep and the goats, or to help the farmers . . . it would be considered

---

*A baron.

as a waste of time, getting educated. Now it's quite the contrary [laughter], I can assure you.

And why were these people in Victoria, again? I'm not sure about this, but I had the feeling that it was not all through exams what sort of career you choose, but rather on the sort of friends or relatives you have, who can pave the way for you; and in the village, we always had a saying for that: "*Dak daħal mit-tieqa*;* that is: "He didn't go in for the job through the door, but through the window." And that label stuck to him for life. These types of people were recognized easily because they were wearing a jacket, of course shirt and tie, and shoes; shoes were something that marked you if you wore them daily, because in the village everybody had shoes, and very good ones, but those were kept for the *festa*, for baptism, for weddings, well . . . for special family occasions. They would wear for the feet what we call *qorq*.[33] *Il-qorq* was some kind of sandals; these were not imported; these were made by the shoemaker, either in the village—some of the villages boasted of their own shoemaker—and we would go, because we lived in Kerċem, a ten-minutes walk—we would go to the shoemaker in Victoria—we called them cobblers because we also very often went there to have our shoes mended—not only our shoes: we never threw anything away.

I remember there was a tinsmith, *il-landier*, in Victoria, very near Sabina Square, and we used to take our pots, our basins, our big washtubs, our chamber pots sometimes . . . if there was a small hole, you wouldn't throw it away! We took it to the tinsmith in Victoria and repaired it as best we could so that it would serve you more. Sometimes the tinsmith would come 'round, and he would put up a stove, and the people would go to him; he would sharpen their knives . . . I can remember a man who used to frame our small pictures; he would bring a sort of carpentry shop in a box; it wouldn't be—how shall I say?—a nice job, a finished job, but we would be pleased by what he did for us.

Now we come to the real upper class, whom we called the *sinjuri*. This was a very low percentage, and they lived in a part of Victoria; at that time, it was called it-Tiġrija. For us, it-Tiġrija, which literally means the racecourse, and it was a racecourse for the public races at Santa Maria; it's now called Republic Street. So, *is-sinjuri* lived in it-Tiġrija, which meant

---

*Literally, "that one entered through the window."

the apex of streets with very good houses: they have symmetric, traditional frontages with a big closed balcony in the middle, two wrought-iron, finely wrought-iron balconies at the side, of course on the first floor; on the ground floor, you'd have a huge door; when it opened, you saw what we'd call a *boxxla.** Il-boxxla* is a glass door—somebody calls it *antiporta*—before the door itself . . . [smile]. Now these people had to have some protection.

They also had a small gate—not like the English ones, but a small gate—and it had a specific purpose, because that stopped the goats from coming into the entrance hall. What goats? you would ask, in it-Tiġrija, of all places! Because in those days, some of the farmers who kept goats and sheep for milk would take a number of goats up to Victoria, and the servants—mostly the servants—went out with containers, enamel containers, to buy milk, and you would see the milkman actually milking his goat for you there, so the goats, hum . . . especially if they smell some kind of food, they would like to go in and see what's in there. So that specific gate had the purpose to not only keep the people, the inquisitive people, out, but mainly it would keep the goats out.

As I said, there would be the main door, and this was flanked by huge windows, not horizontal such as those we have today, but more vertical; the height would be larger than the width. In the summer, they had venetian blinds, all painted green, to keep the flies out and to get in a bit of breeze, a bit of cold air.

There was another thing that distinguished the *sinjuri*, apart from their houses with the beautiful windows: sometimes one had a peep through the lace curtain at the *vetrina*, a sort of showcase, and you could see glass- and silverware! In fact, the people down in Republic Street—called T'Ettru because their father was called Ettore, so we called them T'Ettru[34]—which were in my opinion very well-off and very well known, both because their father was a doctor and because they were lucky enough to get . . . they won what was called the Derby, which was the Irish sweepstake . . . . Well, when I was a student in the secondary school in Victoria, and the school was housed in one of these lovely houses we've just been mentioning, we often walked past the windows to see the wonders of the dining room of this *vetrina*. At least I, and I think

---

*Inner glazed door, generally within a wooden frame behind the main street door" (*Maltese-English Dictionary*, s.v. *boxxla*).

the others, we never felt any jealousy; we never thought that we were less well-off. Now today, that's over; they . . . everyone wants to be up with the Joneses, but that's beside the point.

Micheline: Would you say that, besides housing, there were other typical features or symbols which characterized the *sinjuri?*

Maria: The *sinjuri* were also marked by the way they talked. Most of them talked in Italian. I once went to buy some knitting wool to make a cardigan for my brother—because he was going to university, to the university in Malta, and so I wanted the best of the best for him—so I went to T'Ambroġ.* T'Ambroġ was another well-to-do family, and I remember the old lady sitting on a rocking chair, and I said: "I want some knitting wool and I want the best because it's for my brother, and he's going to Malta University," and that *sinjura* said: "In the university of Malta? They are teaching them MALTESE . . . Maltese is *zalza Russa!*"† [sarcastic tone of voice]. At that time, I didn't understand, but later I understood that she was fighting, supporting the cause of the Italianites, as we called them, the Nazionalisti,‡ the Mizzi, the Enrico Mizzi clan who wanted Italian to continue being the cultural and official language in Malta.[35] Sometimes even in churches—believe it or not— well, we had yearly spiritual exercises . . . there is a small church in Palma Street where my brother kept his offices later on—well, there were special spiritual exercises in Italian for the *sinjuri*, as if they had a special soul, cleaner or more refined than that [laughter] of the other people! This is totally absurd, but that was the case. So you knew the *sinjuri* from their houses, from their clothing, from their way of speech.

Micheline: Would they also speak their own language, I mean Maltese?

Maria: Anyway, if they spoke Maltese, it would be the polished Maltese—the way it is written—because in other parts of the town of Victoria and in the villages, we had a dialect which was richer, you may be sure; it was richer in its feelings and the way it describes things, it describes your emotions; I still like it with its different shades of pronunciation. For example, I come from the village, most of my neighbors speak the village dialect, so I speak that with my friends and neighbors because it would be . . . I would have a sense of superiority—they don't

---

* A family nickname.
† Literally, "Russian sauce," an equivalent of the phrase "Russian salad."
‡ Nationalists.

like that—so I speak like this: *"Id-dôr trejt ħafnej xôl"** . . . [with strong, countrylike pronunciation]. I walk up—a ten minutes' walk—to Victoria and they speak a sort of . . . better-pronounced way, and it says: *"Id-dar trid ħafna xogħol"†* . . . [sounding soft and refined]. If I walk further up, another five minutes further up, and I meet my colleagues or people from Malta, or people who knew me as a head teacher—because that's my job, and at school a teacher always speaks the well-pronounced Maltese—I would change in . . . *"Id-dar trid ħafna xogħol"* [sounding soft and refined], and I skip from one to the other automatically; there's not a switch [smile]. I put on, or off; I make the change—not only me, most of my friends; in fact, there was somebody, and he was an assistant director of education, Mr. Peter Paul Grech; he had been to Rome and he was speaking in a small group: there were Maltese and there were *Għawdxin*, Gozitans, and he would say to the Gozitans: "I went to Rome and I've seen *il-pôpa"‡* [pronounced the Gozitan countrylike way]. He would turn to the Maltese and say [smile]: *"Rajt il-papa."§* And somebody would say: How many popes? [laughter]. Automatically you change . . . even if you are a highly educated person like the one I have been mentioning. You change your tone and the way of pronunciation automatically, sort of . . . you bring yourself down to your immediate neighborhood.

Well, the *sinjuri* would be known even by their means of transporting themselves. The Ettore had a driver for their own use—they had a *karrozzin*, a cab drawn by a very nice, shining horse—and the driver was Micallef Ta' Bendu family, who lived in Archbishop Pietro Pace Street, where Salvatore Busuttil, the painter, lived.[36] The driver had a special job to keep that *karrozzin* and a horse—or maybe he had more than one horse—in very good trim, so that he would go down at a stated time to take up the parents, Dr. Ettore and his wife, up to church in Saint Francis's. So they would be known even by their means of transport.

Anyway I'm sure most of them helped the poorer classes. They employed some village girls as servants—of course with very low pay—but they also fed them; they would give them secondhand clothing, maybe

---

* "A house requires a lot of work." The spelling here corresponds roughly to the speaker's pronunciation; a phonetic transcription would be: *iddo:r treit ha:fnei sho:l.*

† Normal spelling.

‡ The pope (phonetic transcription: *il-po:pa*).

§ "I have seen the pope" (normal spelling).

food which was . . . superfluous—some of these village girls would take a bag full of bread or . . . well, some kind of food—and I must say, they also helped, very indirectly, the economy somehow, the economy of the real poorer classes, poorer families in the villages.

Another class of its own, totally different—we would call it a less fussy class—were the clergy, because—thanks be to the Lord!—we always had many vocations on these islands. We had a special seminary and it was well known, especially at the time when it was run by Sicilian Jesuits: the standard of education was high, and even people from Malta—well-to-do families from Malta—sent their boys here, not necessarily to become priests, but just to have a very good education. Ex-students who made a name for themselves include writers, politicians, historians, presidents of the law courts. You see, in those days, there were no competitive exams to enter the seminary: if someone had a vocation, however poor the family, there was always some . . . the church would help the family along and other individuals who didn't want to show their names, but everybody had a chance. So the very bright ones who went to the seminary had an A-one education. Those who became very bright priests went to Malta sometimes, when it was the occasion for high panegyrics; some of them even went to North Africa and they were very well known.[37] Of course, we had less intelligent priests, but there were very good ones, and they were saintly priests because they were poor. Parishioners would help them by offering agricultural products. They didn't have any commodities in their houses; sometimes they didn't have the right pair of shoes, no servants of course.

And as I'm sitting here speaking to my very learned friend, Micheline Galley, I'm looking at the village of Żebbuġ, and up there, there was a very poor, very wise, saintly priest called Dun Karm Cachia. He was called Dun Karm taż-Żebbuġ.* All kinds of people went to him for advice, both spiritual and worldly advice, whatever it was . . . [noise from the outside—a motorbike passing by] . . . *Excusez-moi*, Madame de Bovary! [said to the interviewer]! . . . Madame de Bovary . . . whoever she was [laughter], . . . there was Madame de Bovary; don't get offended, because I don't know what connection there may be . . . [laughter].[38]

Micheline: Let us start again, Maria. We now have a more accurate idea of the Gozitan social scenery. You mentioned, among other things, that

---

*Of (the village of) Żebbuġ.

the tinsmith used to come to your village now and then to repair utensils or sharpen knives, as well as another craftsman who would frame your pictures. Were they the only visitors to your village coming from the outside? Perhaps you had itinerant salesmen as well?

Maria: I remember the tinsmith very well. He used to come and put up a sort of cylinder in which he had small pieces of wooden shavings, tightly pressed with a sort of hole in the middle, and then that would be his forge for the day; he would have three or four little, long-handled pieces of iron which he heated on this burning cylinder. I remember *tal-petrolju*, the kerosene vendor. You know, housewives used to cook either on a wood fire or on a small kerosene stove, and *tal-petrolju* used to come every week, shouting: *"Tal-petrolju hawn! Tal-petrolju hawn!"**

Another man who came often to our street, or what you'd call our alley—Ta' Ġanton was really a long alley; it wasn't a cul-de-sac—was a certain Wiġi Borġ from Fontana. He'd have a sort of oval wicker basket, with a big handle in his hand, and he would sell needles, pins, thimbles, tape, pieces of soap—I mean toilet soap—and things which a woman would need now and then. For us, that little basket was like a treasure chest, and I always had a good look at what he had brought for my mother especially [smile] because that concerned her most. I haven't any idea of other people who would come as salesmen.

Micheline: If not salesmen, then buyers maybe?

Maria: Oh yes! There was a man who would come 'round actually twice a week, with a horse or a donkey, a cart and wide boxes—wooden boxes or big cages: he would be buying rabbits, poultry, sometimes lambs and sheep or a goat—from the farmers, of course. In our little island, to make both ends meet, if you're a farmer, you must always keep a small amount of animals which would help the budget of the family, and you'd hear this man crying miles away, shouting: *"Hawn min ibegħlu? Min ibegħlu?"†* [Imitates cry of street vendor.] In connection with the sale of chickens, sometimes I used to overhear the conversation, or haggling, as it is called; it always made me laugh a bit, because even over the sale of an old chicken—no longer good for laying eggs, or for any casserole— there would be a long conversation, something like this: "This chicken, this chicken . . . look at it! How fleshy it is! Look at its crown. And look

---

* "The kerosene vendor is here!"

† "Is there somebody who sells to him?" (Note that "him" refers to the buyer himself.)

at that, and look at this . . . ," and the buyer would say: "Hummm . . . this is an old chicken, good for nothing! I'll give you only three shillings!" And the other would say: "Three shillings [high-pitched voice] . . . Let it stay here! You can go! Let it stay with the others!" Well, on and on it went like that, until the difference between the three shillings and six shillings maybe came to four shillings, six pence, but for me it was a pleasure to hear this haggling.

Micheline: Were there no other visitors?

Maria: On a very different basis, we had visitors to our neighborhood, and that would be *it-Torok.** *It-Torok* were salesmen. They came to make some money as everybody else, but for us, especially children, they were, on one side, fascinating; on the other side, a bit terrifying.[39] They would have a hairdress, a fez, generally red, or black with a long tassel coming down over the ear; they would have a sort of shirt-chemise, whitish, longish, with wide trousers. Over this, they would have a sort of *terħa*, which would be a band which they would wind 'round and 'round and 'round and 'round and then, especially if it was wintertime, they would have a long vest, made, in my opinion, of woven wool with brilliant colors—red, black, white and bright yellow. They would be selling *paljijiet*, that is, small straw-woven fans of all shapes: there were square ones, there were circular ones; they had all shapes of them. They were really useful in summertime to make a bit of breeze 'round yourself, and if you had flies 'round about you, they would be very useful to flick away a fly . . . .

These *Torok* also sold carpets, or somebody might use them as a bedspread . . . they were beautiful things, beautiful with those . . . as I said, that rich red, crimson red, black, white, and some other rich blue color. They also sold a *ħasira*. A *ħasira* might be—not might be . . . a *ħasira* was a straw-woven carpet which you could put in the kitchen; it would be the ideal thing. They also had carpets, not as big as the big ones which you could use as a bedspread. Besides that, they'd have exquisite sweets like *lakumja*†—to me, it looked like jelly, jelly wrapped in very fine sugar or flour—and *ħabb għażiż! ħabb għażiż!*‡

---

*Turks. The word *Torok* (singular: *Tork*) was generally misused for dark-skinned people coming from the Moslem countries.

†Turkish delight.

‡Earth almond.

Now if children were naughty, parents [smile] would use the *Torok* to make their children come to their senses because they would say: "If you are naughty, or don't behave, I'll sell you to the *Torok*, when they come 'round." And for us children, it was, humm . . . .

Micheline: Naturally the *Torok* inspired you, then a child, with rather ambiguous feelings, didn't they? But unlike the *Torok*, there was someone whom you would welcome wholeheartedly, someone who, now and then, would come to your house bringing in good news . . . .

Maria: Yes, a very welcome man indeed—in uniform this time—and he would be the postman. I remember a certain Manwel from Victoria—his family is still living in Providence Street—he would come to my mother with a smile, and say: "Today I have something for you, Ġanna." And my mother would come out because, you know, it would be a letter from my father who was miles and miles away in Australia. He might have some other correspondence, but as far as I remember, there were no bills coming all the time as we have here. We only had letters, very welcome letters.

Micheline: Didn't you have also regular visits of the parish priest?

Maria: Of course, every week the *kappillan** with an altar boy would turn up for a little money, or some of the products from the farm, and he would use this for the maintenance of the church; we called this "tithe" or *għaxur,*† because a good Catholic or Christian is supposed to help in the maintenance of the church premises and, of course, for the upkeep of the church and the services. The *kappillan*—there was one, we called him tal-Aħmar‡—I remember when he came collecting in SOME houses . . . As a child, I didn't notice it, but after, I realized what was going on: the *kappillan* sometimes would go into the poor houses and he would leave some money on the table, because in those days there was no national assistance, and the poor people who hadn't any property of their own . . . and sometimes, you know, there was some sickness in the family, or some debts of the breadwinner, and I remember that Kappillan tal-Aħmar would go in unobtrusively and put some money on the table.

Now I remember one particular day when the *kappillan* turned up. I was by that time a student at the secondary school—I must have been

---

*Parish priest.
†Literally, "the tenths."
‡"The Red One," a family nickname.

fifteen—and I had just passed with honors, and even a band had come in front of our house to serenade, to serenade me because I had passed what they called the *matricola*, which was an Italian exam for university admission. I had not even known that the university existed. If I knew, and what it meant, I would certainly have run away from the house straight into that university. Anyway why had that *kappillan* come? I was so surprised . . . the *kappillan* never touched your hand! And he hugged me! And he said: "*Għadditilna! Għadditilna!*" [Emotional tone.] That is, "She passed for us!" I didn't realize for whom I had passed until afterward, of course; later, then you realize what it implies . . . . When you're a child, you just don't understand politics.

At that time, there was the BIG LANGUAGE BATTLE: ITALIAN VERSUS ENGLISH. At that time, the Nationalists were in favor of Italian as the chief language, whereas the Constitutional party—which was led, cleverly led, by Lord Gerald Strickland[40]—was all out for using the English language as the official language in law courts, in government correspondence and all that . . . . But the Nationalists were still thinking of affiliating Malta somehow to DEAR, DEAR MOTHER ITALY. So, in some houses in the best families, Italian was spoken; the *sinjuri* had—as I said—special spiritual exercises during Lent in Italian, humm . . . as if they could get more graces in Italian than if they were in Maltese! Well anyway, the Nationalists insisted that we, school-leavers—I mean from secondary schools—should sit for a matric exam in Italian, and I remember I had worked hard and I had liked it because we had *Gerusalemme Liberata* by Torquato Tasso, and another poem, a beautiful poem: "Lucia, Lucia . . . ." So they argued that if secondary school children could make it and pass this Italian matric exam, they were right. Well, it was very difficult: in Gozo, nobody was successful; I was the only one to pass. So they were so proud of me, these Nationalists . . . .

Now this is a piece of irony because in our family we were not Nationalists at all. We were all Stricklandians because my father had been in Australia in 1916, and as he was not allowed to land in Sydney, he had been transported to New Caledonia. It was Lord Strickland who helped somehow, giving 'em permission later to land and to become Australian—not citizens, but members of the community. So my father was a strong adherent of Lord Gerald Strickland. This is a piece of irony, but still he was proud of me because I had passed the exam that nobody could, ah, ah, ah . . . [laughter]. Well, this is beside the point, but I remember it very well. Somewhere also in Victoria, there was a political celebration in connection with this. I didn't know about it, but later they told me. Well, in Victoria, there was someone from a balcony speaking to a group, and they mentioned me, that I had made it. So, if Maria Calleja, coming from a small village like Kerċem, could make this matric, every . . . not everybody, but it showed that Italian could be used as the official language. Well, the outcome was that, later on, English became the official language.

I remember when Italian was still the official language, and you went to court, and they would be speaking about your case and you wouldn't understand one word. There was a man—there were two men actually, who had been taken to court; they had done something rather unpleasant—and a magistrate said: "*Due anni!*" That means, two years prison, hard labor; and in those days, hard labor was hard labor. So one of them, one of them understood nothing; one of them understood "due," because they played "*uno, due, tre*"* . . . they played cards or something like that. So "due" for him meant . . . and he patted the other, and he said: "Hoy, hoy! Only two days; we've got only two days." And the magistrate said: "YOU HAVE TWO YEARS of hard labor." Well, funny things happened of that sort, but I think isn't right . . . the official language, especially when you are personally involved . . . you should have your own language.[41]

Now we are speaking of the visitors who were coming regularly to our neighborhood. Another officer, not in uniform this time, but dressed with a coat and shoes and tie and a HAT, and he had an assistant, was *tas-sanità*.† *Tas-sanità* was a public-health officer. In those days, unfortunately, there was a lot of fever, undulant fever, *deni rqiq*, in Maltese; abroad it was called the MALTA FEVER, or Mediterranean fever. Well, this undulant fever infected both the Maltese and English soldiers and sailors. It was a headache for both local and British governments. At last, a clever Maltese, Sir Temi Zammit, and an English army doctor, Major David Bruce, worked on this, diagnosed that this fever was coming from the milk of goats.[42] After that, they had some system of precaution. They ordered everybody to boil the milk: after buying it from the goat man, you had to boil it. Later on, we had pasteurized milk. But in connection

---

* "One, two, three."
† Literally, "of health," i.e., an officer from the Health Service.

with that *tas-sanità* man, we kept one goat or two for our own use, so that we get milk from our own farm, so the *sanità* man came to check the blood of the goat: he would pierce the ear of the goat, take a sample which his assistant carried for him; he would take it to a laboratory *tal-gvern** to be examined, and after some time, the answer would come back, and we would wait with trepidation if our goats were condemned or not. If they were found having undulant fever, you had to kill them and burn them; and if not, you would carry on. So I remember that sanitary official, *tas-sanità*. I remember I DIDN'T LIKE that man piercing the ear of [laughter], of the goat.

Micheline: Maria, other diseases such as tuberculosis were a cause of mortality at that time. Do you remember what precautions were taken to avoid the spread of the disease? And individually, how would the people behave toward the patients, for fear perhaps of becoming infected?

Maria: When you are a child, you don't know all these things very much. For me, it was books, making a dress on the sly because my mother did not like the idea of my becoming a dressmaker. She wanted me to become a head teacher, which I eventually did [laughter], as she wanted Tony[43] to become an *avukat*,† which he eventually became. Wonder of wonders, in those days when village people were not supposed to put their heads up, besides the Victoria people or the Malta people! Well . . . I wouldn't actually know, but I remember some conversation— you know, sometimes you overhear a bit of conversation which impresses you—I remember somebody was infected with TB—we called it *mard tas-sider*‡—and that was really bad, that was infectious; in fact, it was incurable.[44] Somebody, humm . . . very rarely somebody who could afford it would go to Switzerland. I think there were hospitals in the mountains, and somebody said some of the rooms didn't even have a roof so that they would be breathing fresh air, fresh Swiss mountain air. There were no antibiotics, it was the fresh Swiss mountain air which sometimes cured the people, and I know a man who could afford it because he was a businessman; he went to Switzerland and he was eventually cured, and lived to a ripe old age. But in the village, there was a family who had TB, and a young man finally died.

---

* Of the government.

† Advocate.

‡ Literally, "disease of the chest."

So, when you had a TB patient in the home, the public-health *tas-sanità* people would come, and they burnt, they burnt all the clothes and mattresses, and they fumigated all the rooms. In connection with this, I remember that when we had the first rooms in Marsalforn,[45] we had some rooms in front down there: two big rooms, a kitchen, a yard and some garden, and I was a bit perplexed because in the garden nothing was growing, and there was a heap of ashes, and I wondered, I said to myself: "What kind of people lived here?" That was not yet the time of barbecue, and they had a proper kitchen typical of those days, with two small fireplaces. And they had left some furniture—chairs . . . and then—and I thank her for that—a lady teacher—she had been my teacher when I was still five or six years old—she came down from Santa Maria—because she lived in Santa Maria Street—and she said: "Maria, I must tell you something. In this house, there was a man dying of TB and he stayed here six months." You can imagine how terrified I was. I left everything; I packed my little belongings and I ran home to tell my brother about all this. I don't think my mother knew about it.

Well anyway, there was nothing dangerous about it because the public-health men had done all the right fumigations and the right precautions so that the new occupants would be quite safe. But I remember I was terrified; for a week I just couldn't come down again . . . . Later on, of course, we gave it up. Eventually we moved from there, because in those days, to have TB was like the end of the world, and I remember something very personal. I was only twelve years old, and I started having a boyfriend. Having a boyfriend in those days, it didn't mean that you go out with him [smile], but I would go out on the public street and sit on a piece of stone, or on a wall, and the boy would come and sit ten feet away from . . . and you'd exchange some words, or a little gift: the gift might be a hair slide; it might be a piece of chocolate or nougat; it may be a handkerchief. Once we were given, I and my cousin Rose—my cousin Rose has married an Englishman; she is now in England—well, we were given a comb, a tortoiseshell comb, blackish, which you'd put in your hair, not only to keep your hair in place, but as a decoration. That was the kind of friendship I had. So an uncle of mine saw me; it was broad daylight on Sunday during siesta time, because my parents would stay in for the siesta and, for me, it was the time to go out a little [smile] on the sly. That would last half an hour, and then I would go back home. But anyway, somebody had told my mother I was speaking with that boy, and in the village everybody knows everybody . . . .

Ahhh! She was really very angry at me, and I remember SHE took a small chair nearby, and she put up the chair like that [gesture of holding the chair above her head] TO TERRIFY ME!

Actually she didn't explain why that was bad. I thought that was bad only because I was not expected to go and speak to a boy, but later on, I heard, I came to know that the brother of the boy I was speaking to had died of TB, and it was unthinkable that you marry INTO a family who had TB, or any other serious disease. In fact, when a marriage was being arranged—because most of the marriages were arranged—the girl would know of it, but it was mostly arranged by the parents; first of all, if the family was from another village, you went to ask somebody responsible if there was any SERIOUS, hereditary disease in the family. You didn't ask whether they were poor, or that or that; but if they had inherited diseases, you would ask.

About two years ago, when I was, humm! over twenty-one [said with a wink of humor to the listener], a man from Xewkija sent a message with somebody to marry me, and I said to the woman who brought this message, I said: "I don't even know whom you are speaking about. How can I marry a person I don't know?" And he sent a note to say: "You can ask about me. You come to the parish priest and ask about me, and if you find one single blemish in my family . . ."—that includes his sisters, his brothers, his father, his mother and all the rest— ". . . I give you two thousand pounds" [laughter]. Of course, I did not carry on with these investigations. Nowadays young people usually meet at one of the many discos in Republic Street in Victoria; they fall in love and get engaged. Mental illness or *ġenn*, TB, skin diseases, or vices like gambling—*logħob tal-azzard**—are overlooked completely. I am sorry to say a good percentage of these unprepared marriages are breaking down.

---

*Literally, "game of chance."

Two of Maria's maternal aunts: (*left*) Evangelista, who was married to Uncle Daniele, and (*right*) Katerina.

Maria's Aunt Lucia, whom she especially enjoyed visiting as a child.

Maria's Uncle Saver and his wife, Concetta, who emigrated to Algeria.

Chapter 4

Maria's Family

When asked about the relationship among the maternal branch of her family, Maria recalls the setting of her early childhood, spent on her mother's family "complex," where each married couple occupied a house of their own. She personally liked Uncle Pawlu's house with its decoration of holy pictures and plentiful store of the year's crops; the sweet-smelling terrace overlooking the scenery was ideal for lacemaking, while the trough underneath served as a bath, to the delight of children, all cousins. Indeed it was a paradise, yet not without a few thorns.

Among the members of the extended family, there were submerged jealousy and occasional tension. The main reason, according to Maria, was the bequest—or rather sale, according to the notarial document—of the house to Maria's mother by her relatives from Algeria; Uncle Daniele responded by "stealing" the crop. Another reason was apparently that Maria's parents were "a bit of higher status." Uncles and aunts, Maria says, should have been proud: social status was normally regarded as the attribute of all in a family. Nevertheless, when traditional role expectations, such as giving help in sickness and with child care, were to be fulfilled, the in-group solidarity was confirmed.

Maria's parents left the family estate, moving to the father's place of work, just opposite the paternal branch of the family in the village. The mother was reluctant to abandon her homestead, the more so because her marriage had been somehow objected to by her in-laws, since the marriage of the eldest son, the provider for the family, was considered a loss. They also showed their disapproval when Maria's brother went to the university; sending one's son to a university was so contrary to the village norms! However, they readily helped the married couple in periods of need, when Maria's father had pneumonia, for example.

All in all, solidarity was maintained on both maternal and paternal sides of the family. But the ties between Maria's mother and her own kin—in particular with Aunt Lucia—were, as they normally are in Maltese families, stronger than with the other side.

Micheline: Maria, shall we now examine a more restricted social group, represented by your own family? First, on your mother's side, the side of the Buhagiar, nicknamed Ta' Pantu. Your mother belonged to a large family of twelve children; eight sons and four daughters. At the time of your birth, the parents of your mother and one of her brothers had died. Among the seven living sons, the three elder had then settled in Algeria, following the example of the Buhagiar of the preceding generation; a fourth would join them later, whereas two younger ones would emigrate, only temporarily, to Australia and return home. Home: that was—as you say—"the family complex of Ta' Ġanton," where your mother continued to live after her marriage. According to what you already mentioned, there was for a time a rather strained relationship with Uncle Daniele, wasn't there? However, would you say that, on the whole, your parents had intimate relations with your neighboring maternal kin?

Maria: With my aunts and uncles on my mother's side, we actually lived near each other. It seems as if that street, or bystreet, Ta' Ġanton, was a complex belonging to the Ta' Pantu clan. My uncle Pawlu Buhagiar was married to a nice little lady from Santa Lucia; they lived in a big tower, one of those stone towers which had been used as watch-out in case you had invaders.[46] Well, the downstairs rooms were mainly kept for animals and fodder, but upstairs, on the first floor, there was a very large terrace, and from there you had a bird's eye view of . . . I wouldn't say all Gozo, but two-thirds of it, and of course that was the reason of the tower being there. I remember my aunt and her elder daughter, Maria, used to make lace on that terrace, with the fragrant smell of lemon, verbena and lavender coming up . . . hum!

Well, there was on the first floor a fairly large room, and the walls were excessively thick: they had two or three *armarji** in the wall, which today you would call china cabinets; some were storage for food, but

---

*Plural of *armarju*, a built-in cupboard.

there was a deep one where my uncle, who was a sportsman, had a gun and a special bag, very lovely, made in macramé, and a little *chapeau.** I also remember they had a little holy picture, because in those days every room had a row of holy pictures; of these four or five holy pictures hung up near the ceiling, they had a nice one—the wedding of the Madonna: on one side, there were Our Lady, who was only a girl of fifteen, and her family; on the other side, there were suitors—young men all looking at the girl; they all wanted her, and there was one in particular who had a stick—just a stick—a dead bough of a tree and it flowered . . . and it was a tradition that, because this *bastun*† had put out one flower— miraculously of course—he was the chosen one. For some reason or other, I liked the blue and red colors, and the high cylindrical hat of the master of ceremonies, the priest or somebody who was celebrating that matrimonial service between Our Lady, who was a young girl of the people from Israel, and her husband-to-be, who is not old at all; he's a bit older than her, but I don't know why, when they show us the picture of Saint Joseph, they never show us that Joseph was young as his bride was.

Now beyond the outer room which I described as partly dining room, partly bed room, partly ammunition room—because I'm sure before that it served as an ammunition room for guards on duty in that tower—there was another smaller room, and there they had *il-barka t'*Alla:‡ they had all kinds of food, fruit, melons, watermelons, potatoes, onions, cheese hanging on the *qanniċ*, which was, as I said before, a special traylike bamboo container for cheese to dry on. And—I'm not quite sure—they must have had a canopy or two, where children used to sleep.

Well, I was always on good relations with the girls there: there was Maria, who was a bit older; there was Rose, who was my age, and I remember WE HAD FUN in the summer, because they had a field near the tower in which they grew vegetables for the family consumption. Well, in this, what-you-might-call back garden, near the well, they had a big circular bath made completely of one stone. Someone had taken the trouble to excavate the stone, which was hard, very hard—it was a *ġebla tas-samm*§—and he excavated it so nicely that it served as a bath. For the

---

*French for "hat."

†A stick.

‡Literally, "the blessing of God," i.e., plenty of everything.

§"Stone of a flint-like nature not suitable for building" *Maltese-English Dictionary*, s.v. *ġebla tas-samm*).

grown-ups, that was the bath for the washerwomen: they would get the water from the well—it was SOFT PURE RAINWATER—and it was easy, without these modern detergents, to make the clothes REALLY CLEAN. And I remember there was a little drainage hole, so that the water could go out—dirty water—and it has a particular stopper, made of stone or wood, covered with a piece of rags. Now it was our pleasure and joy, especially in the summer, to fill the bath with water from the well, take off our clothes, and have . . . [laughter] a bath there. We would share—not share it—but take it in turns; sometimes we did a sort of game: "*Wieħed, tnejn, tlieta, għalik!*"* We would count to know who was the first. That was one of our innocent pleasures of having a bath, ah! [smile] in the *ħawt*.† We used to call it a *ħawt* . . . H-A-W-T . . . [expression of enjoyment].[47]

Another game we would often play, especially the girls, was at keeping shop. We all pretended to be the Tal-Batuta.[48] The Tal-Batuta was a lady grocer in the village, and we used to go to her for sugar, for oil—cooking oil, and in very small quantities—for raisins—I particularly liked the raisins because that would mean that my mother would be making pies—and for pasta. At the right time, maybe a quarter of an hour before the meal, the lady of the house would put into the *minestra* macaroni or vermicelli—well, the pasta which the people preferred—and that would give the men, especially, a good, filling meal after a hard day's work. That evening meal—in summertime, we would have it out on the terrace; we would put our table, and we would sit very often on the floor 'round it all, and in wintertime of course it was taken indoors.

So I remember I always had good relations with my cousins. Maybe I didn't understand what was . . . because later on, I got a feeling that the parents, Pawlu and his wife, Grazia, were a bit jealous of my mother and of our family because my mother, you know, my mother married late, at about thirty years, and before getting married, she had been to her brothers and rich uncles—yes, in Algiers. The Buhagiar had, I think, four or five settlers who had emigrated to North Africa in Algiers. They had big farms in Bordj Bou-Arréridj, and they had a lot of workers, of Arab workers, and my mother had spent some time—I think, thirteen months—with them. She had helped them, and they had given her a

---

* "One, two, three, yours!"
† Water trough.

contract, a notary's contract—it was in black and white—and I still have that book: the cover is pinkish, and the lettering is a masterpiece of handwriting; it's in French, but I can understand just a little. Anyway these uncles of mine, as I already mentioned, left, as an inheritance, the family house, which was fairly large with many rooms, and fields adjoined to it: by Gozo standards, that was something to inherit! So my uncles left that farmhouse to Ġannaroż.[49]

Besides that, these people understood that Ġannaroż was very bright, and my father was a little on the upper end, too. So they saw that Ġannaroż and her family were going to be a bit of higher status than they were. So this insidious—as I call it—jealousy started. I didn't understand at that time. But later I could see that. Now I'm still on very good relations with these cousins of mine: one is in Australia, and one is doing very well in Gozo because she brought up her sons very well: she had three sons; she sent them to the right place, to Manchester, where they started catering; she built three houses for them; now she has just built a huge restaurant and, on top of that, flats for herself, maybe to let, AND she's always on the scene, doing things herself so that the workers don't . . . hum! can't do any hush-hush work. That's the "Pantu" type; the Pantaleone type is always like that, like my mother.[50]

Now Uncle Daniele lived in another house of Ta' Ġanton, a farmhouse with small windows, a *ħarrieġa,** and from the windows you could see an extent of farmland called *il-qasam,†* *il-qasam* Ta' San Ġorġ, where we had many lands. In that place, there was a time, I was told, when my grandmother used to hang a white sheet from one of the small windows as a sign for her sons, if one of the cows was in labor: they would come and help the cow giving birth. Well, Daniele was tall, six feet high; he was dark, very handsome AND . . . a bit rough. He was a bit rough, and he didn't like my mother and my father, but it was my mother the target for him because, as you know, she inherited the common family farmhouse in Ta' Ġanton. I think they never could swallow that, that she had the sole ownership of the farmhouse, and they couldn't touch one stone from it. So with that house taken sort of from under their feet, and seeing that I and Anton were getting on in education, AND my father's

---

*An enlarged windowsill; see note 6.

†Literally, "division (of land)," i.e., a large tenure.

trade was flourishing: he made the windows high up in churches sometimes, he worked as a copartner with a man, Ta' Żerrek,* who was well
known for his craftsmanship, and they had a project together . . . .[51]

So that meant jealousy, and Daniele did not put up with that feeling.
Sometimes he threatened my mother—he tried to terrorize her, and I
remember, as I may have said before, my father would be away, working
in the shop down in the village, and my mother would suddenly shut the
front door; she would say: "Bring the *stanga!*"† and this would be by day!
Sometimes we'd put up sacks, because in that big entrance hall we always
had sacks of fodder for the animals. So we would put some sacks, as if we
were barricading against . . . ah! against enemies. Well, I certainly
remember that.

One nice morning—that's something I'll never forget;[52] as I said,
adjoined to the house, we had a small property called *nofs-siegħ*, and my
father had planted—sowed, rather—potatoes, and the crop was doing well,
and when the potato crop is at its best, it's a beauty because you have all
that green, maybe a little mauve flower; it's not all the crops that do
that; every now and then, you find a little mauve flower with just a tinge
of pollen, yellow pollen, in the middle. Well anyway, in the afternoon,
that was a beauty. The morning after, I went again to fetch maybe an
onion, or parsley, or something like that—it was like a kitchen garden—AND . . . the crop was not there: not one single plant of it, but the
field looked as if somebody had irrigated it thoroughly: it was all mud.
Of course, I couldn't realize what had happened; then I walked on and
I saw my Uncle Daniele's fields, which had been without any crops or
greenery the night before, GREEN . . . and I said: "These are our potato
plants!" This man, in the night, had watered, but watered thoroughly,
the field, pulled out the plants by the root, ah! taken out the roots very
cleverly, and had planted them, one by one, in rows in his own field. I'd
never heard of that . . . .

Another instance I remember, an occasion I remember well, showing
that underneath, underneath, there was a feeling of jealousy or hostility.
Well, I was always making dresses, cutting them out of course, tacking
them, and taking them to my Aunt Katerina, who had a sewing machine,
an old Singer sewing machine. And while I was working . . . I had a

---

*A nickname associated with seduction (from ZRK, which means "to try to grasp").
†A thick iron bar.

sleeve still not tacked on—on the side panel of the machine, AND Daniele's daughter—she's called Maria and she must have been six at that time, six or seven—without my noticing, she GRABBED that sleeve and ran down the stairs onto the street, and she was running straight to her father's house, and for me [sounding desperate] that house was inaccessible . . . . We never entered that house while we were there, while they were there. So I ran [whispered], I RAN like in *The King and I*: "Run, Eliza, run! Run, Eliza, run!" [Laughter.][53] I ran, and how I ran . . . I never ran like that! I ran, and at last, I got hold of my sleeve, and went back . . . ahh! ahh! with it! So my beautiful dress was safe.

Now—this is very funny—for my blue dress, I had some blue buttons, circular, dome shaped, and I still keep them because for me that meant something. Well, only last week, a nice lady from Paris, whom we shall not mention [smile of complicity with interviewer]—I shall not mention her name—she turned up with a jacket JUST-BEGGING for those buttons, believe it or not! So we put, we fixed those buttons there and, miracle of miracles, they just matched the whole ensemble.

Well, that showed the type of relation we had with Daniele and his family. BUT I would like to say something about the wife of Daniele, who was Evangelista. She came from Għarb; she was tall and extremely good-looking: she was fair, but not fair like the English people; she had blue eyes, again not like the English people had; well, she didn't look like a person from Għarb either . . . . So I concluded, and there are several persons who are of the opinion that, sometime or other, the Berbers had invaded Gozo, especially the Għarb area, and mixed with the local women. Anyhow, when my mother was ill or going to have a baby, she would come and wash me; she would give me a bath and see that I was well dressed. Even when my mother had twins, Anton and Sylvia— Sylvia only lived for six months—in the middle of the night, they wrapped me in a coat and took me to Daniele's house. That means they were on good terms at that time: you don't take your child—I was only six—to somebody . . . . So it was not a sort of constant hostility; It would come and go. Maybe another small inheritance would be involved, because Ta' Pantu had lots of lands, and every now and then, this hostility of getting a bit of inheritance would flare up. It was not all the time like that.

Micheline: As far as I remember, there was Aunt Lucia, one of your mother's sisters, to whom you were taken once when your mother was giving birth to a baby. She was living in another village, didn't she, and you were on good terms with her?

Maria: That particular aunt was living in Munxar, because she had married outside her village. It was unusual in those days, but this Aunt Lucia, not because she was unwanted in the village, had married someone from Tal-Patrija* who was extremely rich.[54] That's why Ġamri says:[55] "We have fields, we have lands," because my Aunt Lucia married into a very rich family. Now that one, she was always nice to us, and we would often, I and my mother, walk, walk down the village to Għajn Tuta,† which is a public laundry fountain house—how shall I call it?—it's a fountain with a building around it, and with prepared stone slabs and stone baths, where you could do your rubbing and rinsing, and of course, always with that, oh smooth, soft, running spring water. My mother would go there just to rinse in that spring water her blankets, her winter blankets: it was a must. I still remember the cleanliness, the whiteness as we used to call it, and the *fwieħa*‡ [gesture as if enjoying the sweet-smelling linen]; my mother was proud of the clean scent of the clothes she washed there. Now that water was not wasted at all: when the washerwomen had done with it, it would go into a special *kanal*§ and it would go into another *ġibja*# or reservoir, which the farmers used for irrigation. So nothing really was wasted. The washerwomen would carry a big zinc bath full of dirty clothes, and they would stay there for two or three hours; they had the time to gossip, the time to . . . sort of to make friends and get a little social life along with the washing.

Well, while my mother was busy, I used to pass through Għajn Tuta, walk down the valley, the Xlendi Valley, cross the valley and climb the hill, and then would come suddenly in Munxar. Very often I would meet Reġina, and she would have a batch of turkeys, and when I had a red dress, they would come: "GOB-GOB-GOB-GOB-GOB-GOB-GOBBLE" at you.[56] And Reġina would say: "Never come again in a red dress because turkeys don't like people wearing a red dress." Well, I reached eventually my aunt's house, AND they would always say: "Oh, you MUST have milk." So they would go in their lower rooms and find the

---

*A nickname.
†The Mulberry Fountain.
‡Fragrance (from *FWH*).
§Channel leading drain water into a reservoir.
#A large cistern.

best goat, and give me a big jar of milk, hot, all straight from the breast. And they would give me the good things they would have, and they would treat me well.

One instance I will never forget: later when Anton was getting into university, that meant you had to spend . . . not some money, quite a lot of money ON HIS education because you were sending him to Malta, being clothed like the Maltese upper class. You had to buy books, you had to pay for his rooms which were in a small hotel in Valletta, and of course, you had to provide him with extra food . . . and with pocket money. Anton used to say: "It's the poor who can't bear to go out without any money in their pockets. The rich, *it-tfal tas-sinjuri*,* can stand it but the poor can't go without money." I think that's true.

Well, this aunt, when she knew and UNDERSTOOD what we were doing with our Anton, she said: "Do you need some money [said in a whisper]? If you need some money, I will give you the money [whispered, yet intense]." And I always remember that . . . . Because SHE offered to HELP US in a very important way. We really needed the money for that education, but my father had provided for that, because when you come from Australia, you always bring a nice EGGS-NEST, or a nest egg, I don't know . . . . Well, you always have some amount of money, and my mother was not a spendthrift . . . like me [said in a whisper], and she spent HER MONEY wisely . . . and they never bought things just because the next door had bought them. We always bought what we needed, what we needed as for clothes, for food, or maybe some article of furniture. We were always well dressed, well fed, but we hadn't these, what-we'd-call "fineries." My mother wouldn't buy those because she always said: "If you have a penny, spend only one farthing," that is, one fourth of it, and "always see that you have something saved, either in the bank or *taħt iċ-ċangatura*."† *Iċ-ċangatura* was a square piece of local limestone, and most of the floors were covered with that; some were oiled and shiny, and it was easy to wash; some were not oiled and polished, and even the stairs would be like that.

Anyway that concerns my next of kin: it was, on one side, very friendly, very helpful; on the other side, helpful, and at times there was this slight sign of jealousy, of hostility, but we never kindled a quarrel. Some people

---

* "The children of the rich people."
† "Under the stone paving slab."

would even go to court here, if they have a sort of feud about something. It never came to burst out; we always had the best relations on the surface, but underneath, sometimes . . . . Well, it happens in the best of families, this!

Micheline: Maria, let us turn toward your relatives on your father's side. You told me that your grandparents were still alive when you were a child, and that your father was the eldest of six children. I would like to know where they were living, whether you would pay them frequent visits, what kind of relation your parents had with them.

Maria: I, as a child, often went to see them in the farmhouse, further down Xuxa Street, where I now live. And I would have some sort of food which they had. My grandfather, Toni, was tall and slim; I remember he was always reciting long prayers; he knew a special Salve Regina. My grandmother, Anġilka, was rather short; she was proud of her Salvu, Salvu the carpenter, the counselor, protector of his younger brothers and sister, Maria.[57] As a child, when I looked at Aunt Maria's obese figure . . . I felt a bit afraid I would one day look like her [laughter].

Micheline: That was not the case. Now Maria, can you explain in what way your father was the protector of his family?

Maria: Well, you see, my father being the eldest helped his younger brothers and sister. In the family, they looked upon him as the provider somehow. Even from Australia, he used to send them some money.

Micheline: And yet he was already married.

Maria: Yes. Actually, when he got married, they didn't like the idea at all. It wasn't because of my mother: it would have been with anybody.[58] It was no hostility really, and I remember they helped us often, helped us in the way that when my father caught a pneumonia— we'd call it *purmurija*—and there were no antibiotics in those days . . . so the uncles would take it in turn to come in, spend the night with my mother, so that, if something happened, she wouldn't be by herself.

Micheline: So there were strong ties and solidarity in case of need.

Maria: Well, there was no hostility, but . . . underneath thoughts, as they saw Anton, my brother, going to university, becoming somebody like a doctor or a lawyer, humm . . . one of them said: "What do they think they are? What do they think they are?" Because in those days, it was unthought of that from a village you go to a secondary school, and on top of that, you go to university in Malta; saying "I'm going to university" [laughter], it was like somebody saying "I'm going to the royal family!" In those days . . . . So instead of being proud—they should have been proud—they sort of . . . humm, they didn't like it. You didn't see it, but with your intuition, you could SMELL IT! And you could cut it with a knife, as we say; you could cut it with a knife!

Micheline: Now Maria, the time came when your parents decided to leave Ta' Ġanton and move to Xuxa Street where your father's family was living. Can you explain how things developed until you changed your residence from one place to the other?

Maria: You see, when my father came back from Australia, he began to set up a carpenter's shop in Xuxa Street, opposite Grandma. At that time, the cathedral's treasurer was selling plots thirty-three feet wide for the price of fifteen shillings annual ground rent.[59] So my father acquired a plot and built a large workshop, high enough to take the huge planks he used. Eventually he added rooms for the whole family. When the house was ready, I started moving in my own way: I took a big bread basket, *kannestru*,* and packed it with crockery and cutlery. I put it on my head, as I was used to do when carrying bread from the bakery, and walked proudly down to 20 Xuxa Street. I made this journey several times, so that clothes, books, small pictures were already in the new place . . . . For me, moving from the isolation of Ta' Ġanton to Ta' Xuxa was like moving to the West End . . . entertainment galore!

Micheline: Maria, did your mother share your joy? How is it you didn't show her taking part in the moving?

Maria: Oh, my mother was not eager to live in the new house at all! First of all, she must have hated the idea of leaving her ancestral domain. Secondly, the old farmhouse was on a higher level and from our big terrace, one could see as far as Mellieha in Malta, whereas Xuxa is in a depression with no view at all. But the hardest side of the problem for my mother must have been the fact that she was going to live in the midst of her in-laws: her mother- and father-in-law, her sister- and brothers-in-law, who still considered her as if she had robbed them of their livelihood. Naturally, after marrying, my father couldn't help them to the same extent . . . . Again my mother was a woman of strong principles; she had a mind of her own and she was not easily manipulated. Well, eventually the furniture and heavy household objects were transported to *Xuxa*,† but traveling cases and other not-so-useful objects,

---

*A wicker basket with a single loop handle.

† A place name, *xux(a)* meaning "bareheaded."

including the letters which my father had written from Australia, were left behind unfortunately . . . .[60]

Chapter 5

Parents' Tales and Life in the Center of the Village

By moving from the family "complex" of Ta' Ġanton to the house adjoining the carpenter's shop in Xuxa Street, Maria and her parents passed from the somewhat isolated outskirts of the village of Kerċem to its "lively" center. Maria liked her new environment for the entertainment it offered.

In contrast, she evokes the quiet winter evenings spent indoors with her parents at Ta' Ġanton. However, stories were told and she enjoyed them. They were not tales of wonder. Her parents would rather tell about their own experiences in the countries each of them had gone to (Algeria, Australia), and these tales opened the eyes of the child to the outer world. Other "real" stories would be told about some memorable event of Gozitan life, whether dramatic or comic. At the same time that these accounts raised her sensitivity to human emotions, they gave Maria a clue to appropriate or inappropriate behavior.

In the center of the village, it was the outdoor spectacle that broadened the child's horizon: the street was a stage on which queer-looking, eccentric characters were acting out their lives in a more or less provocative manner, creating effects through their physical appearance, speech, and even the ways they decorated their terraces. The grown-ups paid no attention to this eccentricity, and passed on with a smile, but the children were captivated and had great fun. During the summer evenings, everybody would sit on the pavement, and it was "like a comedy on the street." Such occasions did not lend themselves to gossiping; among those men and women of all ages with children, telling innocent jokes and funny anecdotes was the rule; it had a refreshing effect, like a kind of social therapy.

However, it could happen, Maria relates, that "innocent" laughter turned into pitiless derision in the presence of the person mocked. Such an attitude would have met with social censure in normal times. But the place and circumstances were abnormal—an air-raid shelter during an attack—and a diversion was badly needed.

Micheline: Unlike your mother, you were then pleased to go and live in Xuxa Street because, you said, it meant liveliness as opposed to the "isolation" of Ta' Ġanton. Could you tell me in what way there was, to your eyes, such a contrast between the two social environments or styles of living? Would you describe, for example, your evenings in both places?

Maria: I remember the evenings we had at home. In the winter of course, we would all be indoors in a small room we used for several things, such as having a meal, making the dough for the bakery, and in a special alcove—small alcove—for making cheese out of our own sheep's milk . . . of course, there would be some sort of conversation going on besides the actual meal itself; but as a child, I never remember we had any tales or stories, special stories told to us. We would collect, along the days or along the years, a lot of lore, a lot of knowledge about Australia and Algeria.

My father himself was always telling us incidents which he had gone through in Australia, telling us about his life in the bush when they were preparing the railway, the land for the new railway, and it was really interesting . . . about the time when a very strong wind blew up a whole library, and he had the time of his life picking up books here and there; about the newcomers to Australia who couldn't understand one word of English, and sometimes they would go shopping, and they would dramatize what they wanted to the grocers: if they wanted an egg, they would say: *Kukukukûh, kukukukûh!*" . . . [laughter]. Stories like that . . . . And my mother would, now and then, speak about her uncles in Algeria, about their farms, about the Arabs: how they stayed in a small room, how they baked their bread or food in the middle of the room on the floor, and things like that.

Of course, every now and then, some story, some incident relating to real people—actual real people, would come up—not the gossipy type, because I'm proud to say both my father and my mother never talked really about other people's matters and private lives. They always talked about something you'd call of general interest. Well anyway, I remember some—you wouldn't call them stories, but dramatic events which really took place. One of them, when my father was still in Australia, and of course my mother was living on her own, with me as a child of four or five: in the neighborhood of il-Madonna tal-Patri,* there was a lady called Dolora. She was tall, clean, good-looking. Well, one night a man hid himself under her bed, and she used to stay up late, patching, of course with an oil lamp; so she was patching and mending her clothes, which I remember were always clean. At last, that man was fed up waiting under the bed . . . . As a child, I didn't understand what he was waiting for . . . . She wasn't a rich woman, she didn't have any money, so he was not after riches; most probably he was after raping her. Anyway he said: *"U din, kemm ix-xjaten se ddum tbit?"* "What the devil is she taking so long to sew?" And he went out of his hiding place, and of course he attacked her. She was not killed, but severely injured and eventually he was arrested. I remember his daughter—she was my age—when we were at school; she never mentioned her father, but I knew from my family. She simply said that he was in Malta.

Well, for us, for a small child especially, that story was very horrifying, and after that, I remember every night at bedtime, my mother used to take up the sheets because the sheets would be long and the cover would be long, almost reaching the floor; she would take them up and have a look under the beds. And that sort of suspicion, even in a child—she didn't explain why she was doing that, but it was a little catching . . . how can I explain? I had a little fear—not too much—but a little fear of men, maybe men hiding under your bed [laughter].

Later on, and I was about twelve, ten or eleven years, another tragedy took place in the village. You know, my village, Kerċem, is a small one according to the buildings: in those days, there was a small group of houses, two or four streets, with the church as the focal point, but going with the parish, there were extents of land or fields which we called by the general name of *hemm ġewwa; hemm ġewwa,* that means "there-in," because for us they were the inside of the village. Every now and then, you'd have a well with enough water for a farmer to water his few crops around the well, or, if he had a donkey, to give the donkey a drink. Well, one day there was a young man with a herd of goats and sheep,

---

*The Madonna of the friar. That name was given to the place, Maria says, because of a bas-relief representing a monk praying to the Virgin Mary.

because farming by itself wouldn't pay much, and anyway you always had manure if you kept animals. So there was a boy with a big herd, or flock—for me, at that age, it was a big herd—of sheep and goats. An Englishman later, I heard him saying: "Oh, they are shoats!" He mingled the word—half goat, half sheep—and he called them "shoats."

Well anyway, this young man would spend the whole day out in the country, going from one field to another sometimes because the grass was meager . . . we have little rainfall. Anyway he took his flock in a field near a well, and one of his sheep fell down the well, and he wouldn't like to lose that: he couldn't afford to lose one sheep, or GO-BACK-HOME to his father and mother saying: "I have one sheep lost." So he tried to save it, and he himself climbed, or somehow went down the well. The well must have been deep, and the bottom full of mud—you know, year after year, silt collects, and there was mud—and this man never managed to come out of that well. When the other farmers saw that his sheep were by themselves and nobody about, they went to have a look and see what happened. They tried to take him out, but it was of no avail, because evidently they could do nothing about it.

And I remember the WHOLE DAY, there was a turmoil in the village, and at about l-Ave Maria,[61] I was out in the street to see the proceedings near il-Madonna tal-Patri, and I saw several people carrying a man, all looking solemn . . . and among them, there was the boy's mother [tone of sympathy], and she . . . now this was far away; she must have walked a long distance in spite of her state of mind and physical state; well, she was going down, like somebody in a trance, with her hair . . . down on her shoulders, and she was looking neither west nor east, but looking forward like that . . . . I can still see her walking like that, as if she were a soldier on the march . . . she was so confined in her sorrow; it seemed to give her strength to go on; I don't know because it was a long walk. Of course the day after, there was a funeral, and you know, children look always after something new in the village or something unusual, and I remember lots of people turned up, just to see this boy who had met such a tragic end.

Well, I remember another story which happened in the village, AND it was . . . a laughing matter—I mean, everybody had a laugh at that. This was much later, later—I was a grown-up girl at that time. It regarded politics in a very indirect way. Well, in one village, there was a man who was an MP, that is, a member of Parliament, and because of his . . . station, he could sometimes help people in getting a job. Of course some kind of donation or gift was expected. And there was a man from my village, who was not well-off, but he had some sheep. So he took a sheep, a female sheep to this man's family, and this man, member of Parliament, evidently accepted the gift, ah! and the man of course left it there. He stated what he was looking for—a job—because a job with the government, for most people, meant a soft job; they say *inpappuha*.* The *inpappuha* earn good money and do not work really hard. Anyway the man from that village left, and AFTER A WEEK OR TWO, nothing materialized, and he never got the job.

So although this man was sometimes considered by the others to be a little . . . simpleton, he thought out a plan—very clever one—of getting his sheep back. Of course, without making the man angry, or without anybody knowing what he was doing. So one fine day, he went down to the other village, and he saw to it that the member of Parliament would be in Malta, doing his duty, AND he went very quietly to the wife, saying: "You know you have a sheep, and your husband wants it to be sexed. I have a ram, and I can do that for you as a favor. Can I have the sheep?" So she said: "If my husband said that, yes, of course, go and get it!" [High-pitched voice and more excited.] So very quietly, very nicely, he took out his sheep, put it on the cart in a sort of box. At that time, you know, they had a sort of cagelike box on carts to carry goats and sheep, which were either for sale or for killing, or for sexing sometimes. Well, he took it back home to his village, and nobody was the wiser. But of course, when the MP returned, and his wife told him about it, he said: "Eh! I never gave such orders . . . ." But up to these days, people would say sometimes: *In-naghġa ta' Kelin.*† They sometimes recall this tale. That is ONE THING which looks like *il-musmar ta'* Ġahan for me.[62]

Micheline: Didn't you have another story, Maria, about a sheep which had been promised in a marriage agreement to the other party and never given?

Maria: You'd be surprised at this, but it actually was like this: I know two families, both of the same social status—not very poor, nor very rich—but both very numerous, because families were very numerous, and when a father had three, four, five girls to marry, he was careful about

---

*Literally, "we eat it," it meaning baby food; the verb comes from *pappa*, a child's word for soft baby food; hence the *inpappuha* people are those who have soft jobs.

† "Kelin's ewe" (Kelin is a pet name for Mikael).

what to give them as a dowry, because it was expected from him to supply them with a dowry. And that, whatever it was—whether it was money, animals, a bit of building, a bit of a field—had to be agreed, agreed about, before the actual engagement took place. If it were a well-to-do family and there were some worthwhile property, they would go to a notary so that they would make *il-kitba taż-żwieġ*, the act of marriage, which really meant what the father was giving to his daughter, what dowry he was going to settle on his daughter, as we call it.

Well anyway, it was not a matter of going to the notary at all. The girl who was going to marry was promised a sheep—perhaps they were giving her other things, I don't know—but the husband-to-be was promised a sheep. Well, they were engaged; eventually they were married, because in those days an engagement and a marriage were not far away from each other: if you were an *għarusa*, that is "engaged," you were expected to marry at least in the same year, AND you would go out to *festas* with a chaperon—not only one, but sometimes [laughter] you would have three or four sisters or brothers acting as chaperons! Well, at long last, this man and his family realized that his wife was not being given what was promised, and they broke away, *kisruha*,* they broke away from the other family, and I must tell you both of them were respectable families . . . and they NEVER talked to each other again, just because the promised sheep never crossed over to the other side.

And I remember this lady—because I know her very well—who was not well-off, but she was ALWAYS working at the *bizzilla*,† always working. Well, she had three or four sons, but one of them showed an inclination for education, for schooling, and she sent him to school for how long he wished—in those days, you could leave whenever you were fed up; it was not obligatory—well, he went on in the local village school, and he went to Victoria to the seminary, and of course the family, the husband's family, helped her because when they saw there was a vocation in THEIR family, they would feel proud and they would feel a sort of obligation to help her. In the seminary, the food was rather poor—you know, everybody was of low standard—and if you wanted your son to have a good meal, very often the mothers would walk up to the seminary with a hot meal or a thermos flask of coffee and milk. That was not being looked down

---

*Literally, "they broke it," it being the relationship with the wife's family.
†Lace.

upon, neither in the seminary nor in the families; it was a custom. Well anyway, that lady—and I still respect her for that—although she sometimes went barefoot, and even her husband went barefoot, she did her best to educate her son, who now has a high position, believe it or not.

Micheline: Now, tell me whether your evenings would be spent differently in Xuxa Street. What was your entertainment?

Maria: When we changed lodgings, when we moved from Ta' Ġanton to a more central part of the village, where my father had his workshop, for me, it was like going to a big city because the difference was great with regards to evening entertainments. In summer days, as it is a custom in most villages, we would sit on the pavement or even in the middle of the street because, you may be sure, no cars were passing by. Well, in front of us or near to us, there was Żeppu s-Sultan* [gesture of turning whiskers upwards]; he was called Joseph is-Sultan—that was the family nickname. Not only he was Tas-Sultan;† even his sisters were Tas-Sultan. This Joseph—he was rather shortish and he had a harelip, I remember, and on Sundays, he would wear a big *terħa*‡ as wide as that, with a very bright greenish color, he would put on three, four *ħatem* or rings, and would go up to Victoria and come back nearly drunk. On weekdays, if the *kappillan*§ came along to collect maintenance money for the church—it would be either collecting money or collecting cotton or wool after sheep-shearing time, well . . . or some seeds or corn as the custom was in every village—well anyway, when the *kappillan* would come around, is-Sultan would start behaving in a funny way so as to scare the *kappillan* off, and the *kappillan* would be scared—he would never enter that alley to collect anything.

And one day I asked: "Why is Żeppu s-Sultan always sort of not liking priests?" And they explained to me that one day when he was younger, he wanted to get married, and he had asked a certain girl to marry him. The girl was not really decided what to do, and evidently she had asked advice of a priest, and the priest had advised her not to have anything to do with Żeppu s-Sultan because he was a drinker of wine and he was a bit naughty, and he was not *bil-għaqal*# . . . . So that made him mad, and

---

*Joseph the king (Żeppu for Ġuzepp, "Joseph").
† Literally, "of the Sultan." For the use of *Ta'* in nicknames, see note 48.
‡ Sash.
§ Parish priest.
# "With good sense," i.e., wise.

sometimes he would do the funniest things imaginable. Believe it or not, sometimes he would pick up a piece of wood and a piece of tin, and he would stay in the street, nearly half-naked, and [smile] . . . and bang as if playing music on a piece of wood, or dancing without his pants on . . . .

Micheline: How did the neighbors react then?

Maria: The neighbors—well, those who happened to be on the scene would put up a smile and walk on; but we children stayed on to enjoy the fun. One day, I remember I was HORRIFIED . . . because he lived in an alley; he would do his acts in the main streets; he would bring a big *skutella** or *zingla*,† and in it he had pieces of rats . . . He would do ANYTHING [with a smile in her voice] just to DRAW ATTENTION [still very modulated]. Well, this Żeppu s-Sultan had a roof of his own, and my grandmother's terrace overlooked his roof, and they said: "Look! Look what *burdell*‡ he has on his roof!" I said: "What a *burdell*!" [Uttered in a whisper.] HE HAD a number—say, thirty or forty—chamber pots, because we all had no toilets, but we used chamber pots of course for the bedrooms, made of enamel; when they were useless, we would throw them away, somewhere out of the village. And this Żeppu s-Sultan would bring two or three or four, and he made a BEAUTIFUL BORDER [laughter] on his roof. Other farmers might have *il-qara'*—pumpkins, big pumpkins. In summertime, you might see pumpkins all along the farmhouses on the very edge of the roof. But this Żeppu was like that!

Well, sometimes he would sing something we didn't understand, but this was one of the main characters in my new street . . . . When he was in the village itself, he would be clad like any other one, a farmer. But when he went to Victoria, he had a special nice vest with, as I told you, a big *terħa*, colorful *terħa*, and three or four rings on his fingers, and he would come with his whiskers like that, drawn [accompanied by gesture]; it was Żeppu s-Sultan!

Micheline: You said, Maria, that he had three sisters staying with him.

Maria: Yes. When they were younger, they used to live in Ta' Ganton in the basement of the tower, and their father would tell them to put on

---

*Largish coffee bowl (*Maltese-English Dictionary*, s.v. *skutella*).

†A large earthenware basin (glazed greenish inside), used for cleaning vegetables or making yeast.

‡Of Romance origin (Sicilian: *burdellu*), the Maltese word *burdell* means "brothel," or disorderly house.

their finery, and he would take them up to the cathedral in Victoria, near which there were soldiers. There were barracks, and when they were nearing that guard place, he would say: "Esther, Ursulika, Maria, * għall ordni!*"* That meant: "You girls, walk up smartly because there are men looking!" It was very hard to get a husband in those days, you know. Well, later on in life, none of them got married, and they were living with their brother. Early in the morning, I would sometimes overhear lots of things, as my bedroom overlooked the street. This Sultan would be up at five o'clock, and he would be getting his donkey ready for the fields, and he'd say: "Sika, *ġibli t-tarant, mur u ġibli l-ħabel! Mur u ġibli l-kappestru!*"† I was regaled by this comedy of the Sultan ordering his sisters, who, as I told you, were getting on in years, to help him, and they would never complain because they knew that he could be a bit difficult and do something foolish. So they got rid of him as quickly as possible. That regards the Sultan.

There was another queer character, further down the street. He was not a churchgoer—he wouldn't go to confession, whereas most of us would go to confession every Saturday; in fact, on Saturday afternoon, I would see, not a procession, but a group of men, freshly washed, with something on their feet, a coat on their shoulders, and you would know immediately where they were going: they were going to Saint Augustine's for confession because the day after it would be Sunday and they would go to Holy Communion. Now that man who would not go to confession pretended that he hadn't any coat, nor any money to buy a coat. And there was an old lady, Forta, who believed him, so she said to my father: "Salvu, Salv, do you think that we should make a collection when all the people are here in the evening, and we'll buy him a coat? Or you might have one, still from those you brought from Australia, and you might give him one . . . ." My father always told her not to say anything foolish because my father never had the heart to make a laughingstock of anybody. But in the evening, she would say that again, and the others said: "Yes, you might do that, you might do that . . . ." AND she was the laughing-stock.

---

*"In order!"

†"Sike [short for Ursulika], bring me the trace, go and fetch the rope. Go and fetch me the halter!"

So another time, he said something stranger, that naughty one; he said to her, "Look. Because I feel rather ashamed to go up to the *kappillan*, you know what we'll do? I'll tell you my sins, and you go and tell them to the priest." Now everybody knows that is not proper . . . humm! [Laughter.] And we laughed. These simple things were fun. We had no television of course, no music, no . . . . But I was coming from a place, Ta' Ganton, where in the evening there was no entertainment in the streets at all, where everybody shut his door and you were in, and that's it! Down there, it was a bit more . . . social, if you could call it that [smile]. And that was how we spent our evenings.

Micheline: It seems that you had quite a crowd in front of your house on summer evenings.

Maria: Yes, one by one, even the neighbors who lived down the street would come up, sit down on the pavement, and somehow there was always merriment and laughter. It was like a comedy on the street: one had been to Salonika, and he was always boasting about his medal. A priest, Dun Salv, would be in his rocking chair, smoking a long pipe and saying some funny story; once he had been to Rome on a pilgrimage, and there was a farmer who went with him, and they had been to Frascati, and they used to say: *"Dak l-imbid ta' Fruskuta!"** And Dun Salv would tell us about how the others reacted and the funny things they had done when they were abroad. When you are abroad, and don't know the language, you might make your companions laugh at your expense wholeheartedly. Dun Salv never related anything too personal or offensive. I don't remember anybody mentioning politics; neither anybody mentioning something really degrading. We just had these simple stories until it was time to go to bed. And you would go to bed having your mind sort of refreshed, having a little laugh, innocent laughter. I remember that.

I remember something else—now it's coming to me—and this happened during the war, the last one which was 1939-45. There was a spinster down the road; she was called Zeppa tal-Qara'.† Her mother had gone, her brother had gone, and she lived by herself. And, you know, sometimes when you get older, your mind turns back to your childhood; so she wanted to get married. But of course, she was past marriage age.

---

*"That wine of Frascati!"

†Josephine of the pumpkin (a fictitious nickname).

Some men got hold of that, and they tried to make fun of her in every way. So there was another man, and they told her: "He wants you." And she believed . . . first of all, she was hard of hearing, so she just imagined things.

One day there was an air raid on, a very severe air raid, and the airplanes were going "AR-ROAR-AR-ROAR" above our place, above our village, and in our street, there was a very, very good shelter because the rock is very hard, and everybody had gone down this shelter, including Zeppa tal-Qara', my father, and the young man whom she thought . . . . So, while everybody was saying: "Santa Maria, *ora Pro nobis*. Bieb tal-Ġenna, *ora pro nobis*"* [psalmody tune]—the litany of the saints, because we prayed . . . you could die any moment . . . but, being hard of hearing, when she saw us kneeling, she thought: they are kneeling for some sort of . . . because of my engagement. So, she said to my father: "Salvu, Salv, *Naghtihulu issa?*" She was asking: "Salvu, shall I give him the ring now?" And my father who was a bit . . . frightened—he was afraid of the air raids—would lose his usual calmness. And he said: "*Hallini minnek!*"† That is, "You, go away!" And you can imagine the litany and the laughing, and all that. Then eventually we came out of the shelter—it was not over, but sometimes we would go out of the shelter—and we had to lie down on the ground like that [gesture] completely . . . because something came down: BOMB! We thought we were finished . . . a big bomb came behind the church, which is a bit further up. Anyway these are the little innocent pastimes of our summer evenings.

---

* "Saint Mary, *ora pro nobis* [Latin for 'pray for us'], Gates of Paradise, *ora pro nobis*." "Gates of Paradise" is a way of addressing the Virgin.

† "Leave me [and go away from me]."

Maria's only brother, Anton, who died tragically young from cancer.

A picture of Maria's mother, Ġanna Roża (1883-1970), near the end of her life.

Maria's father, Salvu Calleja, when he was living in Australia, where he went to find work in the 1920s.

Chapter 6

Death of Anton and Her Parents

Throughout this book, a principle of flexibility has been adopted. Too strict a topic organization and chronological considerations have been avoided in order not to harm the narrative flow. With this new chapter, whose subject is unrelated to the previous one, the object has been to preserve the emotional state in which Maria found herself after a discussion she had had at her cousin's house (during a break in our interviews). As we resumed later in the day, she felt the desire to tell about the experiences of her close relatives—her beloved brother, Anton, and her father and mother—and their confrontation with death.

Throughout his life as a student, a young bright politician who deliberately interrupted his political career, and a solicitor, Anton enjoyed prestige and the esteem of his fellow countrymen. As a Christian, he inspired admiration. His spirituality was nurtured by his reading (Teilhard de Chardin and T. S. Eliot, in particular) and, at the end of his life, by the personal ordeal he went through. Strikingly enough, he died on Good Friday (1976), as if in communion with Christ, and was buried by special favor on Easter Sunday, a highly symbolic feast in the Christian church. While he was sick, Maria accompanied Anton wherever he had to go for treatment. The moment she was back home following his death, Maria behaved the way she was expected to: in command of the situation, her emotions in control. A crowd attended the funeral.

Unlike their son, the parents died at home with Maria seeing to their needs to the last moment. Numerous friends—neighbors and priests, ordinary people and personalities—honored the family by their visits during the difficult times.

Maria's father died on a memorable day (October 8, 1948) for the island: a boat coming from Malta sank in a terrible storm; only a few passengers were "miraculously" rescued, as displayed in the ex-voto painting of Ta' Pinu church. Maria's father departed peacefully at seventy, well prepared for a "good passage" and willing to give an account of his doings to his God. Maria's mother, who died at eighty-seven, had her senses up to the very end, and was more determined than ever to do things the proper way, whether it was housework or her last prayers. In a comparable way, both father and mother maintained, when confronted with death, their sense of duty and straightforward Catholic faith. As they had lived, so they died; in perfect consistency with their past behavior, they considered death as the consecration of life.

Micheline: Maria, we were Ġamri's guests yesterday: Ġamri, your cousin, had invited us to his home on the occasion of the village *festa*.[63] And while we—the four of us, I mean: you, Ġamri, his brother-in-law and myself—were enjoying the delicious lunch cooked by Margarita, Ġamri's wife, we had a long interesting talk on various subjects connected with tradition and change in the society. One of the topics we discussed—I am well aware of it—had an emotional effect on you because of Anton, your brother. Perhaps you feel like telling me about Anton.

Maria: Yes. I feel like talking about that because the man from Malta who is working in a hospital as a nurse mentioned some instances of how patients are treated over there, and we discussed it over. We discussed over the difference there is between going away at home, surrounded by your next of kin and your friends, and dying in a hospital. Well anyway, Anton always used to say: "We all die alone. Everybody dies alone."

Anton had been to England in 1965, and of course I accompanied him: we went to Royal Marsden Hospital in London because that was the best place for cancer cure. We saw a doctor—very nice one—and I sat for two long hours—those were the two longest hours of my life—waiting, as somebody is waiting for a verdict, when eventually this doctor with a rosy face came up, and I said: "What d'you think, Doctor?" And he said: "There is no reason why your brother shall not be cured." And that makes your morale better, and you are ready to face anything, as long as there is hope. Well, we stayed in England about two months. We used to go daily to Royal Marsden in Chelsea, which is one of the best residential areas; even artists have their own houses there. Then there would be a bus to collect the patients from the Marsden and we would feel as if we were going on a tour, on a tour of pleasure.

Well anyway, I will always remember the Maltese Sisters of Charity, who used to come every day with a basket full of sandwiches—Maltese bread with oil and *kunserva*,* as we call it—because the Maltese patients, especially the men from the country, used to love that; although wherever we went, they tried to give us the best English food available; for us Maltese, toasts, slices of Maltese bread sort of . . . were so different!

Now, from the Royal Marsden in the center of London, we went down to another hospital in Surrey which is affiliated with the Marsden; to me, it seemed built in a depression, and big basements were lower still underground. Of course radiotherapy includes, I think, strong electricity currents. I never had the courage to go down and see these treatments. I always stayed in the lounge, a big lounge; I had to wait for three, even four hours until Anton came out of the . . . bosom of the earth in this radiotherapy treatment department, and then we would meet other patients and go back to London, sometimes in the dark, sometimes in the damp; everybody would be a bit tired, both patients and nurses, but I always admired the nurses because they did all their best: they followed the doctors' orders minutely; not only that, on our way back to the center of the town—they were going back home, and at that time, there would be congestion of traffic; it was not nice, and sometimes we were driven in a van . . . oh! smelling of petrol fumes and things of that sort—they would try to cheer us up, and they would sing simple songs, but we all tried to sing with them, and that cheered us up. We would reach London, near Victoria Station, rather tired; we used to stay with the Franciscan Sisters in St. George's Drive, and it would be nearly dark because in London in wintertime—we were there from October until January, the winter months—the lighting would be up, and a sort of haze would be all about the city. We would again have some sort of food. If we could face it, we would go out either to friends, or to see a show, or just to have a walk, so that we would forget that we were patients in London.

Anyway, after two-and-a-half months in London, Anton came back cured; even the doctors there were happy because the doctors, the doctor-students, took pictures of his face, and Anton used to say: "What are you looking at? You seem so happy about it." And the doctors said: "But it's

---

*Tomato paste (general sense: preserved fruit).

beautiful, it's beautiful!" [Lively tone of voice.] And Anton answered: "Beauty lies in the eyes of the beholder" [laughter].[64] That was an English quotation and a little bit of dry humor. Well, anyway . . . when we had finished with the treatment, we packed, and we came back home to my mother's delight, who, throughout those months—the neighbors told me—had never looked out of the window on the street, but she had stayed indoors, every now and then going to Our Lady: she had a small picture of Our Lady of Perpetual Succor and she would say: "Madonna, *ġibli dawk it-tfal lura, ġibli dawk it-tfal!*"* That is: "Bring back my children!"

We were not children at all but . . . well, we eventually came back, and Anton recovered a little slowly, and he started his work—it was that of a solicitor—and because of his integrity, he had a lot of clients. In fact, he had more than he really wanted. He never wanted a telephone in the house because he wanted to spend his free time quietly, and he never opened his office in the evening. So he restarted his work. At that time, there were sales of property: old farmhouses from the villagers were sold to English people. I think that, although he was not really fit, those were his peak years of work.

Micheline: He had resumed an almost normal life then?

Maria: Yes, he used to go to swim in Dwejra† beyond the Inland Sea. You know, he used to go through the little channel into the big sea. He used to go to swim to Xlendi, even up to l-Għar ta' Santa Katerina,‡ and [sounding cheerful] he passed a normal life. We used to go out in the car after I came from school—because I was running a school, a secondary school in Qala—and we went back home to our mother whom we never left alone—she always had a companion of some sort[65]—and after a time, she would say: "Now don't stay here all the time. You go and have your time out!" [Laughter.] No night spot for us! But we would have a drive in the country, and the farmers would come to speak to Anton, their friend, and they would give us fruit and vegetables, and not for the fruit and vegetables, but I appreciated that much because I saw that those people really respected Anton.

---

*"Our Lady, bring me back those children, bring me those children!"

†Diminutive of *dar,* "house"; here, a place name near Għarb in Gozo.

‡Saint Catherine's Grotto (a place name).

Well anyway, after ten years of that, Anton seemed to be a little paler; he would be tired. I didn't realize what it was, because with that sort of cancer, if you live near the person—other people might see it coming—but when you live near the person, you don't really recognize it, and Anton was never of the healthy rosy type . . . . He was a bit delicate. Anyway . . . there was a time when he said: "Oh! I have to go for an operation," and I didn't have the heart, or . . . to ask: "What sort of operation?" The only thing I said: "Wherever you go, I come, too."

So this was in Lent 1976, and I had been asked to give a talk in Nadur. As it was Lent, they gave me for a subject: the meaning of Lent. And I remember Anton was lying down, and I sat down, and I said: "Please, help me, Anton, at least to make the chief points, the skeleton of the talk, then I'll fill it up." AND [tone of admiration] he started talking. I got a pencil and wrote what he said because he made a beautiful dissertation about Lent being the time of repairing ourselves, our souls, as if we were going to be reborn, rebaptized, and I remember he mentioned: "*Tinża il-bniedem il-qadim u tilbes il-ġdid.*" That is: "We take off the old man and put on the new man."[66] Well, at the end, I said: "Anton, how is it that you found it so easy to speak about this?" Because he had started talking as if from a tape. He said: "Ah, Maria, you don't understand Christ at all; otherwise you would be able to talk about him."

Well anyway, the day after, I went . . . I had a little shaking of my knees, but I was full, not of what I had read—I usually read several aspects from different authors, so that, in me, I have a stock—but of what Anton had so cleverly and so easily said. So I said: "Good heavens!" when I saw the church—and Nadur church is not a small church—the church was half full of ladies, so I went up—I had a microphone, a stand . . . it was the first time, and I started the talk about Lent, about our preparation for Eastertime, about the risen Christ, and how WE should rise again by believing more in Christ. I remember I never stopped. I was never in a fix what to say next, what Anton had said. Anyway somebody made a sign that it was enough.

Well, eventually I returned home, and Anton was still upstairs in his bedroom, not really in bed, but he was not feeling well. I remember I went up to him to bring him a cup of coffee, or something else, and he said: "How did it go?" and I said how it had gone, and I remember he clapped his hands for joy; he was so happy, and underneath it all, I felt, because he used to tell me: "I should have been a priest, I should have been a priest." So underneath it all, I had the feeling that somehow, though in a very, very humble way, I was doing the thing he would have liked to do himself, but anyway that was a happy occasion.

The next week was Our Lady of Sorrows' week: on the Friday, il-Ġimgħa ta' Duluri,* at about five o'clock, there was a mass in the village of Kerċem, and Anton was asleep. So I said: "I won't wake him up." I put on a decent dress, quietly left the house, and went to hear mass. You see, we have a special devotion to Our Lady of Sorrows. Many people make vows to her and, at the head of the procession, there is always a group of women, mostly women, who go barefoot. And there would be two or three policemen to keep the crowd off because the crowd would have shoes [smile], so that those won't be trodden down. Anyway Anton said when I went home: "Where have you been?" I said: "I went to church [tender voice] to hear mass." And he said: "I would have liked to go, too. Anyway we'll go out for a drive as usual."

And I remember we went to Mġarr—not where the boats are, but on the side of the orphanage—and from that angle, you can see the boats, the fishermen's boats and the big boat coming from Malta, and it is a nice view. And Anton started: "Sister, remember the many times I used to come down to pick you up, when you were coming over from Malta? Do you remember the time when I bought a small dog for you, and you looked down in the car?" It was a little something fluffy . . . . "Do you remember this and that?" And I just hadn't [silence] the strength to say anything. Sometimes I would say "thank you" in a very small way because . . . I was very emotionally involved. Well anyway, we had spent half an hour there . . . . Anton knew he was going because he reminded me of the beautiful things which we had shared.

We passed Xewkija and he said: "Do you mind . . . ?" They usually have a nice procession in the village, and just to take his mind off, you know, I said: "Yes, why not?" But the moment we arrived in the square, we went to the church. And there was still a mass on, and there was a priest—I always remember him, Father Bajada; Father Bajada is known when he goes out, wearing a clergical suit and a blue beret, like the French sailor—well, Father Bajada was preaching, and he said: "Look at that woman!" He was pointing to the statue with Jesus on the cross, and Our Lady at his feet looking up. "Look at that woman! She sees her son dying and she is not even sitting down . . . and she must be very tired.

---

*"Sorrow Friday," i.e., the Friday preceding Palm Sunday.

What a courageous woman!" Well anyway, it was the time for Holy Communion and Anton went up to receive Holy Communion; later a lady from Għarb, Teresa Cauchi, a teacher and incidentally the sister of Bishop Cauchi, told me some months after Anton's death that she had asked herself: "Who is this man coming down from Holy Communion so solemnly?" He must have been in such a semblance of devotion that she was struck by the way Anton was coming down from the altar.

Well anyway, we went home as usual. The next Monday, we went to Malta to Saint Luke's Hospital for what they call a checkup, in order to have your tests, and this and that. And I remember [low tone of voice] Anton: as we were going up the corridor, he said: "These are the corridors of our Passion." [Silence.] Well, that day he had the test . . . the clinical test.

I remember Monique—Monique was a French lady, a friend of ours—and she said: "That's pretty quick." Well, we came back home, and on Wednesday, we went back; we took lots of things with us because we were staying with our friends, Doctor Maurice Ellul and his wife Frances at Tudor Lodge in Balzan,[67] so I had to have lots of things, and we had called the taximan, Mr. Farrugia of Victoria, and after he told me: "I thought you were going on holiday." He never knew what . . . anyway we went to the Elluls', and they gave us a meal, and then in the evening, Anton had to go to hospital. I was so emotionally . . . I just wasn't registering all that was really happening, and later the Elluls told me, because as a doctor and a nurse, they said: "Maria, you were too, too weak to understand what it really implied." And they took Anton's hand and we went to hospital; he changed, put on his pajamas, and I had to leave; I had to go back to the Elluls'.

The day after, of course, I went to see him again, and he said, of all things . . . now Anton was never fussy about food; he used to say: "For me, food is no factor," and he had a special excuse to hostesses; generally we would go to lunch or lunch parties, at Xlendi, at Nina Fitzgerald's house, and Nina used to make special dishes for Anton, so that he would eat, but he used to say: "The amount of food I eat is no comment on the quality"—it was a real apology for not eating too much—now . . . the first thing he said: "Last night, I had a very good lunch of . . ."—we call them meat loaves—and I said: "My! My, my!" [Smile.] I always had done my very, very best to prepare good, delicious food. Well, that was it! I stayed there for some time, and I remember there was a teacher of handicapped children.[68]

Then Father Anton from Xagħra came to Anton's ward; we stayed a little far from Anton's hearing, and he said: "Your brother is very much resigned. He knows what he's doing." Well, he was taken for operation. I didn't like the room where he was being operated, because it was not an operation theatre, but you are not going to tell that to Dr. Harding, who knew what he was doing. Well, Dr. Harding and the assistant nurse stayed there for about four hours. Monique was again with me but I think I was emotionally weak; I couldn't even . . . I stayed there like a piece of stone, and Monique after a time said: "Maria, that's the time to pray." Now it should have been the other way about, but I didn't even realize I had to pray, and I prayed, and they brought Anton out with a drip and this and that . . . . Dr. Harding said: "I found a lot of bad . . . bad matter, which I had to take out." He didn't say that Anton was dying, but he said: "There was a lot which . . . I had to take out." So he explained this to me.

Anyway I stayed there for some time, because you never know when a person is dying . . . it was a difficult time for me because you are not going to say: "Anton, you are dying; let's say some prayers." At the same time, I knew it was a very momentous moment, so I said: "Anton, I'm praying as we used to pray at home: "Our Father who art in Heaven . . . ." We used to say Our Father, and just, "Thank you and we love you." That's the prayer we used to say, and I remember—now I might have been a bit weak, not to see and not to realize what was going on; of course [smile], I wasn't drunk—I remember, very hazily, but I saw the crucifix and Our Lady which were in Xewkija,[69] and I realized that Anton was really dying, and those Two Persons were really at my brother's side, helping him to go the right way. It was just an instant, but I remember it brightly, and I knew it was there. Well anyway, I couldn't stand it any longer because I would have cried or done something foolish I didn't want to—how shall I say?—because Anton and I were very close. If he saw me doing something foolish, I think I would have disturbed him, so I said: "I'd better go home."

Now go home for me meant to go down all those corridors; I don't know how I did it in Saint Luke's, finding the right bus outside and finding my way . . . I had to leave the first bus for the second bus. I was feeling a bit giddy, and I felt, really felt my heart dropping, as if it had dropped inside me. Well, I managed to reach Tudor Lodge where I was staying. The Elluls took care of me; I had some sort of food; they came up to my room, and I slept; without any sleeping pills whatever. My body was so emotionally dried up, I just slept.

Well, in the morning, Maurice—Dr. Maurice, as we should say, but I always called him Maurice—Dr. Maurice and his wife Frances said: "We are going to the village in Balzan to do the Seven Visits.[70] When we come back, we'll go together to see Anton." Well, this is Good Friday now, 1976; I don't know how I dressed. I still remember the "rust" dress and the warm jacket I had, and I went with Maurice; we went up into the corridor in the ENT ward, and I was seeing a group of nurses—there must have been five of them—all looking the same way, and I knew it was Anton's bed, and when I saw their reaction, emotional reaction on their faces, I realized Anton was dead . . . . Maurice must have made some kind of movement, or of . . . that very moment, I passed out; they gave me some coffee and they put me to bed, and I remember the only thing I said: "Well, I knew my brother was going because before I came here, I took out the best mats; I took out the best wine glasses, and it was the last meal we were having together. I had the intuition to do that." Well anyway, Maurice tried to arrange the transfer of the corpse and all that, and he discussed things with me, but all I said was: "Yes, yes, yes." I hadn't the strength to . . . to decide anything. They said: "She is dozing. We do the usual arrangements."

Well we left St. Luke's Hospital and Dr. Ellul put me in a taxi, and he asked the taximan to go to their own house, and the taximan was the same one who had taken us there, and he said: "*Is-sinjur ħalliena, miskin! is-sinjur ħalliena, miskin!*"* Of course, I answered nothing. I remember when we reached the lodge, Frances was at the gate, waiting for me with a big glass of whiskey and hot water to calm me a little, and she embraced me and wept. Well anyway, the taximan drove me to Ċirkewwa, or to Marfa.[71] I think Ċirkewwa was not yet being used.

Micheline: You were then, Maria, on the Gozo boat, on your way back home?

Maria: Yes, I was on the boat, and at Mġarr, there were friends waiting for me, and they took me home. Up to now, I was half awake, but the minute I reached the house, I was [firmer tone] the old headmistress again in command, knowing that it was an important thing, an important occasion for the family, and for Anton. Anton used to say:

---

* "The gentleman has left us, poor one!"

"ALWAYS do things in style; *lo stile è tutto! lo stile è tutto!** So I told the servant: "Marianne, take off all the furniture which shouldn't be here, and get a lot of armchairs, and get the best carpet, and see that everything is in place, because we are having a lot of people here." And believe me, the house was full. As soon as they knew that Anton was no longer with us—it was announced on the radio that Dr. Anton Calleja . . . he was well known as a solicitor—they came and talked to me, and I don't know how, but I was talking all the time of the beautiful things Anton used to say. I was spiritually elevated. I remember Censu Refalo, the bank manager, said: "Anton *kien jitfa' id-dwejjaq tiegħu wara spallejh u jerfa' dawk ta' ħaddieħor.*" That is: "Anton used to put off his own troubles over his shoulders, and he would carry his neighbor's worries." I remember several people said nice things about Anton. In fact, up to now, they remember him. They remember him also for his wit, and of course for his integrity, for his clearness of mind and sense of how things should be done or not done.

Anyway his many friends from Malta accompanied his coffin in a carcade from St. Luke's Hospital to Marfa; then a priest from the village, Dun Karm Borġ, brought him on the boat. After he said: "I had a hard time because the sea was choppy, and the boat . . . the coffin . . . going like that." Anyway this was Friday, Good Friday. Public-health rules are that, after twenty-four hours following death, a corpse should be buried. But I had good friends, and they—I don't know how—managed together that Anton should be put in the freezing system, so that he would be buried on EASTER SUNDAY! This is what I call not a coincidence, because Anton always believed in the light of Christ, and on Easter it is the Feast of Light, of flowers and songs.

But this funeral arrived, and I remember Monique brought me a black hat. Now in Gozo, generally nobody goes in a hat—they wear veils—but I remember I accepted the hat, and I walked in dignity, never crying, because I said: "Anton wants his style. This is Anton's *festa.*"† Then someone said from the lower story: "Maria, there is a man who wants to take photographs of the funeral. Do you mind?" I was a bit shocked, but I said: "Why not?" Why not? This is Anton's *festa*. And they still have

---

*An Italian phrase: "style is everything."

†Any festivity, but most frequently, the word designates the yearly celebration of the parish patron saint.

the photos there. And the funeral . . . I never remember I saw such a big crowd in the square. In fact, Peter Paul Grech, who was standing on a box where he could be seen by the crowd, with his stentorian-authoritative voice, gave orders of how people should march up to the church.

Now the bishop had said: "You're allowed to take the corpse in, as long as you don't do anything funereal, anything sad; it must be the feast of Our Lord Jesus Christ." So Father Martin from Nadur had his usual orchestra and his usual choral group, which are very good, because I said: "I don't want any pompous music with these big trombones and big bass which Ganni Vella usually brings." We always hated that pomposity, but Father Martin's orchestra group and his chorus are just beautiful. And the English people brought wreaths—a lot of wreaths from this and this and that—they brought big bunches of flowers which they just put 'round the coffin, and it was beautiful, and I couldn't [modulated voice] be sad. I wasn't sad; I was elevated spiritually because I said: "Now Anton is going to meet his Friend, in whom he believed so much!"

Well anyway, there's something else I'd like to mention because it is also strange: the priest, Father Gregory Grech, had ordered the bell boys—because on Easter day, at noon, they have a loud peel of bells to show that it is a day of joy—and he said: "Now don't start ringing the bells before the funeral procession has reached the police station down the road." But for some reason or other, those boys had either completely forgotten what Father Gregory had told them . . . THERE WERE PEELS OF JOY, the BELLS, when Anton was leaving the church . . . the bells started peels of joy . . . and they put him in a hearse which is drawn by two beautiful horses—I think it was the last funeral with a hearse drawn by horses because nowadays they have cars, black cars of course, suited for the occasion—and I also remember Mr. Carol Fitzgerald, and his daughter, Deirdri, and his son—Edward, I think—with his curly hair; they were friends of ours; they don't live in Gozo—they come and go, and they were . . . I saw them there on the pavement, saying good-bye to Anton. And I always remember that: it was really nice of them to come up from Xlendi. Well, we went to Santa Maria cemetery in Xewkija; there were the last prayers, but I never went near the grave; I just couldn't stand that . . . [silence].

Micheline: And when returning to your house, you still had, I'm sure, to welcome visitors coming to show their sympathy . . . .

Maria: Oh, the house was full of people who had come to speak [lively tone of voice]. And I couldn't stop speaking about Anton and his Christ.

I remember people paid many compliments about his integrity, about this and that . . . .

Micheline: Maria, you have been naturally sensitive to the marks of esteem and affection expressed by all the people who knew Anton, including British residents. I think there was another English family, you told me once, that came to visit you after Anton's death.

Maria: Yes, just two days after Anton's burial, that English family turned up: a tall gentleman, a nice-looking gentleman, his wife and two children, and I said: "My, my! Some more work for me!" And I gave them a seat in the lounge, and I said: "If you please, who are you? I've never met you." They said: "We are your neighbors in Marsalforn; we own the flat at the top." Ah! I had a sense of relief; I said: "So you are friends. And I treat friends in the kitchen. Come on in the kitchen." And that man sat at the head of the table where Anton used to sit, and I just didn't know what to say; I said: "That was my brother Anton's place. And he used to recite poetry." I was still too weak, but I said the right words, after all. "He used to recite poetry?" said he. And Dr. Eddleston also started to recite poetry, and we laughed a little. And I gave them tea and biscuits. These people, I like very much, and I'm so glad when they turn up. Now Dr. Eddleston seems to be all over the world, lecturing on his subject, which is in relation with skin cancer.

Micheline: So before knowing who they were, you thought they had been clients of Anton. And I presume that Anton's loss meant also for you a great amount of work in relation to succession . . . .

Maria: Well, I had to face the situation, because when somebody dies, then you have to face a lot of paperwork—and Anton was a lawyer—and I had many legal papers to find for the people, but a friend, Ġanni Schembri, came and said: "Would you like a bit of help with your paperwork?" And I said: "Yes, please." And we started cataloguing, making a sort of inventory of every small paper, because in legal papers, you don't know what is important and what is not. I used to work up to eleven o'clock at night. And we had a filing cabinet . . . it was a beauty: Anton's files were a beauty. I was so sorry to pick them up, because you had to pass them on to another solicitor, but they were a beauty of craftsmanship, of orderliness, of very good English, and everything was properly made. So when people came down eventually, especially the English who had property here, and they would have liked papers showing their rights to the property they were occupying, and so on, some of them said: "How is it, Maria, that you have the papers ready?" I said:

"You see, it's because I have an inventory; it's easy like that." I think I went on very well, tackling Anton's legal papers.

Then I had some money I had to share to a family: Anton had left me orders, so I went about doing the right things, thanks to the Lord. I had some difficult tasks because for your what-we-call *id-denunzia,** that is succession duty tax, you have to show the amount of money which you owe to other people: Anton had other people's money; it was in his name in the bank, but you had to show that it was not your personal property, because otherwise I would have to pay taxes even on that . . . . So of all persons, there was a lady . . . she lived in Africa and she was called . . . her surname was Shamiya, Shamiya.[72] And she used to come here because she wanted to build a beautiful villa in Xlendi, and she used to stay at the Electra Hotel in Marsalforn. Incidentally my clerk at school, Frans Magri, owns—or at least, his sister-in-law owns—the Electra Hotel, so he knew all about the Shamiya, and he said: "My, my!" And I had her address in Africa, but it's hard to reach a person in Africa, and to testify that she had a check in Anton's bank account. So he said: "Shamiya is in Gozo." So I went and saw that Sha-Shamiya; she was a lady as if she were preparing to go on the stage [laughter]; she struck me as somebody. Well, she signed the papers I wanted.

Anyway it was a hard time for me, and I had to go to the income-tax people in Malta. Now Anton had died in April, April 16. You had to fill out even his income tax from January up to the time of his death. Unless you had that ready, you couldn't pay the succession tax, and believe it or not, if after some time you are not ready, they tax you so much per day. So you can imagine what a time I had. And I had to have papers. And his death certificate, they couldn't find. Then our friend, Portelli, after some time said: "Maria, after all, are you sure that you have that certificate, because we can't find it, neither in the law courts in Malta nor in the law courts here?" I said: "I haven't reported . . ." because I took it for granted that in the hospital they would . . . , so I had to go, and that was the hardest thing for me to do. I had to go back to Malta to the police station, wait in a queue . . . just to say that my brother had died and that he was buried.

And while I was in the queue, I remember . . . a joke the policemen were passing among themselves in connection with their rise of pay; at

---

*A list of property in connection with inheritance taxes.

that time, there was, as they called it in government circles, a "reorgani-
zation." And, you know, in front of Kastilja,[73] the prime minister's office,
there was a new statue dedicated to Manwel Dimech, in the big square
of Malta.[74] Manwel Dimech was in favor of raising the status of the lower
class, and in his hand, in the statue, he's carrying a sort of roll of paper,
so that these young policemen said: "Our reorganization scheme is
coming, is coming; it looks like Manwel Dimech is bringing it." Although I was not ready for jokes, I still remember what a good joke that
was.

Then I had to sell the car. I had to sell it; I didn't want to keep
it—there was no French Citroën except ours at that time on Gozo, and as
I didn't want to see it here, I sold it to a man from Malta. I did a lot of
things, little by little. I sort of went to my usual—I still had the momen-
tum for work coming from the secondary school, because if you are the
head of a secondary school, you have to work, ah! very, very fast, doing
three or five things at the same time, but with God's help, I coped with
the work I had to do.

Micheline: Maria, when you started speaking about Anton's fatal
disease, you had in mind the opposition between dying at hospital—
which has become the lot of the majority nowadays—and dying at home,
like your parents, who spent the last part of their lives in their familiar
environment. Perhaps you could tell me now about the way your father
and mother went away.

Maria: Let's start with my father. My father died in 1948 at the age
of seventy. I remember a few months—not a few months—quite a year
before his death, he had started having sort of swollen feet and being a
bit too emotional; he would cry a little just for nothing. And if he had
pricked his hands with *bajtar tax-xewk,** immediately there would be a
small wound, a small sore, and that meant that his blood pressure was
not right. It was not usual for us to give a diet to the people who needed
it, and my father was a great eater—he liked his food very much, as I
do—and he didn't want to obey the rules.

Anyway I remember this, this is strange: I had a friend, Matilda, and
we went together to the herbal doctor at Għarb, Frenċ ta' l-Għarb,† as he
was called.[75] I had something in my hand, something very slight, and I

---

*Prickly pears.
† Francis of (the village of) Għarb.

showed him my hand, and he said: "Rub it, and do this and that." It was nothing really, but he told me without ever asking, and I'm quite sure he had not seen my father, or met my father, and he said: "Be a little careful about your father because he has blood pressure, and may be he might . . . ." He didn't put it clear, but later I realized what he was hinting at: he might have a stroke. This is strange because Frenċ ta' l-Għarb could see what was happening to my father in Kerċem. Well, at the moment I didn't realize that he was saying anything unusual; I just went home and told my mother about it, and that was that.

Well anyway . . . I remember one Saturday afternoon, I was going up to church as usual at two o'clock for confession, and I met Mr. Kelinu Scicluna, who was a teacher with me at the school, and we exchanged some words—he was actually going to the lending library in the school, and he would open that for two hours on Saturdays. Well, when I came down from church, I found that my father had fallen down, sort of tripped, on one knee, and I and my mother immediately picked him up and put him on a bed; he had a bed in the corner in the downstairs' room. The first thing I did was to send somebody for the priest to come and give him Holy Communion. Then of course, we sent for the doctor, and he said he might have a second stroke, but my father was conscious all the time. We sent for a male nurse from the hospital, whom we used to pay of course. And we had many friends at that time because it was the time when Anton was still in Parliament. So, being an MP, you know, we were a bit . . . respected, and several relatives came to help us. During the night, my mother was very tired because we had been up nearly all day, and I sent her up to the upper bedroom, and I stayed with the nurse to see what was happening.

Actually the doctor said: "There is little hope that he will ever recover." So we started what is called the *agunija* or "agony"; in the church, a priest or somebody would kneel and pray for the man who is passing away, and bells would be striking, too. Well, I usually sat with my father and my brother. We had a special prayer book, and we used to pray and read the prayers, and sometimes he would pray with us . . . and then one day, there were SIX priests! We didn't send for them, but they came out of respect, just as friends, and that was a good omen to have six priests 'round your deathbed, and I remember father shook hands with them [melodious tone of voice], and he said: "I'm going, good bye, good bye!" He shook hands with everybody, and he said good bye [smile]. In fact, now I remember some days before, he had said: "now I must go and

GIVE-AN-ACCOUNT-OF-MY-LIFE-TO-GOD." He was not afraid, not . . . just like I used to say: "Now I have to give a good lesson." Just like that! Meanwhile, he had told us: "Make for me *il-quddiesa tal-buon passaġġ*."* There is a special mass for a "good passage," they call it. So early in the morning, when our friends got up for the four o'clock mass, and they came in just to see how things were, I told one of them: "Please, tell Dun Salv† to say a mass for my father *tal-buon passaġġ*."

Well, on the 8th of October 1948, father passed peacefully away. He had a beautiful funeral because people connected with schooling came, in respect of me, and people connected with the *avukat*‡ and an MP came out of respect. So my father was buried in great honors, and I think he died like a good Catholic, because that was important after all, whether you are king, whether you are a street sweeper.

Micheline: That very date, the 8th of October 1948, is also associated, isn't it, for all Gozo, with a particularly tragic event?

Maria: Of course. It was a stormy Saturday, and on Saturdays, people who have been on business, or working all the week in Malta, DO THEIR BEST to return home. I don't know why, but we Gozitans, and even the English residents who now live in Gozo, they say the same: "When we have finished our business IN MALTA, we feel like coming back to Gozo, home, as soon as possible." Well, it was Saturday night, and it was very choppy, and the usual boat was not crossing at all. But there was a *dgħajsa*,§ a big *dgħajsa*, you know; it used to carry merchandise from the Grand Harbor[76] in Malta to Mġarr in Gozo, and there was the master of the boat, and some of his crew, and a lot of men and women. I think they were thirty-two people, and the boat master said: "Don't you see? Look at the sea: it would be risky, you would be risking your life, and anyway there is too big a number."

Well at last they persuaded him to cross, and it was really rough . . . . There was somebody tal-Mużew# who was praying all the time, and there were women, perhaps a bit afraid. Well anyway, when they had made half

---

*"The mass of good passage" (into the other world).

†Don or Reverend, a title used for priests and followed by the Christian name (here: Salv).

‡Advocate.

§A boat (formerly with lateen sails) plying between Malta and Gozo.

#Belonging to the M.U.S.E.U.M., a laymen's religious organization founded in 1907 (*Maltese-English Dictionary*, s.v. M.U.S.E.U.M.).

of the journey, near il-Fliegu*—il Fliegu is a very bad crosscurrent between Comino and Qala, even in summer, even if it's calm—there the boat started to be filled with water, and the crew and some of the men started to bail out. But it's no use . . . the water came again, and slowly, slowly, the boat began to sink, and some were already floating, some were drowning, and some managed to save their skin—maybe there was a bit of the boat to which they clung.

Well, many people were drowned that day. Among them, a postman from Victoria, Scicluna, and his fiancée is my present friend. She is Anny. Anny was engaged to the Scicluna postman. That's why she married late, because after that she didn't want to have anything to do with anybody else. And among the casualties, there was a boy from Kerċem who had been my student before. And there was Mr. Paul Zammit—he actually comes from Xagħra, and he is married to Helen Ta' l-Ilma† from Victoria—this Paul Zammit managed to climb on to a rock, on a big rock near Qala, and he stayed there for THREE or FOUR hours, wet, trembling with cold, and, of course, with the shock of it. At last, somebody managed . . . because there was a boy of twelve years who had been saved, and who walked up to Qala, and he gave the alarm. So policemen and other men with ropes and with lanterns went down to save anybody who could be saved. Well, this Paul Zammit evidently was saved: a big strong rope was thrown to him on the rock. You know, there was a space in between. Well, I don't know, but he managed to be pulled up from the rock, and this was at three o'clock in the morning, and the first thing he said, although he must be . . . [sounding breathless], you can imagine in what state he was. But he said: "Let's go to Ta' Pinu and thank Our Lady for saving my life."

Micheline: And in thanksgiving, Mr. Zammit offered a painting which is exhibited in the ex-voto room of Ta' Pinu, and it illustrates his miraculous escape from drowning.

Maria: Yes, it is the picture of this gentleman, of Mr. Zammit standing on the rock, AND THE WAVES . . . HIGH, very, very high, and some people trying to throw a rope. You can find that today.[77] This was 1948, and several people remember it. We were staying in the house, but

---

*The straits separating the island of Comino from Gozo.

† Literally, "of the water(s)," a professional nickname. Her father was engineer-in-chief in the Waterworks Department.

people were coming and going, mentioning this great tragedy, and the hospital had never seen so many mangled bodies, and this, and that . . . all Gozo was there to witness this sort of thing. That was my father's death . . . .

Now I will come to my mother's death. My mother was always very healthy; she was not robust—what we call robust—but she was a healthy woman, always busy about the house. And she was very worldly wise: she had the *għaqal** of the Ta' Pantu tribe . . . [smile]. She thought I was too naive sometimes. Maybe I am, I don't know. Anyway I have survived up to now, and I've come to Paris, and I'm enjoying myself, and I'm doing what you are reading.[78] So with all my naiveness, I think I've got through a lot of beautiful things—thank you, God, for that! Well, my mother was eighty-seven by now, and she started being a bit pale, and with a woman of eighty-seven, you are not worried if you see her getting a bit weak, a bit pale; what d'you expect? But then a specialist, Dr. Fenech, he was a good one from Malta, and he said: "She has the cancer in the intestines." And I said: "Hoy, hoy! We have the 'dog' again." Because we call the cancer a dog. Well anyway, we didn't tell her that, but we took care of her. We always, when we went out for our work, in connection with our work, we always left a servant maid with her, so that she wouldn't be alone.

At that particular time—I had been working as a teacher and as a head teacher for about forty years—I was a bit depressed. I felt as if the school was not given its esteem, its standing as it should have. Anyway I went on sick leave, and so I had the time to see to my mother's needs. The doctor had said with old people cancer is slow. It may be long. But with young people, and the healthier you are, the more galloping; that's the word he said: "galloping." And I remember I had a friend, in front of us—she was only forty-nine, and she was, you know, the peasant type, she could carry a heavy sack like that—and in three months, from December to Saint Joseph's Day, because she said: "Saint Joseph is taking me with him," she was gone. Well, my mother never knew what she was having, but I tried to prepare her; it's your duty. If you know somebody is going, whether family or friend, you should prepare him, discreetly of course, kindly.

So one beautiful day, my mother said: "You've been speaking about *il-*

---

*Practical intelligence and wisdom.

grìżma tal-morda; you go and tell the *KAPPILLAN*† to come" [in a firm and authoritative voice], as if to say: "This is a job I HAVE TO DO, and let's do it!" [Laughter.] So the *kappillan* came. I must admit he spoke a little slowly; I must admit. And my mother started saying the prayers herself, not the prayers we were saying, but her own which were to the same purpose. She was saying something like this: "Lord, all through my life, I might have offended thee; please forgive me for all my sins because I'm coming to you. Have mercy on me." And THOSE were the prayers the priest was saying, BUT the priest was saying them after her . . . . SHE DIDN'T LIKE THE *KAPPILLAN*, who used to SPEAK A LITTLE LI . . . KE TH . . . IS [extremely slow, and sounding exasperated]; she didn't like that. As always, she saw that, the passing over, as a job-to-be-done [sounding resolute], and you don't go slowly about your job [laughter]. Well anyway, little by little, she got weaker, and of course I didn't go to my school. But my mother never lost her senses— she knew she was going, and she said: "Humm, the Madonna hasn't come yet." But after some time, she said: "There is the Madonna. Dust it, dust it," because the statue we had of the Virgin was full of dust. So she was thinking of the Madonna—she thought she saw the Madonna coming— and at the same time, she was thinking of her usual job in the house.

Then in the evening, before she actually went, Monique—she is married to a local man, Dr. Grech, and she is French—so I remember Monique brought a vase with a single rose in it, and she brought her children, too [sounding very tender], and the smallest, Gérard. Well, Monique came to see my mother, and my mother said: "Oh! Monique, thank you . . . *et* Gérard *aussi!*"‡ All the people thought that she was saying some senseless words, but she was speaking French! She was speaking French, because fifty years before, FIFTY years before, she had been in North Africa . . . .[79]

Later on, Dr. Grech turned up and he asked her: *"Int għaraftni?"* That is: "Do you recognize me?" Which I think is silly, asking such a question to people who are either highly feverish or on the point of death. Anyway that was the custom, and I can understand that you don't really know what to say to someone who is dying. It's a squeamish situation.

---

*The anointing of the sick, or extreme unction.

†The parish priest.

‡"And the same to Gérard."

Well . . . you know what my mother said?—and she was at the point of dying: "How can I recognize you? You came in the dark!" which was in Maltese: "*Kif tridni nagħrfek? Int ġejt fid-dlam!*" [Smile.] And I could see from the faces of the people present, if it were not a solemn moment, they would have laughed because this was very . . . trite answer: "*Kif tridni nagħrfek!? Int ġejt fid-dlam!*"

Anyway on the day after—I think it was, well, five o'clock—she passed away. She had a nice funeral; she was buried in the crypt in Kerčem,[80] and I remember I put on black clothes and I again resumed my school career. And when I look back, I think God has provided for her somehow that she wouldn't be alone with a servant, because a servant is always a servant and not family. So on her last days, she was in the home like a queen, and I saw to her needs, and we had a Sister who was our friend and helped us, and mother died peacefully, surrounded with every earthly comfort which you can provide.

The baroque façade of a Church in Għarb, Gozo.

Interior decoration of a Church in Xewkija.

Prize gained by the horse-race

A depiction of the way the *palju* was used in traditional Gozo horse races of the past. (*Print courtesy of the librarian of the National Library, Valletta.*)

Boy scouts carrying the *palju* in Malta today.

Chapter 7

The Parish Church

In Gozo, church and daily life are inseparable. This chapter sheds light on the functions of the church at the individual, social and cultural levels.

The church is primarily, in Maria's mind, a place to meet—besides God—one's priest and neighbors. As a child, the building gave her her first experiences of beauty through its decoration and music, on feast days, particularly, and through the sermons she heard, which she always liked when they were well constructed, based on tangible facts, and spirit elevating.

Each individual has the main passages of his or her life celebrated in the church, from baptism to confirmation, communion, marriage (most frequently), ordination (sometimes), and burial. Maria regrets that nowadays ostentatious celebration, among certain people in town, has replaced the simplicity she knew in the past.

The whole village celebrates their patron saint(s) on the annual *festa*, a typical feature of Maltese life with its great ecclesiastical ceremonies, both inside the church and outside, where long processions unfurl through the streets with their hierarchy determined by precedence. The external celebrations of a *festa* bring together crowds of people who give themselves up wholeheartedly to rejoicing. A *festa* is an occasion to entertain relatives from other villages and strengthen family ties. It is the time for young girls in their best attire to attract the attention of young boys, expect a gift of nougat, and start friendships which might lead to marriage. But for Maria as a child, there was nothing comparable to the taste of lemonade and the sight of traditional horse races.

Today spirituality tends to be declining, especially in towns, and marriages have become fragile. However, this does not affect the "innate" sense of belonging which is attached to the parish church by all parishioners. Each family still takes a financial part in the building and/or decoration of the church. Personal gifts are made as ex-voto. For the grace received on the election of her brother as a representative of his island at the Maltese Parliament, Maria offered a painting to the second protector of the parish church of her village, Our Lady of Perpetual Succor. In Gozo, a church is like a repository of collective wealth, a place of beauty which belongs to everybody.

Micheline: Maria, one gathers that your father and mother had a natural and serene approach to death, almost matter-of-fact, so to speak, which suggests a deep faith in God and eternal life, doesn't it? You already made it clear that for the majority of the people around you, praying and churchgoing were part of everyday life. Could you now explain what social role the church, in your opinion, has been playing in everybody's experience?

Maria: Yes. In those days when I was growing up—and it's still more or less like that in Gozo—but when I was growing up, and I am speaking of the nineteen twenties, thirties, forties and fifties, the church—I mean the building and the activities or services that went on there— played a very important role in one's life, whether you were a child or an adult. We had, especially in the village, no social clubs of any kind; it was the only place where one went to, dressed a little better than usual, where you'd meet your fellow villagers, and you'd meet God especially and the priest; and most important of all, you would feel elevated because the services and the sermons were all spirit elevating. As a child, I looked forward to *festas** because on that day, the church would be beautifully decorated with chandeliers, damask and flowers, and there would be a procession, and we would have the *qubbajt*† vendor, who would have put up his highly decorated stall in the street adjoining the church. There would be *qubbajt* [expression of delight]! *Qubbajt* was a sort of hard sweet called "nougat"; you could have it brown with almonds, or you could have it white. For young people who were friendly, or who were getting

---

*Feast days celebrating the patron saint(s) in the village.
†Nougat.

engaged or married in the near future, it was a must that the boy would buy a good piece of *qubbajt* for his girlfriend.

Now I'm remembering I had a friend, Matilda, who lived down the street, and she was on speaking terms with a boy of Santa Lucia. For some reason or other, her family was not pleased with this, with what was going on, although you may be sure it was very, very innocent. Well, on one feast day, her boyfriend gave her a beautiful piece of nougat, which of course you can't eat at one go, and she couldn't take it home, so she said: "Maria, will you keep it for me?" and I said: "Willingly." You can guess that Maria ate more of the nougat than the . . . [laughter] girlfriend actually ate. Now on another occasion, I myself was given a piece of nougat which I ate, not in the house but on the threshing floor adjoining our land, because we had extensive lands around our farm house. AND . . . my brother, who was six years younger than me, who was always teasing me somehow or other, started SHOUTING as loudly as he could: "Maria *tagħna, l-għarus taħa l-qubbajt!* Maria *tagħna, l-għarus taħa l-qubbajt!*" [Lively and amused.] That is: "My sister Maria, she has been given a piece of nougat by her *għarus!*" A *għarus* is a bridegroom, but it was not a bridegroom at all; it would be a boyfriend.

Well, besides that, the services in the church included speakers or preachers, and on certain occasions like the Lenten sermons, we would have preachers coming from other parishes, maybe from Malta. And I looked forward to those occasions; because I always liked a good speaker who would be a sort of lecturer, and some of them would illustrate the theological point, or the religious point—call it what you will—with a *fatt.*[81] A *fatt* would be a story which could have happened in the Middle Ages or later on, or in the seventeenth century—it didn't matter—or recently; but it was always something which had actually happened. They always illustrated their points from the Old Testament, and I LIKED that story scenery of the Old Testament because we didn't have a Bible at that time, I'm ashamed to say. Now in the home, nowadays EVERY GOZITAN HOME has a Bible which is translated in Maltese, straight from the Hebrew-Greek by a very able friend of mine, Professor Karmel Sant,[82] and they keep it in a prominent place on the bookshelves, so that when the Jehovah Witnesses, who are a sect, turn up and pretend they have the Bible, we are ready with our own Bible to tell them that we

---

*Literally, "true fact, or event."

CAN READ our Bible and you DON'T NEED-THEM-TO-COME-AND-READ the Bible to us [very determined].

Now let's go back again to the twenties and thirties as I am saying. For children, even funerals of children—not of the elderly, but funerals of children—were a bit of fun because when we heard the church bells ringing a *frajha*, so we would gather where the deceased baby was, and follow this small procession.[83]

Micheline: Yet concerning the burial ceremony of the adults, I am sure, Maria, you still have in mind some memories which, you said, had an emotional effect on you, then a child . . . .

Maria: Yes, I remember. One thing which struck me when I was a child was the burial procession of Dun Girgor ta' Damjan.* I was walking, or rather running, to be present for this unusual event: the body, in mass vestments, was not placed in a coffin; it was lying on a sort of stretcher carried by four men. Another burial of a saintly priest which was the talk of the town was that of Monsignor Luigi Vella tad-Dublun.† Can you imagine, Micheline, during a burial service in the cathedral, women vying with each other to tear off a bit of his garments so that they could keep it as an amulet . . . ?[84]

Micheline: These were people out of the common, of course. But as far as the ordinary parishioners were concerned, would their corpse, after the service at church, be carried to the churchyard or to a neighboring cemetery to be buried there?

Maria: No, because in those days we hadn't a cemetery. We were buried . . . my father and mother are buried in the crypt of our church. You see, they had a funeral service in the church; then they would go down some steps and they would go in the crypt. Now the public-health authorities saw that people should better be buried in open-air cemeteries.[85] So we have a section in Santa Maria Cemetery; in fact, my brother is buried there.

Micheline: Maria, before it comes to its end, a lifetime is also marked, isn't it, by other, more cheerful celebrations at church?

Maria: Indeed, and an important one was the bridal ceremony. Whether you were invited or not. If you are invited, you would be more involved, and, of course, you would have your best finery on, and you

---

*Don Gregory, son of Damian.
†"Of the Doubloon."

would see what was going on. It was simple—the bridal ceremonies in the church were very simple. Today it is, I would say, a little . . . overdone! Recently we were present—I and my friend Micheline—in Sannat, where there was a marriage; the bride was from Sannat, but she had been educated, and she got a medical degree in England. She was marrying an Englishman whose mother was Maltese, so you can imagine . . . the guests were partly English, partly Maltese from SLIEMA[86]—where the snobs live—and partly from the Sannat family. But the mother happened to be, the mother of the bride—although she lives in Sannat—she happened to be from Victoria, where they think they are . . . a little better than actual village people. So it was a POLISHED, what I call "polished" wedding. In the church, it was beautifully organized, and it was said in English; I'm glad the parish priest, who came from my village, spoke English tolerably well, and the prayers were of course English, and the songs were English because in Victoria we have an excellent choir. It is from Saint George's, from the Basilica of Saint George. So we had excellent singing. So there again, the church even today, and I'm speaking of 1987, is somewhere where people have a little coming together, where there is a little social life, where there is something beautiful to go to and hear.

After that—to go on with that wedding in question, recent wedding in question—there was a reception at Ta' Ċenċ.[87] Ta' Ċenċ is a hotel, internationally known by now; it's a bit expensive but a good hotel, very good . . . . I'm not doing any advertising, but it's like that. Well anyway, the food—the actual food, the contents and the presentation—were something out of this world. I am of the opinion that the chef is Italian, and the result . . . [expression of enjoyment] was something wonderful. Incidentally we met a gentleman from Sliema, and my friend Micheline naturally said: "Are you from Gozo?" and I would have liked to have a picture of the MAN'S FACE being so . . . feeling insulted, because he was from Sliema and he was thought to be from Gozo. In Sliema, they think Gozo is a bit beyond . . . not a bit beyond, behind progress. Humm, humm! I don't know what kind of progress they have in Sliema because sometimes the modern progress—I would call it more regressive, a regression. Anyway. So you see, still nowadays the church is a place where social life takes place, some way or other.

Micheline: Maria, you said that like all other children, you were looking forward to the yearly *festa*. I would like to know more about your own village *festa*.

Maria: In my village, we had two, because we had a double protector, or patron saint, we would call it. We had, and still have, Saint Gregory the Great and Our Lady of Perpetual Succor. First, Saint Gregory: his feast is on twelfth March, and in those days, on Gozo—not in Malta, but on Gozo—the twelfth March was a public holiday. I mean all work stopped; it was like a Sunday, and if you saw some farmer from another village who was maybe watering . . . for us, for the Kerċemese, it was like a scandal. Well anyway, in Victoria, there was something to see because at four o'clock in the morning, a cannon would be fired to say that the procession would take place. Because in March it could be stormy . . . so, if the cannon at four o'clock in the morning from Victoria, from the citadel up there, would go, that meant that the *festa* procession would be taking place from the cathedral in Victoria to my village of Kerċem. And FROM ALL OVER GOZO, priests, altar boys and *fratelli** would get ready. *Fratelli* would be men, not monks or anything, but they would belong to a congregation, a *fratellanza*,[†] and they would have a white garment, neatly laundered and starched for the occasion; on top of that, they had a sort of cape: if it was the *fratellanza* of the Sacrament, it would be red; if it was blue, light blue or celeste, that would be something to do with the Blessed Virgin; and in Victoria, they had an elite one called tad-Duluri,[‡] and the *sinjuri*[§] generally belong to it. I can't see why they should put the question of elitism in a *fratellanza* with—Jesus save us!—something to do with religion.

Well anyway . . . AND we would have the ordinary people, a considerable number of parishioners, and the bigger the parish, the bigger the crowd of pilgrims would be, and they would walk in order of precedence: the youngest parish would march first, and last of all, we usually had the cathedral parish with the bishop in a very ugly GREEN hat, and I remember Bishop Pace who had a weak-looking face, and with that green hat, I didn't like him at all because it made him look a little as if he was already half dead. Well anyway, Saint Gregory's *festa*, for us, would be something!

Micheline: Do you know the origin of the procession?

---

*Lay members of a religious confraternity.
†Religious guild.
‡"Of Sorrows."
§Rich people.

Maria: Well, that pilgrimage on Saint Gregory's day was related to a vow,[88] because—they say—there was a plague on Gozo, and the people promised: "If the plague stops, and our population is not totally taken away, we'll go every year on pilgrimage from the cathedral to the small church of Saint Gregory in Kerċem." Now when the small church near Lunzjata Valley was no longer existent,[89] and the Kerċemese had built a new one, it took place at the new one of course. That was RELIGION WITH A LITTLE JOLLITY—how shall I put it? Because there were prayers, but after that, everyone had a bit of fun: there would be band marches, drinking of wine and merrymaking, a special meal at home, and a lot of flirting for the younger ones.

But what I remember particularly is that my mother always liked me to be dressed in the peak of fashion. Once she bought for me a FINELY knitted dress—oh! it was chic; you may be sure it was chic! Sometimes she even ordered my dresses from England; we had a special catalogue called "Oxendale" and she would order . . . . Once she bought me a ROYAL BLUE taffeta dress, and the people looked at me [lower tone of voice suggesting the people's surreptitious glances and hostile feelings] . . . yooow . . . . My mother's relatives in Algeria would also send all sorts of things;[90] so she would change them somehow: she would go to a good dressmaker in Victoria—Ta l-Armla,* she was called—and she would describe how she wanted them changed; I once had a VERY LOVELY silk—off-white, we'd call it—dirty white, self-patterned shawl. It would be a shawl for an evening, and they converted it into a lovely blouse with small—how do you call it?—with small balls at the bottom, like Micheline has in her bathroom,[91] just like those, and it was beautiful . . . . Well, that's beside the point, but I must always speak of clothes because I have become—of all things besides being a head teacher, a dress designer, and I'm proud to say I design my clothes; the material, I get it from Pjazza it-Tokk,† and the remnants—believe it or not—come from Oxford Street, from the best shops there!

Micheline: So, Maria, Saint Gregory's Feast was a big occasion, not only for the people of Kerċem, but for all Gozo, wasn't it? But nowadays, is Saint Gregory's procession still taking place as before?

---

* "Of the widow" (a nickname).
† The central meeting square in town.

Maria: Unfortunately not. About twenty-five years ago, a dispute arose between two parishes on a point of precedence,[92] and the traditional procession was stopped. They decided to put it off, WHICH-IS-A-PITY! And now it takes place in the village, but not on a diocesan basis. There is only a very small, penitential pilgrimage on the Saturday before.

Micheline: But you have a second patron in the village. Therefore you celebrate another *festa*, don't you?

Maria: Yes. In the summer, we had, and still have another *festa* in honor of Our Lady of Perpetual Succor, tas-Sokkors* as we usually call her . . . . The main picture in Kerċem church, the titular picture, depicts Our Lady in heaven looking down on St. Gregory the Great kneeling in prayer. In the foreground we see victims of the plague, some corpses and a few men kneeling in supplication. The background shows the Gozo Citadel and a long procession coming down from the cathedral to the main square, It-Tokk. The painter, Salvatore Busuttil, cleverly combined the two patron saints in one magnificent picture.

Actually the miraculous picture of Our Lady of Perpetual Succor in Via Merulana in Rome looks more like an early icon. And a picture like that hangs in the sacristy of our parish church. I had the pleasure to offer it in 1947. I had made a vow to Our Lady. I had read the story and it had impressed me so much, so I said: "If . . . if." Well, in 1947, there was an election in Malta and Gozo, an election of the members of Parliament, of a new government. And in Gozo, WE HAD, very sanely and very wisely, set up a Gozo party, a political party which was neither left nor right, so that the Maltese couldn't use us; we had a political party with the members, with the gentlemen who stood for election: ALL GOZITANS! Then that was something which could put Gozo on its feet, because I'm ashamed to say that Gozo was ALWAYS THE CINDER-ELLA OF MALTA. They would come to Gozo just ON THE EVE of the election, promise a lot of good things, and even if they were elected, they never really . . . did what they promised to do. Now I'm proud to say that my brother, Anton Calleja—he was only twenty-five—had just come out of university. Sure, nobody knew him really because he had spent most of his time in Malta, in the British Institute and in the library, teaching and doing all sorts of things. Well, he was one of those who stood for election.[93]

---

*(Our Lady) of (Perpetual) Succor.

My father himself was, you know, political minded; he was pro-Stricklandian, that is, pro-British, and he was getting on in years, had a little high pressure, blood pressure, so I said: "Our Lady, please give us a good result, so that Anton will be elected." It was not for the power or for anything, but just so that my father would be pleased. I knew he would be pleased. And to save him maybe from a stroke. SO I MADE A VOW [melodious tone]. And . . . he was elected, to make the story short.

Micheline: So, Maria, your vow being accomplished, you offered your ex-voto gift, didn't you?

Maria: I did, naturally. I went up to Victoria near Saint George's, and there was a barber who, besides being a hairdresser, used to make beautiful lace designs for the lace-makers: they were black and green, a special kind of green, AND he was a good painter as well. So I went up to him with a picture of the Holy Mother of Perpetual Succor, as I had seen it in a special book, which a teacher of mine had given me, and I said: "Please, can you do me a largish picture as big as that, say four feet by three feet, or five by two and a half, something like that, because I want to offer it to our church?" And he said: "Yes." And he cleverly did it AND he put a gold frame to it, and that's only for SIX POUNDS! This is in 1947. And that goes to show how the prices of things have gone up, and-up-and-up-and-up-and up . . . . Well, Our Lady of Perpetual Succor is there, and it has a story of its own.

Now, tas-Sokkors, as we say, tas-Sokkors loomed much in the horizon for us children. Because we'd have a new dress, first and foremost. On the eve of the *festa*, we'd have the band march in the village. We would have fireworks, AND WE WOULD BUY *luminata*.* That is, we would have a glass of lemonade, of *luminôta, luminôta, luminôta* . . . [rapt in her memories]. Now there is a small alley near the church, and two men from Victoria came with a sort of half-barrel, which was filled with ice, big chunks of ice, and in the middle they would have a sort of zinc cylinder, and in it they would put water and lemon, maybe a little sugar, and they would turn it 'round, and 'round and 'round, and they would have glasses ready, and with one penny, YOU-COULD-BUY-ONE-GLASS-OF-*LUMINÔTA* . . . [expression of ecstasy], which for us children, was . . . [laughter]. There is a certain drink which could take you

---

*Lemonade. Note the countrylike pronunciation in the next sentence.

up to heaven—I don't know its name now—but there is a certain drink which can take you up . . . [laughter]. That was *luminata* . . . .

Micheline: On *festa* days, I presume that the horse races were also an attraction?

Maria: They were indeed for all of us, men as well as children. We wouldn't miss the races for *mitt skud*,* that is, for eight Maltese pounds! Actually I wasn't interested in the horse racing as such, but it took place on a road from the police station, where it still is, up to a lovely old house, which, I think, in the English language, would be called a manor house; it belonged to a well-to-do farming family who even had a *xrik*.† Now unless you have good lands and many workers, you couldn't have a *xrik*, a sort of partner, cofarmer, or foreman of works. So they had a small room adjoining their manor house—let's say that—and on it there would be twelve beautiful flags—rectangular highly colored flags called *paljijiet*.‡ One is a *palju*, and there would be twelve of them of silk material, either one-colored or patterned, and believe me, they were BEAUTIFUL! I don't know where they brought 'em from because certainly in the shops of Victoria, you couldn't find such material. Now they would fix them up so that every winner of the race would get a *palju*.

To see the races, I just had to pass from the backdoor of our farmyard, to cross one field or two, and here I was in the right place to watch the races. So aah! on the day, I felt a little proud because I was in the center of things, so to say. Well, in the evening, there would be a special service in the church, culminating in a procession, and maybe your parents would buy again some *qubbajt*, and of course we had a special dinner at home on that day. So we always looked forward to a *festa*. And you would meet your friends, and when you get older, you might have an eye on admirers, and many boys and girls would find a partner on *festa* days because you would be in your best dress, you would be in your finery, and it would be a little time of leisure, when you could walk up and down, when you could be looked at and look at people. It was just the time for beginning a serious friendship.

---

*A hundred *skudi* (the *skud* is an obsolete coin worth twenty pence).

† A partner (from *xirek*, which means "to associate").

‡ Flags, generally made of silk or damask, given as a prize to winners in a horse race (*Maltese-English Dictionary*, s.v. *palju*, plural: *paljijiet*).

I'm remembering I have a cousin called Konsilja; she is in Australia now, and she had another friend from the Sciberras family: they were of the same age, and in order to be conspicuous—because I'm sure it was that—THEY PUT ON A HAT . . . . Now to put on a hat [laughter] in Kerċem's *festa* was something! But I can still see them [enjoying her vivid memories]: Konsilja had a playful smile in her eyes, and those two girls walked up and down as if they were on a stage, walking up and down the principal street with that hat. . . . I can still see them, and Konsilja was dressed in yellow, and this is ages ago . . . . Well, she got friendly with the Rinoll boy, and they eventually got married, and, you know, because jobs were scarce at that time, they emigrated.[94] Emigration was without quota in those days; you could emigrate. So they emigrated to Australia, and incidentally this very summer, on the *festa* day, I met one of her children, a boy called Paul like his grandfather, who is my uncle.[95] And this boy is smart. Anyway I asked him: "What is your job?" He said: "I'm an electrician." But an electrician of some standing, because I remember his mother describing that he would have a special post, and if there were something wrong with the lifts in the principal hotels or principal organizations, he would be on call. So he must have had some education.

Well, you see, on *festa* days, many hearts are mended, many hearts are broken [smile] sometimes, and friendships start. As for me, I was always on the lookout, not for serious friendships, but for the complacency of having somebody looking at me [smile] the right way. I was always out for an admirer, but nothing serious. I never wanted to be really involved in something which would implicate me . . . . Ough! [Exclamation accompanied with slight shudder] . . . .

Micheline: Well, Maria, you have shown the important part played by the church in social life.

Maria: But the church for us means more than a social life. We have our spirituality . . . it gets its life from the church, especially from the sacraments: the church is the house of God, and you went there to be baptized when you were still a baby; later you received the sacrament of confirmation; and later you got the sacrament of Holy Communion; when you grow up, you may be ordained as a priest, you may be married, and when you are ready to go, and actually go . . . , you have a funeral in church.

NOW, alas! it does not always mean all that—there are people who . . . sometimes it's only on the surface they have this religion; it doesn't go down deep, and when they find some obstacle, sometimes politics—because politics now are getting rather hot and rather dirty and rather . . . sometimes, for reasons of politics, sometimes they go abroad, and you know, in a big city, you don't feel the need of going to church unless you are really religious, and sometimes they come across people who HA-HA-HA-HA them for their beliefs and all that, and they say: "YOU STILL BELIEVE IN HEAVEN; YOU STILL BELIEVE IN HEAVEN!" [High-pitched, mocking voice]. And so they leave religion. Sometimes in my village, I'm ashamed to say, there are a lot of things going on which would be unheard of in my younger days, such as . . . not abortions, but you know, fidelity to one's marriage partner has been broken unashamedly. So that goes as far as the church has to do with people in my village.

Micheline: Now, Maria, let us go back to Anton's election. I would like to know how the good news reached you, and how the people reacted.

Maria: I remember that long vote-counting night in 1947. In our house it was as if we were keeping a wake—when somebody is being buried; in those days we had neither telephone nor radio. The news from England and from Malta came to the Banca Giuratale in Victoria.[96] It was relayed on a loudspeaker. I remember one neighbor had just come down from Victoria at about 11:00 P.M., and he said: "They are saying that Tony is going to make it." "You, go away!" I said [angry tone of voice], because I knew that the first count was low. Well, 'round about midnight, a man from Victoria, Feliċ Ta' Sillato, came and said: "Toni *tala'*!* Toni *tala'*! Tony is elected!" I just couldn't believe it: "Toni *tala'*! Toni *tala'*!

The first thing I did was to wake up my father very gently and tell him the news [expression of great tender attention]. You know a shock, even of joy, can be harmful. I didn't want him to get the good news from other persons. So he put on his clothes, and THE NEXT MOMENT, the house was full of people [rhythm of speech suggesting excitement in the house], and I gave them drinks—very little, because not all the neighbors were our friends. There were . . . some friends of ours, and some not. And I didn't buy a lot of drinks because in the village everybody knows what you buy. So I didn't want to buy a lot of drinks in advance. You see, if he hadn't been elected, we would have been ashamed. I didn't even

---

*Telagħ or *tala'* means "to go up"; here it means "is elected."

put up the curtains . . . because we have a set of curtains for special occasions, and a set of curtains for daily use. I hadn't done anything in preparation for an occasion.

So at twelve o'clock, midnight, we had a house full of people, having drinks. They came to congratulate us and all that, and we wept a little [smile]; you know, it was like something unheard of . . . in a Kerčem house, a FARMER'S, a CARPENTER'S HOUSE! Well anyway, I thanked the people. Then we shut the house for a little while, and then at three o'clock, I got up and I said: "I must go and hear mass." That was the first thing I did, and when I went home, there were friends, and I'm remembering one called Rosanna, and she said: "Can I help you with something?" And I said: "You know what . . . ? Go to the public garden or send somebody to the public garden and bring some flowers." Because I always had the feeling, even today, that the best decoration of a house, however simple it is, is some flowers, and in the back gardens, one doesn't grow . . . in gardens in those days, you only grew VEGETABLES [laughter] or either some kinds of prickly pears to give it to goats! You don't grow flowers, humm! You would have seen my mother's face if you said you were . . . [laughter] planting flowers in the back garden!

So I said that, and I told another one: "Go and order a box of whiskey and a box of vermouth and a box of that . . . from Mr.—he's called Ritz because his nickname is Rizzu, and he calls his shop and his hotel "The Ritz" [laughter], R-I-T-Z. And, of course, my neighbor friends helped me to put up the lace curtains; they were true lace curtains! Somebody brought the flowers, and by the first boat, about ten o'clock, my brother turned up, because he had been in Malta: when you have your votes being counted, you have to sit by your ballot box and see that you are getting what is due to you. So when the counting of actual votes and the election results were out, Tony came home, accompanied by friends, and for us, THAT was an occasion . . . and I remember a small neighbor boy of ours, who was only six and now is manager of the waterworks: he CLAPPED his hands and he shouted: "*Viva l-avukat viva!*"* [Laughter.] It was something special in those days.

And then of course, Tony started his political career. He would go to Malta often, and there would be a sitting at night; sometimes he re- turned very late from Malta, sometimes he had to spend the whole night

---

* "Long live the advocate," or "Hurrah for the advocate!"

over in Malta, and they were poorly paid: one pound for one sitting. Well anyway . . . Dr. Boffa[97] had such a high opinion of him, after hearing his maiden speech, that he offered him the Ministry of Agriculture. You may be sure that Anton, being surrounded by farmers, would be a good minister of agriculture—more than any Maltese, because in those days the people who stood for election would all be of some profession, either medical or legal, so they wouldn't know about agriculture. But my brother said: "If I could have the Ministry of Education . . . ." Later on, they offered what has now come to fruition, the Ministry of Gozo. They said: "We give you the ministry for all Gozo." So some friends of his, you know, said that he had not actually begun his career as an *avukat*, and so somebody advised him and said: "Ton, you know in politics, you are in one day, and maybe after some years, you may be out. And you haven't actually started your career . . . ."

I remember that was a tough time; there was a tension in our house. We couldn't advise of course; he was still young, and it was a serious decision whether to be minister for all Gozo, whether to drop your political career altogether and start a career as a solicitor. Well, I'm glad he did that because politics, humm! and people in Gozo, if they have given the vote to you, AND if some of them pretend that they have given the vote [smile] to you, whatever favor it is—whether it's a job, whether it's an extension of their field, whether they want—the permit to build their house right in the middle of the street—whatever it is, they expect you to bring them that favor from the minister. Now Anton was not the type to go to the ministry and LINE a minister's pocket.

So Anton, I think, must have decided the right thing: he decided to drop politics and begin the career of an advocate. He actually kept rooms in Palma Street, and he has been dead now eleven years, and he is still remembered for his integrity. You'd be surprised; last week I went to another lawyer because I had a little problem, and in the waiting room, there was a man whom I had never known, and he said: "You are from Kerċem. You had an *avukat!*" I said: "Yes." He came up to me and said: "Ahhh! If I had taken his advice, I would have won the case . . . ." And he said such nice things. Up to this day, without my soliciting any opinion whatsoever, people whom I've never known come to tell me something like that.

Now I will tell you an incident which I liked very much: three years ago, I was coming up from my bathing in Marsalforn, because I like to bathe in Għar Qawqla*—it's a fairly big mouthful to spell or to say: Għar Qawqla! When it's fine, you can swim in the big bay, and that beats everything. When it's choppy, you have to swim in the smaller bay, AND if it's very, very rough . . . you may be lucky enough to have the services of a nun, WHO brings down a rope, and she ties you to this rope, and she keeps on very tightly so that you can swim, and if it gets very rough, she can pull-you-up. Have you ever heard of that? [Laughter.] This is in 1987, and here my friend Micheline has experienced THIS . . . .

Well anyway, about three years ago, I was coming up from my bathing—a bathing which is a daily must in Gozo if you are spending your days in Marsalforn—and two men were coming up with a small truck, and they had sacks of *bettieħ*; *bettieħ* are melons, and I adore melons because they are good, they keep, and with our local cheese, which we call *ġobon maħsul*,† that's unbeatable, like *quelque chose pour commencer* or *quelque chose pour finir*‡98 the whole meal. They're unbeatable. Well, I bought a sack of melons, and you know that's heavy, and the man who eventually came from Għarb, kindly brought it up to my flat, and of course I paid him, and when I was paying him and we were talking a little, his head was just in front of a photograph of my brother which I keep there in the flat, and I JUST couldn't escape the question: "Do you know this man?" He said: "No." I said: "That was an *avukat*." "An *avukat*? I've never gone to court," he said. "I've nothing to do with *avukati*."§ Then he had a second look, and he said: "I KNOW that man! That man gave me a good advice once." And he told me the story:

One man from Għarb, Mr. A, had a cow for sale, and this cow was all right except that it had one small defect, which could be visible to anyone who wanted to inspect the cow from head to tail, from under, from above, from left, right and center. Well anyway, Mr. A had a cow for sale. Mr. B liked the cow, and they were in the middle of the bargain; it was HALF, nearly . . . you would say 90 percent concluded. But Mr. A was a very conscientious man, and he was afraid that Mr. B hadn't seen the fault of the cow, so he went to my brother, and he said: "*Avukat*, this

---

*"An inlet and cave on the south of Marsalforn" (*Maltese-English Dictionary*, s.v. Għar Qawqla).

† Marinated cheese.

‡ "A little something to start" or "a little something to finish."

§ Plural of *avukat*, "an advocate."

happened so and so; what am I going to do? I don't want to lose the sale because it's a good bargain, and at the same time, I don't want it on my conscience that I have sold something with a fault." So my brother said: "Have you got a friend?" He said: "Of course!" "So tell your friend to go to Mr. B, the buyer, and tell him to say this: 'Mr. A is selling a cow, but . . . humm, listen: it has a defect, and he doesn't speak of it.'" So there and then, Mr. B said: "That's done!" and there and then, when the other left, he took the money and went straight back to Mr. A, the seller, because he thought that Mr. C was going to buy the cow, and he would have been there to scare him off, and the sale went through. And you know what the defect was? The defect was that the cow had one breast, or udder, a little larger than the other . . . but evidently the seller was a conscientious man, because that's not a defect at all.

Chapter 8

Maria's Teaching Career

With her choice of a profession, Maria refused the role traditionally assigned to a woman in the social network—that of a housewife—and took her fate into her own hands. To do that she received the support of her parents, and later, that of her younger brother, Anton. For the father who had known poverty as well as the hardships of emigration, the only valuable wealth was knowledge, not money. Maria was aware that employment provided a woman with essential economic independence, but she never regarded her work as a purely money-making exercise. For her mother, accepting as a personal challenge the necessity of fighting in life was unquestionable. Like her, Maria became a fighter, determined to attain professional achievement in spite of all the difficulties she had to overcome, not to speak of the pain of being far from home when attending courses in London. Each step on her long trajectory was experienced as a victory to be proud of.

An enthusiastic, conscientious pedagogue, she used to collect up-to-date information from various sources, including British magazines, and adapt the material to her local audience. She practiced dramatization with her schoolchildren, convinced that playing was a means of education. In a sense, her teaching was the fruitful result of an Anglo-Gozitan graft. But she wanted to do more to benefit her island, and was eventually given, thanks to her fabulous energy and pragmatic nature, the opportunity of organizing a school of home economics, which became a model praised by Maltese officials. Public consideration was a great reward for her.

Maria felt fulfilled in her profession. However, she managed not to give up completely the pleasure a Gozitan woman finds in taking care of her house: career and household were then somehow harmonized.

Micheline: Maria, it must have been a great satisfaction for your father to see before he died his son succeed in all that he had undertaken as a young politician, then as a lawyer. Another source of joy and reward for your father, I am sure, was your personal achievement. Would you now tell me about your life as a teacher, as well as your career ascent.

Maria: So I had that job! I had the job of . . . how shall I say? . . . a schoolteacher, which is demanding. Micheline, the job of a schoolteacher is very demanding if you take your vocation in earnest: you have to read, you have to be always up-to-date with methods because they are always changing. In the old days, they didn't change OFTEN, as they change nowadays [smile]. But I was always seeing what things were up, and I was always ordering magazines from England—I mean educational magazines—and I would take these to school for the pupils because they had so little firsthand experience. They had only what the village and the immediate environment offered, and that was that!

So I supplemented that by pictures and other visual aids. And what's the use of having English books talking about railways, talking about the height and the width of rooms in England, and how to calculate the length of wallpaper to be used[99] . . . and about so many things, and about the THEATRE . . . when the children's theatre consisted only maybe of a small room, a garage maybe, put up for the occasion, with some clumsy and primitive acting? So I used to collect these informative magazines and get the children around my desk, AND THEY WOULD LOOK-AND LISTEN wide-eyed, as if I were the man from the moon [laughter]! And I would tell them: "Now *ara*,* look! THIS is a railway. Look how these are going and coming!" You see, because LEARNING means two things: you read and you learn the basics. BUT second to that, it means experience. And in the village, they had no cars; they would leave the village rarely, and they had no firsthand experience except, of course, with animals and farming. But of the outer world, a big city for example, what it would look like—that would be out of the question.

So what I'm coming to is that you have to do homework, and you have to correct; I used to take the exercise books and correct them one by one,

---

* "See!"

and on the following day at school, I would call the children: "*Grech, ejja daqsxejn hawn!*"* near my desk, and correct them, and tell them why they . . . . Now that means a lot of work! And every now and then, we would have an inspectress from Malta with a hat, and [smile] when in Victoria, they saw a lady with a hat at church because she would stay at the Duke of Edinburgh Hotel, and she would go to the seven o'clock mass, either in Saint George's or Saint Francis's, and the teachers from Victoria—in my school, there were many teachers from Victoria—so they would know that the inspectress was here as soon as they saw a lady with a hat: "Ah! Our inspectress!" So the first thing: they would come earlier than usual; they would send the girls home to get the uniform, because the uniform was something for special occasions, and they would smarten up a little. The head teacher had a lot of red bows made of crêpe paper—you know that paper, wrinkled paper for the girls' hair. AND we would see that our notes of lessons were quite in order. Well, I was once—how shall I say?—so "emotioned up" that I didn't give the proper lessons I usually give when I am on an everyday routine . . . .

Well anyway, a teacher, for us and all of us—I'm not speaking of myself only—I'm proud to say that the teachers in those days, although they had no real training in a training college of education, they were conscientious and they worked hard. And we were interested in the children, not only as pupils but . . . in the children, and I think we did a wonderful work. And I'm grateful to my head teacher, Evelyn Fiorini, because we were given first-class education, as I said, and I tried to do my best and I think I did that. Because even now that my ex-students are grown-ups, they respect me, and they greet me with a friendly smile or word.

Micheline: Naturally all marks of respect and friendliness mean a lot to you, Maria, now that you have retired. But during your professional life, you also had, I am sure, testimonies of affection from your pupils. On one particular occasion, as far as I know, the schoolchildren's reaction toward you went straight to your heart, didn't it?

Maria: True! The finest thing in my educational life I remember well: once I was given a transfer to Victoria by mistake because there was another teacher whose name was like mine, Calleja. But in those days, NOBODY DARED TO DISOBEY ORDERS . . . even though one felt

---

* "Grech, come a little up here!" Grech is a surname.

one had been wronged somehow! So I stayed for a week in Victoria. Finally Miss Cortis, the head, told me: "Maria, you go back to your school, where you belong!" and I went back—say at three o'clock in the afternoon, when it is still schooltime—and my class overlooked the road, and it had louver system windows, so that the cold current of air doesn't reach the children. And . . . when I was near, underneath the window— because the window was a bit higher than the actual street level—I saw my schoolchildren; most of them were boys who didn't like school; it was hard for me . . . I was not scolding, but preaching all the time . . . . So they were not a nice bunch, but they were there, behind the window, LOOKING at me and shouting: "*Ġejja . . . ara reġgħet ġiet! Ara reġgħet ġiet!*"* And I think that was the most rewarding compliment for me because—as I said before—they didn't like schooling, but they received me with such a welcome. I couldn't have a better welcome, not even if they had brought the band of Ta' l-Istilla† or Ta' l-Iljun‡[100] . . . .

Well, one fine day, Maria Micallef[101]—she was an excellent headmistress in the secondary school in Victoria—came and said: Maria, what ARE-YOU-DOING here?" Sort of: "You are wasting your time here, and why don't you come up to my school?" And I said: "Yes, I'll come," without thinking about the salary, about the promotion, about anything, because I felt it was doing something better than I did. And I went to Victoria secondary school, where I started teaching English and mathematics to the younger, in the lower forms, and I was happy then. But there was a friction in the class—believe it or not!—because some of them belonged to Ta' l-Istilla, and some of them belonged to Ta' l-Iljun. Once I took them for private lessons in my house at Kerċem: I put them around a big table, and I started teaching math; it was near Santa Maria time, when this movement is a bit more alive,[102] AND they started quarreling. They started quarreling, and they shouted so much that the women who are usually out in the street working lace thought that somebody had been taken sick, or there was something serious.

Well anyway, I started teaching those lower forms; then I was sort of promoted and given the senior, or upper, classes, who were sitting for their G.C.E. ordinary level: I had to teach them English and history,

---

* "She is coming . . . look she came back! Look she came back!"
† "Of the star."
‡ "Of the lion."

and—mind you—English meant a Shakespearian play like *Twelfth Night*; it meant a lot of difficult poetry which I was not at all familiar with, and I had to study that, so I spent the whole weekend correcting exercise books—piles and piles—and preparing for the next Monday. Because you don't go into a class of GROWN-UPS . . . they all came from good families, and I felt sort of more responsible; one of them was the bishop's sister, Teresa Cauchi. One of them is Pawlina Ta' l-Ispanjol.* Another, alas, had to go to Switzerland, because she had TB, and she died in Switzerland, and I remember her mother went 'round the village asking for charity: "Please, can you give me some money because I have to send my daughter to Switzerland, and I don't have all that money?" And I remember somebody said she even sold her rings, and for a Gozitan woman, to sell her rings—it's like selling your eyes or selling your ears [smile] . . . .

Well anyway, I had a nice group of students whom I meet up to this day, and who respect me. I was a bit happy there . . . but the headmistress was not tactful enough. Once I said: "I'm afraid I can't work up that syllabus; it won't be ready for Christmastime." And she said: "You are not building Rome!" And somebody said: "You should have said 'Rome was not built in a day, either.'" But I kept my tongue. She was not diplomatic. If she had just helped me a little . . . . Anyway, and my salary was never raised; I never had a promotion in spite of working so hard. So I started looking at the senior teachers: they had been correcting piles and piles of exam papers, and I would be correcting papers, too . . . . AND I used to watch them walking up the street like . . . elderly women. I was still young in those days, but I said: "Humm, humm . . . I don't want to be like THAT when I get old."

And anyway, I hated my weekends, all doing schoolwork, because I always liked my house to be a little smart. On weekends in Gozo, it's a must: even the girls who work in factories, just all of us, at the weekends do a little housecleaning from top to bottom; I hated the fact that I couldn't do that, although my mother—you can be sure—was keeping the house quite decently, but I still . . . I didn't feel the loss of not going out to a party, or not going to a disco just as they do nowadays, or to a cinema, or meeting a boyfriend. No, that I didn't miss at all. I missed the fact that I couldn't take up the stairs' carpets and give them a good

---

* "Of the Spaniard" (a family nickname).

sunshine, and a good beating in the sunshine. That I was missing—being a woman, sort of . . . I'll put an end to this.

So I had a friend, a teacher in Għasri—Carmena—and she said: "My head teacher is retiring because she is getting near sixty, Miss Masini." And I took a bit of advice from my brother—although he was younger, I always discussed important matters with him—and he said: "Yes, I'll help you. Do that." So I asked for my transfer without my head teacher knowing. Maria Micallef wouldn't leave me, who was—I'm not bragging—a good teacher; she wouldn't leave me. So I got my transfer and was given instructions: "As from that day . . . she would go there, and be in Miss Masini's shoes." That is, she would be acting head teacher. Anyway that meant I would have only one class to teach, having to run the school. You can imagine WHAT Miss Micallef said to me! Everytime I met her, she would . . . not insult me, but say something unpleasant. Well, I made it and I went to Għasri.

Going to Għasri from Republic Street, the first week was a bit hard because it was QUITE different: the children were quiet, not very well dressed—clean, but not very well dressed—and you see, the atmosphere was as if you had gone to some . . . in the World of Beyond. Even my village was a little smarter than that. But after some time, I got used to the situation. For teachers, I couldn't have better teachers. They were nice and hardworking. One beautiful thing I remember . . . because in Victoria there was a British Institute, and they organized a drama festival competition, and the schools were taking part. I said: "From such a small bunch, what can I do?" And I found something from Dickens—just a short scene, just one scene from Dickens. I chose one girl and two boys, and I trained them; I bought some clothes from the Pjazza,[103] as usual, and I sewed the right clothes, and you may be sure we were one of the best. George Xerri, who is still director of Astra,[104] made beautiful comments.

Another nice thing I remember: we used to organize a little drama in a big room—it was not a hall, because the school premises consisted of a house, a country house—so I would pick stories from their Maltese book, and I would set them in dramatization form, so that they would really understand what they were doing. My teachers would get some old hats from their cupboards. I would fish up something . . . and the children were being educated. They were having a good time, and you may imagine we the teachers, also had a good time. I remember once one of them entered so much in the spirit of what she was doing that she went improvising. Now in those days, when you are doing drama, YOU DO EXACTLY [tone of command] as you've been trained to do, EVEN the actions, EVEN the movements, even if you walk up and down, but SHE was so captivated that she started improvising and doing things, going up and down, which we liked so much. And that is real education.

Well, I stayed at Għasri some time, six years or so. As I told you before, I was only a teacher acting as a head teacher with only one pound compensation for all this. So I said, at Għajn Sielem, on the other part of Gozo near Mġarr, there is going to be a vacancy because the head teacher was of retiring age, and I said to Anton: "I would like to go there." And my brother said: "OK, I'll speak to the minister." At that time, Anton was in Parliament and he was respected by Miss Agatha Barbara, who was then the minister of education. Well, I got the transfer, TO THE AMAZEMENT of my teachers, because in Gozo the nearer home you are, the better you are. In that case, I was asking to be far away from home. In fact, I had to get up at six o'clock, leave home at about half past six to catch the seven o'clock . . . it was not a bus; it was a charàbanc . . . to get transport to my school. SO I stayed at Għajn Sielem, and that was a NEW confrontation for me because the Għajn Sielem children were very . . . at first, difficult to discipline. You know, the lady before me, being old and being from the village . . . there was a bit of lax discipline, but I managed, by God's help, to get it down to normal.

The first thing I did—believe it or not—was this [smile]. Because I had to get on good terms, not with the children only, but with the parents, and in Għajn Sielem, they are well famed for being smart and self-assertive . . . . So it was Parents' Day. Parents' Day would be open day in the school, and the parents would come and discuss their child's progress with the teacher in charge. Well, the first thing I did, I went and bought two bottles of Martini, one black and the other dry; it was only six shillings in those days. Now you have to pay two pounds and five shillings. Well . . . and I bought some biscuits. Because otherwise they wouldn't come for Parents' Day—I mean, they didn't care much. But the word went 'round the village: "*Is-sinjûra qed tagħti ix-xorb! Is-sinjûra qed tagħti ix-xorb!*"* [Laughter.] AND they came. They came, and I started to talk with them, and dialogue with them, to make them a

---

*"The *sinjûra* [headmistress] is offering drinks."

little understand—how shall I say?—what I was like, what I wanted, and that I was in earnest, and the school was going to stand on its feet . . . .

I also remember some funny things, Micheline. One of my teachers was engaged to be married, and the gossipers in the village knew about it. On Parents' Day, a woman with disheveled hair came straight to my office, and instead of asking me about her daughter's progress, she bombarded me with questions: "*Din iċ-ċuċ minn hawn . . . min hi din iċ-ċuċ li se tiżżewweġ?*"* Because in those days, having a salary of your own, and being able to be independent, it was considered foolish of you to go and get married, and be the SERVANT . . . of a man. Because a married woman was always sort of servant: she had to cook, she had to look after the children, she had to work hard, she had of course to serve . . . to see to her husband's sex problems, and there was no delicacy about that whatsoever, and no family planning! In fact, they were breeding like rabbits. Somebody from England in the colonial office made a report saying: "THEY breed like rabbits." Because a child would come every year. Well anyway, it was considered rather foolish to get married . . . . The woman said: "*Min hi din iċ-ċuċ li se tiżżewweġ?*" "Who is this foolish one who is going to get married?" And I said "That one!" The woman retorted: "That one, what a donkey; *kemm hi ċuċ*! She is a donkey to be married . . . ."

Well, after that, the woman told me about herself. She said: "When I was young, and I used to come to the school, the head teacher used to give me a pail and an umbrella, and I used to go down to the beach to get a lot of sand in the pail." Because for the younger ones, they would have a sort of tray—they would fill it with sand, and to start writing, they would trace letters or signs in the sand with their fingers, which I think was very, very wise. Because you have the sensation, and you could put the sand together in its place by just a little movement . . . .

And you can imagine that woman, who—as I said—was a bit disheveled, going down to the beach with an umbrella [laughter] and a pail of sand . . . . Well, I had a good time there, too; I had a good time that means . . . slowly—it wasn't easy, but gradually—I got the school ship-shape, both the premises and the school population, because everything had been stolen—I don't know why; the doors wouldn't close because they had not the proper closing equipment; bit by bit, I got the premises in

---

*"This fool, where is she from . . . who is this fool who is going to get married?"

order, and the school discipline in order. As for the teachers, we went on well together; we went on so well together that, if one of them had a boyfriend and her family wouldn't like her to go and SPEAK to the boyfriend, she would come and say [with a tone of shyness in her voice]: "Madam, can I go out JUST for five minutes, because my boyfriend is coming over from Malta? I'll go and cross the path and speak to him just for five minutes." And I knew this girl, and I knew the boy, and I closed my EYES, and I would say: "Yes, but don't tell anybody . . . ." So it was like a family to me, and we got on very well. We had a small kitchen at the back and we prepared the meals: we always had hot meals, but, you can imagine, quickly done, so that we never wasted the children's time; we were still the old type . . . .

When I go to Għajn Sielem now and meet the people there, they say something nice, and when you are older, when you retire, it's a big compliment and a lot of compensation. Even just a smile . . . . Now back to the time when I was a teacher in Għajn Sielem. I used to go every day up and down in the bus, and I would have a look at a school, a small school in Republic Street which was called Housecraft School, because in there it was set up like a house, and children from all over Gozo would go and learn how to cook a little, table manners, how to clean, and things like that. It was called the Housecraft School, and in those days—I'm speaking of 19—in the thirties—in those days, especially in the villages, table manners and setting up a proper kitchen with a sink, and setting up a bathroom . . . few people had a bathroom—they would have a toilet, but not a bathroom. So setting up a proper kitchen with a sink and a cooker and a fridge . . . not even in the school, we had these amenities because it was still the state when we were a bit . . . you know. Well, progress was a bit slow at that time. So anyway, EVERY MORN-ING I would see the school there, and I would say: "Humm . . . this is a job!"

Anyway I was not getting what I had fished for because the reorgani-zation scheme never materialized, or rather it materialized much later. But the union of teachers and the minister of education at last agreed that there should be a formal exam, the exam TO BE a head teacher, and it was to be a stiff job because you had to give a lesson in front of experts, including the director of education from Malta. And at that time with us, people from Gozo, who were still feeling a bit . . . SHY of people from Malta, not because we were stupid or not clever enough, or not prepared enough; there was always that feeling that you were watched by the people from Malta [laughter].

Well anyway, you had to give a practical lesson which you drew up by lot; and it could be difficult because in Malta they had already started choosing big titles such as: "The Migration of the Population," or "The Distribution of the Population" . . . . What a lesson to give in a primary school! And I had to study more or less to prepare myself for lessons throughout the school population, from the five-year-old to the fourteen-year-old, because you never know what the lesson is going to be. Well, you had to draw your lot, and they would give you just ten minutes' preparation, and you had to bring the visual aids or other aids, whatever you can get hold of. You also had to undergo a written exam in many aspects of education, and I remember I used to study and get up at four o'clock in the morning because at seven I had to leave for the school, and I liked to study in the morning. Well, I was forty years of age, and still looking after the house and everything. The exam included a criticism lesson, and for that we had to go to Malta to Floriana School, I remember: a teacher would be giving a lesson and you had to criticize her; you see, it could be adverse criticism, and it could be good criticism. Well, you had to show how good you were.

I remember in the practical lesson I was lucky, because I HAD GIVEN THAT SAME LESSON in Maltese a week before to that same class. I was very lucky. In the written exam, there was no difficulty for me because I am good in writing and I had prepared myself well. And in the criticism, I could see what was wrong and what was right. And I remember this, Micheline: when I saw all those men and women in Malta going in for the criticism lesson, and there were two hundred of them, two hundred of them, and they said: "That man has already a degree, and he's studying in London . . . ," I said: "*Ċwieċ, kollha ngħaddikhom!*" or, "You asses! I will pass you all." I said this in my heart of course. I said: "*Ċwieċ,** I will be the first; I will be the first!" I sat for the exam with that frame of mind: that I'm the best. And believe it or not, in the women's section, I was first. And THAT comes to show what a frame of mind can do. Well, I was prepared, very well prepared. But when I saw all those coming in, I sort of felt the challenge in me that I was not going to be downtrodden by those. I said: "*Ċwieċ, kollha ngħaddikhom;* I will pass you all."

---

* "Asses."

I remember when the results were about to be out, my brother was on a holiday in Spain with Marcel Mizzi and Joseph Calleja—he's not a relation; he's a friend—and I remember he told them: "I had better go home, because if Maria fails in this exam, I can imagine in what state she will be." So he shortened his holiday and the first thing he did in Valletta, he went to the Education Office to see how it fared with me. So he came home, and I remember we were in Marsalforn—in summer, we always go—not in the modern flat we have now, but in the little house further down the beach. We had a little dining room, and people came to congratulate me because Maria had become a real head teacher, not an "acting head teacher." Well, I think that was a nice experience.

Micheline: You had then become a head teacher?

Maria: Well, the first thing you have to do if you are a real head teacher—you have to go to London to a college of education to get practice and to observe, practise and observe, in many schools 'round about London. I was lucky to go to Digby Stuart College of Education; it's a University College of Education near Froebel College, and it was run by the Sisters of the Sacred Heart. Well anyway, I had to leave home, and that was very hard for Maria to leave her mother and Tony by themselves because I was the right hand of the house after all. Well, I went; somehow I went . . . . And, Micheline, I had a calendar and I was noting the days one by one. I was having a good time there, and I was happy whenever I had good lectures; I still have my files of notes neatly written. I used to say to myself: "My, my, is this Maria writing all these notes?" Anyway I had a good time, but I still was homesick because we Gozitans like our home; we are like that.

Anyway the year came to an end, and I came to Gozo to my family. And then I said to Anton: "Go and see if I can get that Housecraft School . . . ." In London, I had taken "home economics," as they call it nowadays; and I had a good report, so why not? The director of education then said: "There is a vacancy in Xewkija, so you go as head of the primary school, and you go to the Housecraft School so that you run both schools."

I thought that was a bit hard at the beginning, but I had good reliable teachers, things went well, and I stayed for three years in Xewkija. Then education authorities said: "Maria, you'd better go up to the Housecraft School and improve it along modern lines." And I DID improve it: I SOMEHOW borrowed part of the lyceum complex and I turned it into a modern up-to-date school of home economics.

I observed that there were no craft centers, and no craftshops in Gozo. As girls from all the primary schools in Gozo were coming to the Housecraft School, I could see from my "vantage point of view"—call it what you will—that there were the intelligent ones and the not-so-intelligent ones, and that we had more . . . not-so-intelligent ones; all in all, it went to 25 percent who could have teaching jobs or clerical jobs, so I said: "What are these 75 percent going to do?" So I decided to start something on the lines of a trade school; such schools were nonexistent. I discussed this with my caretaker—who knew a lot about weaving—and with my two teachers who were good at dressmaking, at embroidery, at knitting, at crochet, and were cooperative. We—I included—all made our own clothes! And we were always smart.

You see, we were worldly wise about money because we had a low salary, and we always had somebody to help—nieces or nephews or brothers. That is why most of the female teachers didn't get married. Not because they were not good looking; not because there was not somebody who fancied them: *Aħna ngħidu: Għal kull qoffa hemm id-demel.*"* That is, "Every female can find a partner." Remember, Micheline, the teacher we met on Saint George Festa? That one was one of my teachers. Well, she did bring up her sister's family, and now her niece is a teacher with a degree and she is getting married to an Italian architect. You see . . . ?

Now in that Housecraft School, I discussed everything with my two teachers because in any organization, a head without a staff which is cooperative can-do-nothing! So I discussed with them and they liked it. So I went to the new lady director of education, Margaret Mortimer, and discussed things in her office. She thought about it and she said: "I think what you are saying is reasonable, and I will give you my help. You go and draw up a plan of a school, and how it should be, and the equipment you should have and all that, and even sort of a timetable and the subjects to be taught . . ." because it was an entirely new thing. As regards education, I always could take a challenge; I never said: "Humm, what a tall order!" I went home and would roll up my sleeves, find a table and a cup of coffee [laughter] and start working, and never discussed that with anybody, mind you. I might look up English books of education

---

*Literally, "We say: 'For each basket [large wicker container], there is manure [or fertilizer].'" This is a variant of "*Kull qoffa ssib miżblitha*": "Each basket finds its dunghill" (see Aquilina 1972, 205, n. 122).

because in those days—I'm speaking of 1956–57—they were very good; it was a marvel.

Well, they liked what I did, but for the premises, I'm afraid it was a hard thing to get. I said: "Why not enlarge these and build another story on top?" The architect Mr. Joe Mizzi came, and he liked my sort of trying to get on in spite of difficulties, and he tried to help me. But the architect Mr. Huntingford and his foreman said: "Maria, this is a complex; this is not a solitary building, and we are not going to ruin the aesthetics of the whole. So if you can manage with this, carry on. But we are not ruining this." Well, we started something and it went on for two years . . . .

One thing I remember: we had in summer, at the end of the course, an exhibition of dresses, of crafts, of this and that, and believe me, Micheline, it was an A-one. Believe me, it was an exhibition TO BE PROUD OF anywhere. Well, I was having help from the Education Office to bring sewing machines, to bring irons, to bring this and this and that. And once, two ladies from England, who were in home economics, came and said: "This is a very well-put-up school! In England, we don't have such a high standard." And on another instance, there was a professor at the university—he was English—and he took his student architects to Gozo, and my teachers took them 'round. They went 'round, and when they went to the laundry room, he said: "Take out your notebooks and make sketches of this because this is A-one." Micheline, that's a big compensation for all the hard work, because it's hard work getting people to understand what you are doing, and I'm lucky they understood and they were cooperative.

I remember once there were some workmen, Public Works men. Now in Gozo, and I think anywhere else, the Public Works employees go a little slow; they do their duty, but they don't go about it . . . with sweat going down from their BROWS, "with the sweat of your brow," like in the Bible. And they told me once—it was the time of the boom of building houses and villas and bungalows to sell to the English; they were cropping up like mushrooms—so, they told me: "*Jaħasra, sinjûra, għax ma tmurx issib għalqa u tibni villa?*" "Sinjûra, why don't you go and buy a field and build a villa, and sell it to the English, because you are quite good at doing this sort of thing?" Well, instead of building a house like the English, I converted my house in Kerċem because I knew Anton liked it there, and when he came home, he would say: "I have been to many houses, but when I come in here, I feel relaxed!" And when we used to work a little in the garden, he would be happy. I didn't want a villa; I didn't want a posh house, but I wanted a functional house where we could relax and where I could entertain on simple lines like that.

Now, let's go back to education and my school. I had visitors from the Desk: Mr. Mintoff sent people from the Desk in Castille—they call it the Desk—well, he sent officers from Castille to Gozo to see what THIS SCHOOL was doing, and they reported that IT SHOULD BE EXTEN-DED. AND it was finally decided that they should move to Xagħra, and that's why at Xagħra now there is a proper trade school. And I like that very much because, as I said before, girls with a lower IQ should not spend their school life up to sixteen doing the same lessons as the others, because it would be a hell for the pupils, and for the teachers, a waste of time. Now they are doing fine work at Xagħra in that trade school: macramé, dressmaking, tailoring, and all sorts of . . . well, things which are useful to a girl, both for earning some money, and later on in life as a housewife.

And what did I do next? While that was being discussed, that trade school business, another political issue regarding education came about. There were the Nationalists in office and they said: "We should have secondary schools for everybody." Because up to now, secondary schools were only for the 25 percent of higher IQ. The lower ones, the 75 percent of lower IQ, were out: no school at all. Well, they said: "We'll have secondary schools for everybody." And they were opening thirty-two new schools: four in Gozo, two for boys and two for girls, and the rest in Malta. And for that, they wanted new head teachers. And although I was already a sort of head teacher, you had to undergo another exam, AND at the age of FIFTY-FOUR, I had again to start studying and preparing myself for a gruesome exam for a headmistress. Well, I had always had an eye on what was going on in education: I read the reports, the English quarterly reviews, and even in my brother's newspapers, there would always be an article or two on education, because we always got newspapers such as the *Daily Telegraph* and the *Observer*. Well, so I was what you'd call up-to-date with modern education, and we had a preparatory course by Mr. Michael Morgan from the College of Education in London. And we had local lectures. I remember I used to cross over by the first boat every morning and come back by the three o'clock boat, have a meal, rest a little, perhaps study a little, and the morning after again . . . .

But I liked it. I used to thrive on this, at the age of fifty-four! I used to like it. Well, there were some other Gozitan people, such as Monsignor Gauci, Mr. Joe Micallef, Mr. Gorg Xerri, and from Malta there was Mr. Francis Ebejer who is the famous novelist, and many head teachers of course. So I was competing with some two hundred teachers and head teachers of various ages, various academic background, various intelligence, and maybe various nepotism or chances of "entering through the windows." Eventually we sat for the exam. It was what we call an interview, a gruesome one. You had to go to Malta, sit in front of five different people, and they would ask you very difficult things regarding education, and you wouldn't know . . . . The examiners included a sister, an English nun of Mater Admirabilis College, and as I had been used to hear my young colleagues saying how headstrong she was, I completely forgot about being nice and affable and started arguing, insulting the English way of housekeeping into the bargain! Anyway they seemed to like my approach to interviews for they kept me going for one-and-a-half hours. You may imagine in what state I found my poor brother who was waiting with trepidation outside the exam room! Anyway I passed and was given charge of Qala Secondary School in Gozo, which was my finishing school [smile].

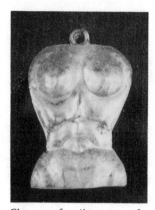

Close-up of a silver torso of a woman, an ex-voto at the Folklore Museum in Gozo.

Some examples from the Folklore Museum in Gozo of anatomical ex-voto in silver. Several are linked with childbearing and breast-feeding.

A votive offering donated by Anna Giglio, the wife of Notary Franc Cauchi in 1769 "for obtaining a beloved daughter," which was restored by the nephews and nieces of the donor in 1841. This ex-voto is in the Immaculate Conception Church in Qala.

Chapter 9

The Question of Marriage

N ow that Maria can look back upon her professional life, she tries to analyze the reasons why she did not get married—beyond the fact that she did not "need" to, being economically independent. In her opinion, the main cause was that she thoroughly enjoyed her work and felt free and fulfilled in her school, as well as in her house. A second reason is her belief that her fate was ordained by God. She perceived her job as a vocation which resembled, somehow, a priest's ministry.

However, Maria expresses herself freely on the subject of marriage in her society. When she herself was of marriageable age, she saw housewives confined to their houses, literally tied to the sink with all the washing to be done, always busy feeding and nursing their numerous children, and cooking and serving their husbands' needs, including the sexual ones. Birth control was unknown. On the other hand, if no child was born during a reasonable time after marriage, it was the woman who was blamed; in the man's mind, infertility had to be due to his wife only. Things have changed with time, but there occasionally may be a childless woman who still endures bad treatment from her husband, and Maria is revolted by such a woman's submissive and obedient behavior.

If a girl was unmarried, pregnancy used to bring shame on her, as well as on her family, unless a marriage was soon concluded. If it wasn't, the girl, by losing her integrity (chastity), became a prey to gossipers and was exposed to social and sometimes cruel sanctions.

Nowadays attitudes are different. Childless couples resort to medical treatment and, if necessary, to adoption. Mothers have two or three children on an average. Yet to Maria's mind, women today are creating new forms of dependency, for example—to satisfy their social ambitions—by cramming their children with knowledge and pushing them toward accomplishment, thus making the children victims. For Maria, robbing children of their childhood is a true crime.

Micheline: Maria, you have, step by step, achieved and enjoyed professional fulfillment. On the other hand, you did not get married. On one occasion, you expressed the opinion that when a woman acquires economic independence, she normally keeps apart from married life. I would like to go deeper into the subject of marriage as seen from your angle. Can you explain why personally you chose to have a profession instead of getting married?

Maria: It was, I think, not a personal decision really, but something which grew along in my subconscious mind, as I watched other girls getting married and what they were having out of that. First of all, on my way to school in Victoria, I used to see the husbands of married teachers with a small basket and money purse, going around in the marketplace, just to buy a few vegetables, a piece of meat, and maybe fish; and that meant that their wife was at home, washing clothes or washing dishes; that their wife was not even entrusted to manage the little budget that goes with family shopping. First and foremost, I watched that. Another thing I watched was that when a girl got married in Gozo . . . in those days, the houses were not so well equipped with the gadgets—time-and labor-saving gadgets they have now; you had to wash by hand, and the standard was high; I'm pleased to say, so that meant the lady of the house had to get up at five o'clock and soak clothes, so that by eight they are already on the washing line. Then she had to prepare the children's clothes . . . to send the children to school immaculately dressed. And of course, her husband would ask: "Where is that? and what is this? and bring me that . . . ." Because men were not expected, as a general rule, to give a helping hand, neither in the kitchen nor anywhere else.

Another thing which is the most important for me, the determining factor of my being left on the *xkaffa*,* being left on the "shelf," as they say, is because I liked what I was doing at school. In whichever school I was, whether it was a primary one, whether it was a home economics one, whether it was a secondary school, I am thankful to the Lord I was always

---

*To be left on the "shelf" (*xkaffa*) means for a girl "to remain unmarried."

very, very happy. So there was not the immediate need of getting rid of a job. I was very happy. In fact, when my friends, or Anton's friends used to ask about me, Anton, my brother, would answer: "It's Maria's last year at school, and it seems as if it's her first because she's happy working, and she has got a project on, a very intriguing one, and her school got second of all the schools of Malta and Gozo, and she went on television to collect the prize for her children and her staff." So I was a lucky one because schooling was easy for me in whatever line it was.

Another thing: when a girl gets married, I always say: "She has nothing to lose; she is getting a bit up some way or other." But I was so independent, and I had a bit of family, although a strange one—I had my mother, I had my brother—so I was not feeling lonely or uncared for, or in any way unfulfilled. We had that . . . unusual family, but I had family of some sort or another. And in fact—you know my father went a bit early and Anton was still studying—so I felt I was the provider of that family, not only economically, I'm saying. I saw to it that they were well fed, that the premises were always in good working order; I felt like a foreman. In the summer, instead of going away for a holiday, I would see if there were any leaking roofs or if the doors needed painting, something like that, and I felt useful, and I felt happy.

And the most important thing of all, when you look back upon your life—from my age, I can look back, and through my experience and through my reading—I consider it that . . . well, a book I often read by somebody called Strong, she says, "THE CURRENT THAT KNOWS ITS WAYS . . . ." It's no use planning your life because the Lord God, who loves us all immensely, is somehow always there to guide you without even your knowing. Sometimes I ask even myself . . . because any woman would like to have somebody to admire her, to help her . . . and there were SOME, some of the boys I liked very much, but when they approached me just to say a simple question, or to pay me a simple compliment, I would DO exactly the REVERSE of what I had planned to do: I would look proud and look standoffish, as if I didn't CARE a hoot for what they were doing. And of course, if you start on that basis, you are finished and it's no . . . .

So when I ask myself that, and I remember Patience Strong—that's the lady who writes beautiful books; she was a doctor and a good Catholic—and she writes that whether we know it or not, whether we are conscious of it or not, there is a current, there is the Lord, who sometimes guides you, and you are doing WHAT-HE-HAS-PLANNED-FOR-

YOU because after all, this life—this sixty- or seventy- or eighty-year life, or ninety—will come to an end, and then your real life starts, which is eternal life. And God doesn't ask you how many houses you have built or how much money . . . . He asks and sees if you have done as he has planned it for you . . . and evidently for me, it has been planned to TEACH, because I'm still teaching all the time; even in my kitchen I teach; even if there is a more learned person than me, I think I'm teaching.

Micheline: So that was your choice, or rather your "line," wasn't it?

Maria: Yes, you see, it was not an actual choice, but throughout life you are being guided by someone, and it was not an actual choice, but that was my line . . . and I think I was always a bit happy. Every now and then, you get a disappointment, especially if you are going out with a girlfriend. And there would be someone who would be eying me, trying to catch me. And I wouldn't react as I should react. And my girlfriend, who would be a bit less naive than I was, she would somehow cheat me and get that boy, so that I would be losing the girlfriend and the admirer.

Micheline: So, as you said yourself, you were like all young women sensitive to men's compliments.

Maria: Yes, I would be NATURALLY—I would be VERY pleased.

Micheline: Maria, I remember that you mentioned once some nasty remarks coming from your neighbor about a boyfriend who supposedly had left you.

Maria: Yes, yes. May I tell the story?

Micheline: Yes, please.

Maria: That was 1948, when Anton was in government and everybody expected that he would do miracles. So a neighbor of ours wanted to be employed as a caretaker in the schools. For some reason or other, this employment never came. And she was working as a part-time, not fully employed, caretaker in the school, where there was a teacher WHO somehow fancied me a little. And after some time, after some time, he started going out with another one. Now she went into the back garden, which could be audible from my home, and she started *l-għana*,* because *l-għana* was a means of insulting people.[105] She wouldn't come up and say that to my face, but from the garden, she started singing something like:

---

*Song, i.e., a traditionally improvised song.

U l-għarus li kellek inti
Jien naħti li ħaduhulek . . . .

That means: "And I am the cause that *l-għarus*"*—it was not an official fiancé, but it was somebody who fancied me—"I am the cause that your fiancé left you."

I was hurt, not because of that boy—I was hurt because she sort of insulted me [expression of disgust] and my brother in a low way; because that means you haven't the courage to speak up and you are insulting people . . . . *Għana, spirtu pront*† was considered by the law as legal insult, and you could even take somebody to court; not like that—what that lady did was not real insult which you could put your finger on, but you would be hurt a little. If it's not a compliment, everybody would be hurt.

Micheline: Therefore, Maria, social opinion was important for everyone?

Maria: Maybe, maybe . . . .

Micheline: I mean that what people thought and said about you mattered a lot. Remember, you quoted the case of a family in which one of the sons started going out with a young girl. You told me what happened to them and, by way of consequence, how the young man's brother was, so to speak, threatened in his vocation . . . .

Maria: Oh, yes. I know that story . . . Yes, of course, in a small community where everybody knows everybody and where mistakes happen as in any group—humanity is always humanity—but social opinion mattered a lot, regarding what happened in your family, to your cousins, to your aunts and to all your family-tree members. Well, I remember this story: there was a good-looking girl, rather smart for a village type, and she was going out, or meeting—because you didn't go out; you would meet your boyfriend either in the early morning—in fact, I know couples who used to go to four o'clock mass, so that after the mass, they would have a little time just to talk together—or after l-Ave Maria; l-Ave Maria would be the Angelus that would be about 7:00 P.M. Well anyway, a couple were going out together, and the girl got pregnant before she was even officially engaged; she wasn't even engaged, and because of that, there was a lot of litigation between the two families; each side felt that

---

*Bridegroom-to-be, fiancé.
† Literally, "prompt spirit," i.e., impromptu singing.

this pregnancy had put a blight and a shame on the whole family, and that this might have an influence on the future of the other children, girls as well as boys. Evidently somehow the matter was settled: the boy married the girl, but the whole village would know and ask when is the baby coming; they would know when it was started, AND they see every little inch of change IN-YOUR-BODY-AND-IN-YOUR-HAIR [tone suggesting the scrutinizing, insistent look of one's neighbors; Maria concludes with a laugh].

You know, in the village, it's terrible; it's like that. If you pay attention to them . . . the best thing is not to pay attention; it is to carry on what you are doing; otherwise it will kill you. Anyway this case was settled because the couple were married. Another lady I know has been very unlucky . . . . She was carrying on with somebody, and she also got into trouble, but she was not married, so she had been single all the time, and I am afraid some of the men and the boys tried to make fun of her, and I think that's cruel [sad sounding]. She doesn't seem to mind, but . . . they shouldn't do that. Other cases, I can't remember, but I'm sure we had many cases of girls getting into trouble.

I remember another case: there was a peasant girl—well, we are peasants, village girls—and part of her job was to go out in the fields. Now, there was a deep well in one of the fields, a little away from the houses; it was called "il-Bir ta' Trumbettier," "the well of the trumpeter"; I don't know why "a trumpeter." Evidently they had lands there, and in this big field, there was a deep well and the water was very soft, and sometimes when you had shorn your sheep, you would have to wash the whole fleece, and the best thing for it was to be near a well, so that you can rinse it over and over again. Well, this village girl was doing some sort of work, and nearby there was a young man with a herd of goats, and he tried to rape her. This was not a love affair. He tried to rape her . . . . That I can remember, too.

Micheline: Maria, let's talk about married women and, in particular, about their situation when, for some reason or another, they cannot give birth to children. Of course this was felt to be, and still is, to a certain extent, like a calamity, whatever the country. But in your society, how have you tried to solve the problem? And nowadays how is a childless couple facing such a situation?

Maria: Yes. After marriage, of course, naturally it comes to having a family, to bringing up a family and to have children. And sometimes the couple would be childless for a year. If they are childless for a year, they would start making vows to the saints, to Madonna Ta' Pinu, to Saint Joseph.[106] Well, everybody has respect for saints. They would start making vows. And I think it was not yet the custom to go for medical advice, because sterility can be the fault of the woman; it can be the fault of the man as well. But most of the time, it is the woman who got the brand of this. In fact, they would say: "*Il-mara li ma għandhiex tfal, il-mara li ma għandhiex tfal . . . .*"* That would be the epithet under which she would be known, "*il-mara li ma għandhiex tfal,*" and maybe it wouldn't be her fault at all. It could be something wrong with her husband.

Now later on, they started what they call the Cana Movement. The Cana Movement are a group of people including a priest for moral advice, including a doctor for medical advice, and somebody who would be sort of a social worker. Most of them go to England to be trained, and then to advise people who are getting in trouble with their marriage in some area or other. But when I was young, there was no Cana Movement, and people had to go to Malta, first of all to specialists, but in fact they didn't go there at all. It was considered as a great . . . how shall I say? . . . tragedy that no children came out of marriage.

I know a lady who somehow got out of this very cleverly because she and her husband—they are both well educated—started helping others: they joined what is called the Legion of Mary, and they worked a lot for the others, so that they don't feel as if they were useless, and they mix a lot in society, and they made up a beautiful house where they can entertain even the best people from Malta, and they are looked upon well in the village and in Victoria, and I think that's a clever way of getting out of your . . . which is not a tragedy after all, but getting out of your little disappointment in life. I think that if people forgot themselves— because if you are in that situation, and it has become totally hopeless, the best way out of it is to try and forget yourself and help others.

Now in more modern times, I'm remembering another couple. They were a rather well-off and respected couple, but they were childless. And I'm sure none of them liked it. They went up to England for medical advice, and they came back after some time, some months, and the lady became pregnant, and now they have . . . humm! a tall, strong boy. So several people try to heal the situation in different ways. I lately heard

---

*"The woman who has no children."

of someone else: when someone meets a husband who is not educated enough, and who does not show respect to his wife—sometimes they are even cruel, and sometimes they BEAT them—this is in modern times! And maybe, as I said before, IT MIGHT NOT BE THE FAULT OF THE WOMAN who is childless. I am sure HE should be examined and not the wife. Well anyway . . . [smile].

Micheline: Would he accept to be examined?

Maria: I don't know because I don't know the private details. But I know he goes to see another woman, and when he comes back, he beats his wife, who is always crying and praying for him . . . she is a saint. She cries and welcomes him in their home, and she cooks for him, and she does all the rest. And I think that's the-life-of-a-MARTYR! and not of a woman. In the 1980s. That's as far as I can say.

I know of another couple who, as I say, are extremely well-off because they put up a lovely house—you would call it a school, not a house . . . . Nowadays in Gozo, the houses, humm! are not houses, are not homes; the houses are PALACES, you would say. Well, by the standard of their house, they are well-off, and they were wise enough to adopt a girl, I think, or a boy—I don't know well—a child from the orphanage, because at Għajn Sielem, there is a small orphanage, Lourdes Home, run by the sisters, and they often have as many as thirty babies. Of course, this orphanage is supported by the church and charitable people. Anyway they went and adopted a child from the orphanage, which is very, very sensible.

Another one I know, she's called Regina, and she lives at Xagħra although she is from Victoria, and this Regina married a bit late. When she and her husband saw that they couldn't have any children, Regina decided to adopt a child. And do you know where she got this child from? She GOT THIS CHILD FROM BRAZIL! Because in Brazil, there is a priest—I think he's bishop there—from Sannat, and he managed the whole dealing. I often heard Regina speaking about it before she actually got the girl. She had the photo; she had the papers ready, BUT—believe it or not—an admiral's wife from Brazil went to have a look at the bunch of orphans, and she wanted to adopt one, AND SHE PICKED THE ONE that Regina wanted [sounding scandalized]. And you know, you are not going to disappoint an admiral's wife evidently . . . so Regina had a lot of . . . how shall I say? . . . disappointments. But eventually she got another one, and I often saw her playing the piano in musical competitions. This girl has black curly hair [tone of admiration] and BLACK

EYES, and she is sweet . . . a darling. AND SHE SINGS . . . [suggestive of singing], and she acts when she is singing like a grown-up, and she can play the piano; sometimes she plays the piano together with my cousin's son, who is Massimo. Sometimes this child, Regina's girl, and Massimo play together at a concert at the conservatory because they are taught to do it together, and believe me, he is fair and very . . . demure, and SHE IS, you know, brunette, and they are a nice couple together. And that Regina looks happy, and she knows everything about education, step by step.

By the way, all the mothers in Gozo, they overdo it; they are overdoing it. In the old days, it was . . . you finish your school as soon as possible, so that you come and help either in the home or in the fields. Now it's the other way about: they get a small family—one, two, three—and they give them the best education. And they start COMPETING, and—which I don't like—they fill the children with this sense of competition even when they are at the ripe old age of six, and they start giving them private lessons. And it's such a big headache to educators that the present minister of education, Nationalist of course, Ugo Mifsud Bonnici, is doing something so that the children are not overtired, and that there is no need for private tuition at a young age. Because these poor children of Gozo, as I see them, are being robbed of their BEST—of the best years of their childhood. They have to wake up; they have to go to the doctrine, catechism lessons; and then they go to school; then they go to a private lesson; then they go to another meeting; then they have to do their homework [rhythm of speech showing uninterrupted daily activity]. And I don't know why they give them BIG numbers of exercises at one go, compositions at one go—THIS-IS-NONSENSE!

I never agreed with that, and I'm saying this in public—in the middle of Paris, rue La Bruyère[107]—so . . . Jacques Chirac, listen to me and don't let your children be robbed of their beautiful years of childhood. After all, playing is a means of education. It's how children learn: through play, through imitation; they are imitating what the others are doing. That's the best way of education. They are having a bit of FREE air, which is so good in Gozo and it's free, and they are shutting up the children in their rooms and in other institutions . . . they are robbing . . . that should be STOPPED!

Chapter 10

A Spirit of Competition in Society

In the Maltese islands, there is a specific word, *pika* (pique), to denote a relationship based on rivalry, which is typical of traditional folk poets when engaged in song dueling. This type of competition promotes mutual emulation and implicates the honor of each opponent. Nowadays in Gozo, competitiveness has reached all the levels of social life, according to Maria. It can take various forms; some she considers negative; others, positive.

The first case concerns women who tend to vie with their neighbors in a struggle for prestige through the display of showy expensive items, or signs of wealth, in the decoration of houses, in clothes, jewels, and so on. Their family gatherings turn into "fashion parades," thus losing their meaning as ritual celebrations. Materialism is a threat to morals. Of course, the attitude toward money has changed considerably since the island started to enjoy prosperity, coming mostly from emigration, then from tourism. But the need to outdo one's neighbor and be different involves, paradoxically, the leveling of society in general. Being a person of marked individuality, Maria condemns that sort of modern conformity.

On the other hand, competition existing between, groups of people, rather than individuals, is, in her eyes, utterly fruitful from an aesthetic point of view. Among those groups or associations are the "band clubs," which, because they are in charge of the outdoor celebration of their respective parish *festas*, strive to organize a more spectacular feast than their neighbor. Their rivalry (keen at times) constitutes a considerable force, which is channeled into the production of theatre plays, among other things. All the community takes part on a voluntary basis, including those who act on the stage; on the day of the performance, everybody shares a feeling of pride and a sense of togetherness.

There are still other spheres of Gozitan life where the spirit of competition is kept alive by, for example, the holding of a yearly exhibition of agricultural products, or by the creation of football clubs in each village.

Micheline: Maria, you have started showing how women compete with each other through their children in the sense that they want their little ones to do better than the neighbor's. But would you say that there are other motives of rivalry between them, and that there exists a spirit of competition on a wider scale, not only between individuals, but also between certain groups of society?

Maria: Yes. This spirit of competition seems to pervade ALL levels of life in Gozo [assertive], as I see it. Let's take women, for example, because it seems to be more obvious in women than in men. Let's take their house. It's a status symbol to have your house immaculately clean, to have curtains a bit different from the others, to have furniture being bought from a firm such as Ta' Fino or Ta' Joinwell.* In fact, I heard a lady whose husband made the furniture himself because they couldn't afford to buy it, and she said: "Ta' Joinwell? It's only white wood covered with formica!" Now that is extremely foolish, but that's because she was a bit jealous that the others were buying ready-made furniture from a good firm in Malta, whereas they had to make their own furniture. Now I remember one lady once went out in the street with the bill from the person who had sold her the furniture, and she went about the street showing the bill, saying: "You see, MY sitting room costing that much!"

I know it's silly, but it is very, very highly competitive, and I'm glad to say, even with regard to cleanliness, there are NO lazy women in Gozo. You wouldn't go into any house and find dirt because they all want . . . it's a must that you keep your house immaculately clean, and on Saturdays—even nowadays on Sundays, I'm ashamed to say—especially the women who work, they clean the house from top to bottom, and they keep their children well clothed and perfectly clean. In fact, about some years ago, I met a lady—she was from Oxford and her husband was an architect—well, this lady said: "In connection with my job, I have been all over many countries to see how the children were being treated; I

---

*Literally, "of Fino" (Fino being the surname of the owning family) and "of Joinwell" (the name given by the owner to his firm).

have been up to Russia . . . ." And this lady said: "I have found that the best treatment to children is being given in Gozo." I well remember that. And she said: "I like their uniforms, their school uniforms all immaculately clean and well ironed." So that shows our women are competitive. They are even competitive about their husbands. Not in the way of competition as to the respect, or love . . . . Of course, everybody is jealous about her husband; nobody likes the husband to go and carry on with . . . although it's being done. Now in modern times, some husbands are carrying on with other women, and women are carrying on with other men, which was an unheard-of thing! This is something very, very modern, and I think it has something to do with the soap operas they give us on television, like "Dallas" and "Dynasty." But that's beside the point.

So there is competition about the children's schooling, about the houses . . . humm! you should see the buildings. And NOBODY does his house exactly like the other one. So I'm afraid we have a hodgepodge of architecture now, and they don't mind the architect—they have a plan of their own; they want the house to be *comme ci, comme ça*,* and they have the architect just to get the permit, because they wouldn't be able to build the house without the architect's signature. So the traditional structure is being completely abandoned, and it's neither here nor there, and you rarely come across a new one which has the good signs of aesthetics and you would like it; at least, I don't like it. Now, adding insult to injury, they ARE using aluminium, AND THE MORE ALUMINIUM YOU HAVE, the richer you are. I think something should be done because the look of Gozo is being completely changed. Another thing which they are competing about is the *bankina*,† the pavement which some of them are covering with bathroom tiles. A friend of mine has said: "Now they are bringing the toilet out in the street" [smile]. So there is a competition of many things, and it should be directed because things are looking serious, about architecture especially. I don't like that.

Now another sort of competition is about dress. Humm! about dress, and gold, and jewelry. For a *festa* especially. Now nobody is proud that he's a dressmaker like me—I'm always proud that I can make a dress out of a seven-shilling remnant from the Pjazza—but they have to go either

---

*French for "so-so."
†Sidewalk.

to Republic Street, because there are some six or seven ready-made clothes shops, which is, for Gozo, unthinkable. Or some of them go to Malta, so that nobody has a costume, a dress like theirs. And for some social religious occasion like Holy Communion or confirmation, it's a fashion parade, and they make their children lose the sense of what they are doing. It's a fashion parade with makeup, with gold, with a small hat, with a thirty-pound dress from Malta; well, with this and that. And on top of that, a party [sounding flabbergasted] . . . a party at home, which you would be proud to have at your wedding, Micheline . . . [smile]. AND A VIDEO; they must have all the proceedings done on videotape so that later on, it could be shown. A video I don't know; I don't have a video, but I understand because they hire a man, and I think that's expensive. Again this competition is growing out of all sense of proportion; it has no sense of proportion at all. And you don't say Mrs. So-and-So can afford that, and I can't afford that. SOMEHOW OR OTHER, the social status has become a conformity; there are no well-off and not-so-well-off, but I think this is foolish because there is always a difference in the . . . how shall I say? . . . in the budget of families: some can afford it, and some JUST CAN'T, but they want to show off . . . . Anyway . . . .

There is another sort of competition in the village itself. If the village has a smaller village, a hamlet attached to it, such as in Kerċem—we have Santa Lucia, which is like a smaller village, with its own church, with its own priest, with its own feast—it has already started having a competitive spirit of one part of the parish with another. In Għajn Sielem, they, too, have this very strongly because there is this small, not-so-small, church of tal-Patrijiet* side, and there is the actual Għajn Sielem parish church. So, there is a competition for *festas* between the two sides of the village.[108]

Now in Victoria, there is another strange . . . I call it healthy competition this time. It's a healthy competition between two bands: one is called Ta' l-Iljun, the other, Ta' l-Istilla.[109] They both have a nice theatre. Ta' l-Iljun have the Aurora Theatre down Republic Street, and Ta'l-Istilla have the Astra Theatre—it's called like that, Astra. These bands were at first connected with churches: Ta' l-Iljun is connected with the cathedral church of Gozo, which is dedicated to Santa Maria, and

---

*Literally, "of the monks."

Santa Maria is on the fifteenth of August, and it's a big *festa*. And the Astra people are connected with Saint George's Basilica—actually their *festa* is on the 23rd of April, Saint George's Day, but now they celebrate it later on. They both bring special bands, the best bands from Valletta: La Valette and King's Own, and they have other bands from Malta. And we have visitors from Malta, so the Saint George's said: "We'd better put it on later in the summer so that, at least, the people wouldn't be faced with the problem of crossing over in winter." It's a little crossing, I know, but if it's stormy, it may spoil your *festa* and everything . . . .

So in both theatres—because I've been to both of them—they PRO-DUCE VERY GOOD PLAYS. We have very good directors, and they know their job. We have very good scenery, and it's all made cheaply because it's all made on a voluntary basis. They don't employ anybody. And about some years ago—believe it or not—they produced operas, and for the principal singer and actors, they brought members of La Scala Theatre in Milan. You can imagine how expensive all that is! And even their tickets were expensive. But even like that, they said they barely, barely covered their expenses; I think they've come to their senses and are not doing that any longer.

Anyway besides those operas, every season in winter they have lovely plays; sometimes a man I know, George Xerri, who was a teacher in the Lyceum Complex, translates. He translates into Maltese plays from either Italian or English, very high-class plays, and he's a very good translator AND director. Mind you, he finds the best actors and actresses, and you would forget you are in Gozo. Outsiders—we also have outsiders— although it's in Maltese, English residents often come to see our plays. And they wonder at the talent, the amount of talent they see in Gozo, whether it's in the costumes—because they make their own costumes, mind you—in the acting itself, in the production, in the SINGING, and we have our own choirs such as Maria Frendo's choir, and we have the Aurora Choir; they, too, are nice. And there is a high competition because the theatres are always full; and I know some of the audience don't half understand what's going on, but THEY SUPPORT IT so that they say: "Oh! Ta' l-Istilla was full." They go there just for the prestige of the theatre. I could see sometimes it's a bit intellectual what goes on the stage, and I see it's above them, but they go there to support their band, whether it's Astra or the other.

On other occasions sometimes, they bring over groups from Malta, theatrical groups. The people from Malta produce a play, AND it would be an A-ONE PLAY [expression of delight]. But look at the theatre: it's nearly empty because the supporters don't feel any obligation to go; it's the Maltese; we couldn't care less [smile]! But on the whole, this competitive feeling is healthy because there is something going on, and they are learning, because indirectly we all learn from play or from the stage, whatever kind it is.

There is another theatre in Victoria called Don Bosco because it's Don Bosco Oratory, and it was started by the Salesians, and the Salesians were always good at educating through the stage. It's not competitive; I wouldn't say it was competitive with anybody, but there is always a spirit of belonging, and the actors are all very proud of making a good show; the shows there are marvelous. Last year they did a ROCK opera: ALL GOZITAN! Everything: the lyrics, the music, the costumes, the scenery . . . the only thing they did in Malta was the recording, because when they have something like that, they go and record it in Malta, and that's the most expensive of all. The rock opera was called *Ġwanninu*. Ġwanninu is a pet name for John; it was the life story of Giovanni Bosco, AND THE WAY THEY DID IT WAS MARVELOUS. With me, as a guest, I had Countess Barbara Strachwitz; she comes from Germany, and she knows all about this, because she's a writer herself, and she is a cousin of Graham Greene, the English writer, and she knows what she is talking about, and she said: "Maria, this is wonderful, this is wonderful, this is wonderful." And that shows what a HEALTHY spirit can do, even in such a small place like our own tiny Gozo . . . .

In Xewkija, too, they have a good parish hall, and EVERY YEAR they produce a show.[110] Generally it's written by someone in Italian, and Mr. Joseph Vella very ably translates and puts the local language, the local exclamations, and all this . . . to give it a local color; and there is Maestro Farrugia from Victoria and his sister for costumes; AND the archpriest, because the Archpriest Dun Karm is producer, is everything . . . and I don't know how he does it because when I am invited to go and give a talk in that complex, I can't manage it rightly because they are talkative and very ill-behaved, but that parish priest can stand all that shouting, all that going on, all that pushing . . . maybe for five months, because it always takes months . . . nowadays the last show I saw, they even had actors and actresses from Malta who specially came to take part because they said: "It is a very good show; we want to take part."

All over Gozo, even in our Kerċem, we have shows every now and then. Sometimes, as a fund-raising activity—sometimes they get the whole show from Malta; sometimes they do it among themselves: we have a small society, a drama group, choral acting group. So this competition goes on and on in every sphere, and even among the farmers: in the morning, at four o'clock in the morning—believe it or not—from my bedroom, I always can hear discussions, and they are discussing their products and where they are going to sell them, and why the government is putting the price low; it's not a litigation, but it's a healthy, very healthy friendly competition so that everybody would like his products to be as good as the neighbor's. Another sort of competition . . . .

Micheline: As far as farmers are concerned, perhaps one should mention the holding of an agricultural exhibition every year with prize awards . . . .

Maria: Yes, you remind me that next week, next week Saturday is Santa Maria, and on the eve . . . at Villa Rundle, in the public garden down Republic Street, there would be an agricultural show—crafts and agricultural products—and you may be sure that is highly competitive because the farmers get the best specimens of their fruits, vegetables and seeds and all that; there is also a section for crafts, weaving and hand-knitting and all that . . . it's highly competitive. There is also a show of animals, such as cows, pigs, and hens, and rabbits, and horses. Of course everybody is proud to show off their animals . . . .

Another competitive spirit that has lately grown up is about horse races. In fact, the government had to provide a big horse track near Ta' Xħajma,* between Xagħra and Nadur; they have built a high wall enclosing—I'm ashamed to say—a highly cultivable land, and somebody said: "That high wall shouldn't be there at all!" and they should have at least planted some trees to surround it. But the race horse owners are keen on it, and they spend a lot of money on bets. A neighbor of mine has a horse called Kysko; it was a champion in Malta, at the Marsa racecourse, and someone would have paid as much as twelve thousand pounds, and he didn't like it; he kept the horse. You see that's another sort of competition.

Of course there is football; in every village, there is a football team, and in the summer they play water polo. Well, I think, all in all, though sometimes it may be carried on too far, for keeping houses, for educating the children, for keeping that community activity—producing something

---

*Place name at the limits of Nadur.

A votive dated 1859 in the Tal-Hlas Chapel in Malta. An inscription (*left*) reads: "I, Teresa Farrugia, gave birth to four children; all of them died. I implored the Blessed Virgin and I have a fifth one, alive and in good health" (translated from the Italian).

in a theatre takes a lot of people, and all are doing their very best on a purely voluntary basis—I think, all in all, it's HEALTHY. It's keeping up the standards of social life in Gozo.

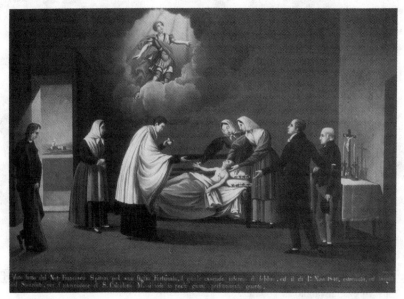

An ex-voto painted by Clemente Busuttil (1840) in the Manresa Chapel in Gozo. It represents the miraculous cure, through the intercession of St. Calcedonius, of a dying child (Fortunato, son of Notary Spiteri) after he received the sacrament of the anointing of the sick. (*Courtesy of Mr. Joseph Attard Tabone.*)

Chapter 11

Further Personal Considerations

Maria goes back over her personal attitudes, trying to define her idiosyncratic personality. First, she feels entitled to be proud of herself: she gave every satisfaction to her parents and enhanced the family prestige; she was a respected head teacher and showed solidarity toward both neighbors and friends. In a sense, what she accomplished was even more than was normally expected of a woman. However, in her relations with young wooers, her behavior was in total contradiction to her natural character and good manners; she is aware that her uncontrolled reactions came from the unconscious.

In fact, her life course has been marked, since childhood, by a succession of contrasting features: unlike the majority of girls of her age, who shared the chores and child care with their mothers at home, she went to school. Later, instead of getting a dowry from her father (marrying one's daughter(s) was a heavy burden for the family at that time), she became the "provider" with the money she earned herself. Then, being an unmarried childless woman, she dedicated her motherly love to her younger brother.

Of course her parents had a crucial influence on the modeling of her personality. Funnily enough, the mother who resented the buying of serials by her literate husband—for her, it meant throwing money away—decided to provide education for her two surviving children, Anton and Maria. After losing three baby girls, she declared in the depth of her heart and in an almost prophetic way: "I'll make Anton an advocate, and Maria a school headmistress!" From then on, she acted with this aim in view. The father inculcated in his daughter the pleasure of learning. She inherited his taste for the theatre and admired the ingeniousness he showed in his craft, in particular during the war, when one had to adapt to the circumstances. Between all these sometimes-contradictory forces, Maria maintained—as reflected by her life history in this book—a harmonious balance within herself.

Micheline: Last time we let our conversation develop gradually from the question of marriage to that of competition in society. Shall we come back to more personal considerations in relation to your life as a woman?

Maria: Yes.

Micheline: Maria, whilst being a teacher, and later a head teacher, as well as a devoted daughter and sister, you have been, and still are, a lively, cheerful person who enjoys putting on a nice dress, entertaining friends at home or going out to them. You like company. And according to your phrase, you did not lack the complacency of having an admirer, yet did not want to be "really involved." This sounds apparently as a contradiction. Can you explain that?

Maria: Well, as any other girl, I naturally put on my best finery for special occasions, mainly the *festas*, and you always had somebody—I mean some boy—who would . . . try to catch your eye somehow, or try to be your admirer. But to say the truth, I never did really like the boys in the village. I don't know why . . . I was not snobbish, but I had the feeling that with my education, they wouldn't be the good partners for me. But anyway, there was one in the village called Girgor, and we carried on for some time. When I say "carried on" . . . we just met on Sundays, and we used to go, with my cousin, Rose, and her boyfriend, perhaps walk together down to Xlendi and exchange a few words, or exchange a few gifts. But when mother got wind of that, she didn't like it, and she stopped it altogether!

Later, when I finished my education, people from Victoria came to me, asking me to give private lessons in their own homes to their children, sitting for important exams. And some I refused, and some I accepted. And I remember there was near Saint Francis's Square—there was a boy, tall and dark looking, whom I liked. At least, I liked what I saw because I had never spoken to him. I liked what I saw. And the girl to whom I was giving lessons said: "Thomas wants to speak to you," and I don't know for what reason, I REACTED in a very . . . angry and rude way. I can't explain this because this happened several times. Now I would have liked very much to be on speaking terms with such . . . to have him just for a friend. Because he was good looking, and he was smart, and he was a bit taller, because I always liked tall men, not the short ones . . . whom I never liked. But WHEN just the chance came to begin this friendship, I remember I spoke a . . . rude word which I don't normally speak! I don't normally use rude words like that. I said: "*Għidlu jmur jieħdu f'għajnu!*"*¹¹¹ which is . . . rather rude for a girl, an educated girl . . . .

And that of course, for a week at least, stopped the relationship; because after, we met somewhere, and he smiled at me, and I smiled at him, and we started a friendly relationship like this, by letters—believe it or not. We met in the street, but I wouldn't stop. We used to exchange letters by hand. He would give me a letter, I would give him another, and at HOME, I HID those letters.¹¹² And on *festas*, we would stay near each other just to enjoy the sight—not the company—the sight of each other. Maybe a small present would be exchanged, and that was the sort of friendship that we had. It lasted for some months. Then I disliked him for something he said, and I got fed up.

Later on of course, as I grew up, I would mix with teachers, and maybe head teachers-to-be because in my group there were some very intelligent people. One of them was very serious, and he is still a very serious man, but I made fun of him. I said not in his face, but somebody told him later what I had said of him: "A Chinese man is coming to our class . . . ." And it's NOT in my temperament to make fun of, or to say unpleasant words to, or behind persons . . . and I can never explain this.

Another man, Albert, who later on became a head teacher, liked me. He was a nice man. First, he was not after me, but after my friend, Ġorġa. I was sort of a go-between. But this friend of mine didn't correspond; then he started sort of being friendly with me. He was nice looking, but I still couldn't bring myself to sort of . . . extend my friendship to him because I said: he didn't want ME at first—he wanted the other—so why should I lick him, sort of?

Another one, Frans—he's dead now; he died a few months ago—he was to become a head teacher, and we were about nineteen, twenty years old . . . this was not among children. He gave me a beautiful something: it was like a triptych, or what would be today like these folding cards. In those days, it was a very nice present, and he gave it to me while the

---

*Literally, "tell him to go and be taken in his *għajn*" (*għajn* is euphemistic for *sorm*, i.e., "arse"). The phrase *ħadu f'għajnu* is quoted as "(vulg.) he went to the dogs" (*Maltese-English Dictionary*, s.v. *għajn*).

class was nearly empty, while the other students—when I say students . . .
we were already teachers; we would go . . . on Wednesdays for continuation class, yes, "continuation class." Well anyway, this man came up to
me very nicely, and he said: "Look what I have brought you today . . . ."
And out of the corner of my eye, I was seeing the other one I've just
mentioned, and he was looking a bit puzzled to see how things were
carrying on, and I COULDN'T stand anybody seeing that I . . . would
accept somebody's favors, or call it what . . . So I said: "*Mur tiha
l'nanntek!*" That is, "Go and give it to your grandmother."* And of course,
treating a man like that was . . . humm! Later on he tried to make eyes
at me, but I had my heart set on somebody else. I was after—I was after
the man who wasn't after me. The men who were after me, I sort of
[laughter] ignored them. And with regards to this, there was a *sinjur*†
from Republic Street: he was a bachelor, and he could well marry; he was
well-off. So somebody asked him: "Mr. So-and-So, how is it that you
never married?" And he said: "*Għax dawk li rrid ma jridunix u dawk li
jriduni ma rridhomx!*"‡ Maybe I had a little temperament like that gentleman.

But strangely, when I was in London on a *Peregrinatio pro Christo*,
which means you are on a week of apostolate organized by the Legion of
Mary, and you go abroad to help in a parish; not to convert—to convert
would be a big grace—but to speak about one's relationship with God,
and to see if you can put in order marriages, broken families. Well, on
a *Peregrinatio pro Christo*, near Brixton in the parish of Saint Simon and
Saint Jude, I was walking . . . you see, London is a big city, so you are
given a map and you have to walk and walk and walk, and you can't be
praying all the time. So sometimes you gossip a little, and I got on very
well with a lady from Malta who was a head teacher—nice person, and
very friendly—and without my telling her anything, she was saying the
same things I am saying more or less: that whereas she was such a nice
gentle person who could share a joke, both with men and women, would
act rudely, quite unlike her everyday manners, to men who sort of
approached her in a nice way, but you'd feel that they were approaching

---

*In other words, it is just about good enough for an old woman!

†A gentleman.

‡"Because those whom I wanted, they did not want me, and those who wanted me, I did
not want them."

her for more serious friendship. I think this . . . I can't explain this. But when that lady said this to me, I was amazed that somebody intelligent, well mannered, nice, could act in the SAME MANNER as I generally do. I can't explain this. Perhaps a psychiatrist would explain it to me. But I'm seeing from every day's experience that the girls who do not have a good education, and whose IQ is a bit low—for them it's SO easy to be nice, and smile, and say just the right words. They needn't be very clever: JUST SIMPLE WORDS to make it easy to start a friendship with a man. I can't explain this. A psychiatrist would.

NOW let's go forward . . . . Later on my mother used to take me to a family in Xewkija because, from this Xewkija family, one of their sons, Joseph, was married to a cousin of mine who was in Algiers. We had uncles and we had cousins in Algiers, and of course you get friendly— they were nice people, those of Xewkija. So Joseph's brother was about my age: he had had a good education at the seminary in Victoria, and we started a friendship, just a clean friendship with no . . . love at all—at least I didn't feel anything like that—AND when it was his time to get a job—usually you would expect one as a government employee, such as a clerk—a man from Malta got the job. It was always like that: the Malta people always had what we call *il-qaddisin.* * *Il-qaddisin* help you to get a job, just because you are somebody's nephew, or somebody's . . . well, the other guy got the job, and this man, my friend, was very disappointed, and the only way out for him to get on was to go to Algiers near his brother. And he got in business—I think THEY were in the business of buying and selling horses—and they got on well in that; they made good money out of that.

Well anyway, he wrote to me as a friend—how shall I say?—as a friend, and I would write to him, and one thing leads to another, and there was the war on, so one fine day he said: "Maria, I'm coming over so that we'll arrange . . . a marriage; we'll get engaged." And I, very foolishly, didn't think about it seriously; I encouraged him; I shouldn't have encouraged him because I didn't in the least feel anything about it. I know my mother was worried, because my mother had been in Algiers already, and she knew it was not the life for me at all; she was very worried, not because of the boy—she had nothing against the boy himself—but life in

---

*Literally, "the saints"; metaphorically, influential persons. Hence the proverb: *"Bla qaddisin ma titlax il-Ġenna"*: "You can't go to heaven without saints" (Aquilina 1972, 13: 37).

Algiers, among the Arabs and all that . . . she had been there, so after giving me such a good education, she felt I was ruining my life, and that I wouldn't be happy. And my father was very, very upset.

Well, I had even started filling my bottom drawer: I used to buy nice shirting from Gharb; for three pounds, you could buy a bale and make TWELVE good sheets, beautiful sheets; I still have them in my bottom drawer, because I never used them . . . . Well anyway, this boy came over on a warship because there was the war on, and there were no regular services . . . on a warship, and he came to my house, and I sort of . . . somebody said: "Why don't you go out for a walk with this man who came up?" And I started going out for a walk, but I would come back very, very, very sad, and very upset [lower tone of voice]. In the morning, I would ring him up and say: "I'm sorry, I can't go on with this any longer." Then he would come again. Well . . . it went on like this for some time, and I was feeling very, very confused, and I was worrying my father and my mother.

Well, at last we promised each other that it was no good, and we cut off the relationship . . . I was not sorry that it was cut off at all; I felt relieved. But during this indecisive mood, I got myself a little—how shall I put it?—sick. I had a strong headache, and there was no right medicine for that at that time, but I think I had done something foolish. After that, I was careful not to encourage, or start anything of the kind, unless I was completely sure of myself. In most other areas of my life, I'm proud, and I'm thankful to God that I've made well. I've made my parents proud and myself proud, and I've helped my neighbors whoever they were, whether they were children at school, whether they were people outside . . . I think I did well. But in that area, I was a complete CA-TAS-TRO-PHE [laughter]. So please, let's . . . not speak of that any longer . . . I still have an admirer or two, and I feel complacent about that because a lady always feels complacent, but it's a very innocent . . . flirtship—call it what you will—just a flirtation, VERY, VERY innocent. And let's stop that, stop that.

Micheline: Anyhow, Maria, as an unmarried woman, you were not feeling lonely or uncared for, were you, since you had at home your own family, or—as you said once—"family of some sort," between your parents and your brother, Anton? Perhaps you would like to recollect memories, and show what relations you had with each of these close relatives.

Maria: Yes, yes, yes, that's a safer field of life. First, I'll talk about my childhood, of course in the Ta' Ġanton farmhouse, with my father, which consisted in those days of my father and my mother. My father, as I said before, was a carpenter, having his workshop further down in the village; so he would be about the house early in the morning—I wouldn't be awake yet—and in the late afternoon. My mother was always in the house, except when she was at church, or near her friends a little further up near il-Madonna tal-Patri.* Later on we had babies. In fact, in 1921,[113] my mother had twins, a boy and a girl: the boy, Anton, somehow survived, but his twin sister, Sylvia, when she was about eight months old, caught what, at that time, was a common disease in babies: enteric fever, something to do with the intestines.[114] After that, we had two more girls, Josephine and Carmela; I remember my little sisters . . . they were good looking, healthy, and suddenly they would swell up; their fingernails would become blue as the blue you use for washing in the laundry, and they would be dead in two days. That was common. Well, Anton survived, and we went on well together. Sometimes, as children, we would have a fight over a piece of cheese, or over some kind of toy, and it was natural.

With my father, I think I went on very well. First of all, he started to educate me, as you know. He taught me how to write; he taught me the ABC with his thick, flat pencil, the reddish one—a carpenter's. And he wrote the ABC on the back of our door, so he taught me to say A, B, C . . . or rather *a, b, ċ,*[†] because in Maltese it's different from English. He would talk to me about stories of this and that—not fairy stories, but stories which always broadened your mind somehow, especially those about Australia. Sometimes he would take me for walks, and he would explain the things around us. HE was like an educator to me [expression of tender gratefulness]. In fact, at school, I was doing rather well; the other children would say: "Humm, humm . . . she has her father who teaches her at home, and we have nobody."

Well, in the evening, my father would bring some of his work home as an after—how shall I say?—after-hours job. He would bring chairs because he used to make a lot of chairs which were used by women at church, or which were used by the women who would order the right

* A place name.
† Phonetically, a, bə, tʃə.

height for lace-making, so that, when you sit down, you would be in the right position for lace-making. Besides, when three or four of them are sitting in a row making lace, it would be nicer for them to be at the same level: when turning their heads to gossip a little, they would be [smile] at the same level. Apart from those *bizzilla** chairs, my father would make sometimes chairs for pubs. Well anyway, the seating of the chairs would be made of *soghda*, or rather *seghda*,† which was like entwined straw. So my father would get about four or five bottomless, seatless chairs, and he would bring long skeins of this *soghda*, and we would help him to fix it. He was good at fixing the seating: he would wind three or four times, then put a long skein, then wind . . . you have to pull because you are not cutting and joining; IT MUST BE ONE COMPLETE sort of thread, so to speak. So that needed someone to help the pulling when it was being woven, because it had a certain pattern. I liked that pulling; for me it was playing while I was helping my father.

Another thing I liked about my father: he used to bring a certain big book, which I didn't understand at the time; it was a geographical atlas, and without any glasses at all, he would take a wooden stick and tell me all the seaports and lands which he must have seen on his way back from Australia to Malta, and he would know them all by heart, and he would always tell something different about each one. I remember that in one East African port—it must be Addis Ababa—he bought—we still have this souvenir—a fan made of palm leaves, which the natives must have made. I remember he said: "It's strange; we could dialogue with those people . . . ." Somehow he was happy he could dialogue in East Africa.[115]

Incidentally Dr. Joseph Grech,[116] a doctor who worked in Nigeria, once saw a man, an African who came to him from a LONG DISTANCE, and he tried to dialogue with him: he tried English, he tried the local African, he tried French . . . well, they tried many languages. And at last Dr. Grech said: "*Int ġej mil-boghod? Ġej mil-boghod?*" in Maltese; that is: "You are coming from a far distance?" AND THAT MAN EMBRACED HIM, and then started talking. This is strange. And when Dr. Grech, after forty years, mentioned this instance, this nice story, it reminded me

---

*Lace.

†Dialectal pronunciation of *soghda*, "material out of which the seats of some chairs are made, formerly in common use in the churches of Malta and Gozo known as *siġġijiet tas-soghda*" (*Maltese-English Dictionary*, s.v. *soghda*).

of what happened to my father on the East African coast.

Anyway that's how I was introduced to geography, and through him, I got an idea that the world does not consist of Gozo only, that there is a world outside. Funnily enough, I knew little about Malta because we didn't go to Malta in those days, but I knew a lot about Australia [laughter], and about the journey up from Australia to Malta. So sometimes he would take me for a walk and explain things, or he would tell me a little story, a story which had actually happened, and that always had a sort of educational effect on me. Now that's for education sort of: partly experience, partly oral—how shall I put it?—not having any practical value for the time being; it was all stored in my mind, and I thank him for that, but for every day-to-day living, there was my mother.

My mother saw to it that I could wash plates, that I could sweep, that I could go and draw some water, and drawing water . . . [laughter]. We had two wells in that house: one in the farmyard—sometimes we would use it as a refrigerator, as I said before—and we had another one outside, in the fields surrounding the house. Those two wells would not be used either for washing clothes, or drinking, or for cooking purposes, only for watering the fields. So every now and then, my mother would say: "Go and get a pail of water!"—like Jack and Jill [smile] from the public fountain, which was about forty yards down the road. At the junction with the main street, there was a big well which the government had put up. Before that, we had a fountain, like what you see in the movies, in the westerns: a fountain with a LONG semicircular piece of iron, and you have to go up and down, up and down in order to draw the water. And of course, for us children, that was something!

So I had to get the water from the right place, I had to know how to wash the dishes, I HAD TO KNOW HOW TO GRIND THE COFFEE, Humm, humm! and roast the coffee, and that was real good coffee. I went shopping for her. I went shopping for her to the grocer's in the main street of the village, and sometimes, you know, children are children; they would be playing beads or hazelnuts—at Christmastime, we would be playing with hazelnuts and not beads—and sometimes I stopped a little, you know; I delayed myself a little and didn't go home at the right time [expression of shyness]. Well, that was how my relations were, you know . . . with one, my father, I had education, which I liked very much—it was in me; I liked it instinctively; on the other side, my mother's side, I didn't say I disliked, but it was my DUTY to do that, and I learnt to do things, and I thank the Lord because later on in life, you never know what you are expected to do.

Then Anton was no longer a baby; he grew up, and we used to make some game together. I remember one carnival,[117] I decided, of all things, to dress him up as Napoleon: we had in the drawers a big, large, new, completely new, bluish pair of knickers—china-pottery blue—and I took hold of a newspaper, because in our home [sounding proud], there were always newspapers. My father was a reader, and he would get newspapers somehow. He would order fascicles, that is, printed serials. A man from Malta would come around the house and say: "I brought your serials." MY MOTHER . . . euh [sounding as if she is holding her breath] DIDN'T LIKE IT. The money . . . she looked upon the money spent on serials [suggesting a reproachful expression in her mother's eyes] . . . as throwing money away. Well anyway, we always had newspapers, so I took hold of one newspaper or two, and somehow I made a hat by folding in the Chinese way. I think the Chinese, or the Japanese, fold paper to make it look like a boat or a rabbit . . . well, we had learnt from somewhere how to make a hat, a triangular hat, and we called it Napoleon's hat. And I still see it; Anton was very proud . . . [laughter]. We went out just to have a bit of fun.

Of course, at Christmastime, we had our presents which were put under the pillow, you see . . . and we were told that il-Bambin,* if we were good, would bring us more than usual. If we were not so good, we wouldn't have as many presents as usual. Anyway, considering the low standard of living in the village and all over Gozo, I think our standard was a good one. We had food, we had clothing—better than the others, as I was saying—we had a little amusement . . . .

Micheline: Would you say that, generally speaking, boys were, to some extent, more taken care of than girls? Did you happen to feel personally a difference of treatment as compared to your brother?

Maria: Looking back and reminiscing, I think that, by all the parents in those days, a boy was somehow preferred to a girl. Because in those days, when you had a girl, you had to bring her up AND LEAVE HER A DOWRY when she is of marriageable age. Marriage had nothing to do with LOOKS OR LOVE or anything. Marriage had to do with how many . . . if you had a house, or fields, or money![118] So the poor man having a girl, or four, or five, humm! whereas a boy would be welcome

---

* "The Child."

because he would be somehow a breadwinner, and not expected to be given a dowry. I can't complain of that. I used to feel it very, very indirectly. In spite of that, my parents saw to it that I was educated.

And about six years ago, a cousin of mine, Konsilja, turned up from Australia. We were having a meal together, and she told me what my mother used to say: "I'll make Anton an *avukat* and Maria a *sinjûra*!"* And I said: "What?" Because this was prophetic, and it showed will-power. Now coming out of that small village, without any suggestion or any help from the upper class—because that makes a big difference— SHE JUST FELT . . . she saw that we were intelligent, and SHE FELT THAT SHE WOULD HELP US. And she did help us. She worked hard, THAT WOMAN, to give us a good education. Further on, when we grew up, things changed a little because my brother had to go to Malta as a university student.

Micheline: At that time, Maria, it was still uncommon for a carpenter's or farmer's son to be studying at Malta University, wasn't it?

Maria: At that time, it was taken for granted that only the professional people like doctors and lawyers would have their sons at university. It was unthought of that village people would dare enter the sacrosanct university. Anyway if you decided to send your boy to university in Malta, you had to provide for board and lodgings. So number one: we had to see that Anton had the best clothes available. Number two: Anton had nowhere to go, and we had to find lodgings. We had to see that Anton had the right food, the right pocket money, and all that . . . Later on he stayed with Maurice Ellul, whose family came as refugees to Victoria during the war;[119] so the house in Valletta was empty, and my brother stayed with his friend there, and they fixed their own meals, you see.

Micheline: But during the war, you must have found it difficult to supply him with food. Was your father in a position to exercise his trade then?

Maria: Yes. Thank God, my father earned good money. He earned good money, especially when the war started, because they needed long handles for a certain kind of instrument to cut the rocks for shelters; and those were selling like hot cakes! So my father would go up to Victoria every Sunday, with a cartload of these, and he always brought a lot of

---

*"Advocate" (Anton); "head teacher" (Maria).

money. People would also come to him for what would be today a small winepress, but at that time, it was needed for grinding corn, and my father was ingenious. He also made a *patilott*: a *patilott* would be like a cylinder, and it would be tightly filled with remains of wood, and that would act instead of fuel. During the war, we didn't have any fuel, or at least very, very little, rationed. Anyway I was feeling myself the provider, and I didn't mind it, and I was PROUD that our Anton was going to university.[120] I made shirts for him because there weren't any ready-made shirts in those days, and especially during the war. So I made shirts for him, and my mother would wash them immaculately, and I remember that *sinjura* from Malta who said: "How is it that Anton's shirts are so well made, and so immaculately clean every time?

Micheline: Anton was cherished both by his mother and by his sister, wasn't he, Maria?

Maria: Certainly my mother who had an only boy, only son, was proud of him. She looked after him very well, and she cherished him, especially when he grew up and started bringing all those prize books: every exam he would need the donkey; we would say: "You need *il-ḥmar** to carry all those prize books!" And she saw that he was going to be witty like her, and that [laughter] pleased her a lot. She thought that I was more like my father, who was very straightforward—a straightforward, sincere person—and I am like him. She was not like that—not that she wasn't sincere, but she always saw that nobody was trying to cheat her, or outwit her, or making use of her. Well anyway, Anton was cherished by her, especially when he went to university, and she was proud to say: "I have a boy at university studying for an *avukat*!" When a difficult exam would be over, a band would come and play in front of our house, and all that. She was very proud of our Anton. She cherished him.

I, as a sister who was older than he, also cherished him. The woman in me, the mother in me came out like that: I was fond, very fond of Anton, and I always tried my best in every way to help him along. Not with schooling—he was so good, and so proud—and yet I was a teacher, but he never asked me to help him just with one word. The only time I helped him with his schooling was—I remember it clearly—during the war; he was in Kerċem, typewriting from notes, and he said: "Maria, you can dictate to me while I'm typing so that I can go on more speedily,"

---

*The donkey.

and I remember that well: we had a door open—we were on the first floor—and from Sannat, we heard a strong, unusual noise. In fact, they were bombing Sannat; the big German bombs were coming down. So because of that connection, I always remember that.

Anyway I helped Anton with his clothes; for example, he would be buying a new suit, and he would get a sample from Malta, and he would say: "Do you like it?" And of course, I did my best to choose the best for him. AND he would say: "How much do you think that's a yard?" and I would say: "That's three pounds, five shillings!" and he would start making the cross in wonder because I would have said the right price . . . it happened several times. Anyway I would help him CLEANING his study; I would help him fixing books on shelves, things like that. I would help him of course getting food to be stored in Malta, to be stored before he went to Malta; and once, during the war, I said: "I'm going to Malta and I'll take something to Anton." As I said, Anton was staying with Maurice and with another friend, Joseph Cefai . . . . Two weeks before, my mother had bought a good leg of mutton, and she had roasted it for him and sent it with other people, but it never reached Tony . . . . During the war, you may remember . . . they must have devoured it!

Anyway I remember I took cauliflowers, and tins of sardines and tins of butter, which we could get from the ration—not from our own ration, but some people would get the rations from the grocer, and they would sell them—not double price, but quadruple the price . . . and we would buy eggs from the farmer and ONE EGG COST TWENTY PENCE; twenty pence is like saying twenty cents today! Now in those days, it should be much, much lower, but in order to fill a fairly sized trunk with eatables and the right food, I think we would spend twenty pounds . . . I am speaking of 1940 . . . . Well, I remember one fine day, I went to Malta, and at Marfa, I had to go on a small warship and then, sort of to climb up to another ship before landing, because Marfa was full of warships and boats, navy things. Well, I made it to Valletta all right, and I remember it was the Festa ta' San Pawl.[121] Anton was staying in a hotel—that was before he went to Maurice's house—and I had made some nice pictures with a collage, applied paper . . . that was a way of cheering him up and going to see his room. Incidentally I remember the next room was occupied by a man from Yugoslavia; he was a friend of Anton, and he must have had some hole overlooking, and that man said: "Who was that girl that came today?" And Anton said: "She is my fiancée. What do you think of her?" And he said: "She's good looking, but I think she is too serious." [Laughter.]

Well, that's how I helped Anton. Later on, when he was putting up an office in Palm Street, I would go and help him fix the curtains and the rugs, and I would help in cleaning the floor [sounding devoted and happy]. Of course, when he was not feeling well, I often stayed at home, and I used to answer the telephone, and sometimes, because Anton was a very good lawyer, he had many clients who would even come home—which he didn't like at all—but anyway, I would go, make the go-between, seeing what that client wanted, and I would go up the stairs and say: "He said this . . ." and I HAD TO REPEAT EVERYTHING VERBATIM! And Anton would say: "Tell him this and that . . . ," and I would go down and say that. I think I helped him in many ways.

So all in all, it was that relationship, and later, when he became sick, I think I helped him very, very much. I needn't go through that [silence due to emotion]. I think this poem written by Anton and obviously dedicated to me sums up what I have been trying to say:

> You are for me:
> Barefoot walking on a lone seashore,
> A fire on a cold winter evening,
> Remembering a cherished poem;
>
> Beautiful, gentle, and good;
> A November sunset at Dwejra,
> Resting in a cool place in summer,
> A great happiness.

Chapter 12

Naming a Street After Anton

It is somehow fitting that Maria's life history should be completed by the description of the public ceremony organized in 1988 to honor her brother, Anton. In order to enhance the cultural life of their island, the authorities undertook to rename several schools and give the name of "Anton Calleja, Man of Letters" to one street of the village, Kerċem. Anton now has an official rank among the notables, men of culture who devote their leisure time to studies—a tradition particularly well represented in the Maltese islands even today.

Anton's renown as a writer was already ensured by the publication, on the one hand, of his correspondence in a Maltese review at the university and, on the other, of his literary work collected by Maria in a book entitled *Frak Mill-Hajja, Fragments of Life*. Even the epitaph on Anton's tombstone gives evidence of his veneration for the poetry of T. S. Eliot.

As soon as the date of the ceremony was announced to Maria, she transformed her house into her "headquarters," to prepare the *Soirée d'Honneur* appropriately. She decided that musical and poetic intervals should be included among the speeches in the memorial program: in her mind, joy must be associated with remembrance.

Once more Maria bears witness to the values which are held in great regard among the people of her island.

Micheline: Maria, we are resuming our conversation in the same familiar place, your kitchen. Nearly one year has passed since last time.[122] This year I came at the right moment, almost by accident, to attend a ceremony which has just taken place in Kerċem. You welcomed it heartily, Maria. Will you explain what it meant to you, personally?

Maria: To make a long story short, they have a committee here in this village, and evidently they wanted to name a street after my brother, Anton Calleja. About two months ago, one of the members, Fredu Stellini, called at my house and, with a smiling face as he usually has, he said: "Maria, we are naming a street after your brother. And it will probably be the lower part of Santa Lucia."

Micheline: Very close to Ta' Ġanton, where you and Anton spent your childhood?

Maria: Quite. Well, from that very moment, I started preparing because I felt there should be a ceremonial, whether on a small or on a big scale. So I started by looking up the electoral register, where I could look up the names and addresses of the families of the street which would be bearing my brother's name. That was already a big job. Because here the surnames are a headache . . . . There is a surname like Grech, which is common to lots and lots of families.[123] and even the Christian names sometimes are similar, and you know, you don't want to mix people because you would be in the frying pan [smile].

Well, I had other preparations to make because I would send invitation cards. As this ceremonial would have nothing of the kind that went like that before—I mean there was nothing to copy—I had to IMPRO-VISE, to invent all the wording, the printing of invitation cards and even the very name of the ceremonial. I finally decided to give it the nice-sounding name of *Soirée d'Honneur*, but I had to fill it up . . . . At that time of the year, they were even changing the names of schools in Gozo, such as the lyceum complex for boys, the lyceum for girls, and the trade school in Xagħra, and the head teachers invited me, so I made it a point to attend and opened wide my ears and my eyes. More or less, street naming and the naming of the schools would run on the same lines. And I carried home all the papers, such as programs, invitation cards, and I kept them for reference. So I'm a little indebted to my friends, head teachers [smile].

Anyway the program itself would ipso facto include speeches, and speeches, however good they are, if they follow one another with nothing in between, would be boring, to say the least! So I decided that the program would include musical intervals, and I happened to have a friend in Victoria, Antoinette, whose son, Reverend George Frendo, conducts a choir called Laudate Pueri, including his sister, the well-known soprano, Maria; they even go to sing in the old Manoel Theatre on important occasions,[124] such as when the secretary general of the United Nations,

Mr. Javier Perez de Cuellar, was present. They came and sang so well that they gave a touch of class to my *soirée*.

Another interval I included was the prologue to a short play, called *Kull Bniedem Huwa Hija,** that was put up at Qala Secondary School for prize day, after I had worked with my pupils on the theme: "the poor in the Third World."[125] And for that play, I had asked my brother: "Please, will you write something as a prologue to this play?" It was a short, but meaningful play. And he started walking up and down, and I was running after him with notebook and pencil [she mimics the scene], and he dictated the most wonderful prologue which people classified as poetry. That was beautiful . . . so I felt that should go in this memorial program, and I started training girls from the neighborhood. I trained them here in my own kitchen, and I explained to them what they would be talking about—they would be talking about African people asking the Europeans to help them develop their richness that is inside their earth. And the result was good, as you could realize: they gave a nice bit of choral speech. Besides that, I included the reading of testimonials from Maltese, as well as English, friends.

Micheline: All this requires a lot of preparation.

Maria: Yes, it took all my energy. Well, Maria started working, and when Maria works, first she prepares some kind of food because Maria the Greedy [laughter] must have food, and then she starts phoning . . . I turned my house into the headquarters. I don't drive so I had to organize everything by phone. And it worked, and finally the GREAT DAY came.

Micheline: I can testify that your three hundred guests, or so, were much impressed when they found themselves opposite a beautifully decorated open-air platform for a sit-down, and the program began.

Maria: They just stood openmouthed. They did not expect that.

Micheline: Naturally the commemoration had started with the unveiling of the street name by the minister for Gozo, Mr. Anton Tabone, and its blessing by the parish priest. As far as the inscription is concerned, the mention of "man of letters"—or rather, *letterat* in Maltese—after Anton's name shows that he was commemorated primarily for his contribution to literature, wasn't he?

Maria: Yes. Anton is remembered by the people always holding a book in his hand, or under his arm. Well, he wrote articles, he translated

---

Every Human Being Is a Brother.

Ibsen's *A Doll's House* into Maltese, he made poems in Maltese and English.[126] He liked, and quoted T. S. Eliot all the time. This is why on his grave I put an inscription which is a quotation from T. S. Eliot:

> With the Drawing of Christ's Love
> and the Voice of His Calling,
> to Make an End Is
> to Make a Beginning.[127]

Before putting it, I consulted Dr. Dillingstone, who is an authority on T. S. Eliot, and he was friendly with my brother—Dr. Dillingstone has a beautiful farm in Għarb, near San Dimitri[128]—and he said: "Maria, you couldn't have put a better epitaph for your brother!" And he said: "Next week I'm going to lecture on T. S. Eliot in CAMBRIDGE, and I'm going to quote your brother."

Micheline: As regards Anton's personal writings, you did a great deal to bring them to the public by editing *Frak Mill-Ħajja.** Can you say how you got involved in the making of the book?

Maria: Well, sometime after Anton's death, when things started to quieten down, Professor Dun Karm Sant[129] turned up with some of Anton's letters. These letters had been written some years before, when they still were students, and there was the war in Malta. So they had exchanged letters, and Professor Sant said: "Do you mind if I publish these letters, because we are doing a special number of the *Leħen il-Malti?*† The special number was in honor of Professor Aquilina on his retirement.[130] Well, I went through the letters, and I said I would be proud if I see them in print. After that, Professor Aquilina—incidentally he is a relative of ours, too—well, he said: "Maria, you should do something; you should collect some of Anton's writings." And he indicated where and how I could get hold of these. And Mr. Marcel Mizzi, himself a poet, said: "Maria, you must collect Anton's work and put it in a book." And some other persons said the same.

So I set to my task with pleasure and gratitude to my brother, who had given me such wise, happy companionship and help, brotherly help. I helped him, but he helped me a lot; he used to come to Qala—now

---

Fragments of Life (1982).

† The name of a Maltese paper published by the University of Malta.

Qala is five-and-a-half miles from Kerċem—to pick me up at 12:30 after his office work, to go back to Kerċem and have a bit of lunch with my mother, so that we would still keep the family together because we were a small family: Mother, Anton and me. And he would take me back to school unless there was some other teacher going the same way. No other man would do that, but when you are with a person, you don't really realize . . . eh! how well-off you are! Anyway I started that book with joy.

Micheline: And the book came out as planned. That was in 1982. Since then, Maria, you have been living the existence of a retired person in this village, Kerċem, which may at times seem to you a little too quiet, especially in the winter season. Yet you have never ceased to be active in one way or another. You always have a lot of social commitments. You have been traveling abroad: you went to Lourdes, you went to Rome, last year you came with me and stayed some time in Paris. Your neighbors would say that you are always on the move . . . .

Maria: They would say: *Dik il-mara dejjem tiġri!*"* [Laughter].

Micheline: You seem to be always involved in some project. Recently you have been building and decorating a flat in town, in Victoria, and you thoroughly enjoyed it, although you doubt you will ever leave your village to move there. And now this present joint book! Remember, Maria, two years ago, it suddenly flashed upon us, as the natural outcome of the long talks we had had together, that "we should make a book." By all means, it has been a long, demanding undertaking for both of us— although from different angles—yet very rewarding, surely for myself, hopefully for you too. Perhaps when we started, neither of us appreciated clearly and fully all the implications: psychological, emotional . . . . Maria, would you express your views and feelings on the matter?

Maria: Certainly, Micheline. I quite agree with you that reviewing my life, at least the salient points, has proved to be an exciting and reward-ing experience. Because we have been friends for such a long time, I felt it easy to talk to you so spontaneously about myself. I had a feeling of elation for being able to fish up, from the marvelous computer of my mind, the petty, sometimes pathetic, sometimes meritorious experiences of a lifetime.

Since I retired from government service, I have not been idle at all,

---

* "That woman is always running."

The honorable minister of Gozo, Dr. Anton Tabone, unveils the street name which commemorates Maria's brother, Anton.

but still I feel an urge to start or join a voluntary movement concerning the elderly, the sick, the lonely and the trampled on. How does one go about it? I feel confident that, as I always say, "The Lord provides!"

I have a feeling that this activity will somehow brighten up the picture of myself I have been painting, consciously or unconsciously, throughout my lifetime, and with which I shall meet Christ, when ultimately I come face to face with Him.

Commentaries

1. Marsalforn, a small fishing harbor, has become the most popular sea resort for Gozitans as well as, more recently, some people coming from Malta; those among them who can afford it have a flat of their own and spend the hottest days of the season there. On summer evenings, cheerful crowds of people of all ages gather on the promenade by the sea to enjoy the breeze and the company of their friends. Nowadays Marsalforn is also frequented by foreign holidaymakers; new modern constructions, including additional stories built on the roofs of the existing houses, are changing (and damaging) the general appearance of a charming little place.

2. Mr. Joseph Attard Tabone, a retired police officer, is now devoting his time to his passion: research in history and archaeology, as well as protection of the environment. As suggested here, he rescued from fire some documents which happened to be connected with Father Manwel Magri, a well-known pioneer of Maltese folklore.

3. The family nickname, Ta' Pantu (*ta'* before surname or nickname indicating the family one belongs to), is supposed to have originated from a Corsican family name, Pantaleone, which, as Maria says, was, in the course of years, "twisted 'round the Gozitan way and became Pantu." Maria explains how, in her opinion, one Corsican man named Pantaleone would have been introduced into her family (on her mother's side): "As you very well know, before Maltese and Gozitan emigrants went to Australia or America, many of them, including my uncles and great uncles, emigrated and settled in Algeria. As Corsica was a French colony, many Corsicans also went to live in Algeria. A certain Corsican gentleman, by name Pantaleone, married one of my relatives—and evidently they had quite a number of descendants . . . ."

Maria's version seems to be strengthened by the information collected from oral sources among elderly people by one of her relatives, Mr. Grima, but up to now that research has not been available. More accurate data—at least on the question of marriage between Maltese emigrants and other European communities in eastern Algeria during a limited period—are provided by an inquiry made for the Società Medica d'Incoraggiamento di Malta by a medical doctor, Dr. E. Moreau (manuscript kindly lent by J. Attard Tabone), who established statistics for the period 1832–51 in the Bone area. It appears then that, with the second decade considered (1842–51), although the greater part of the Maltese (156) still married within their own community, a few cases of marriages with other European women, preferably Italian ones (nine instances, in contrast to only three French ones), were registered. Not surprisingly in a traditional society, there was not a single example of a Maltese girl marrying a foreigner. But things changed gradually, and perhaps the marriage we are concerned with, between a certain Pantaleone and Maria's ancestor, took place much later; at any rate, we are aware that it was mostly at the end of the nineteenth century when a large number of Corsicans—whole families sometimes—emigrated. That may have been the case with the Pantaleones, who apparently, as far as I know, have left no descendants alive today on the island of Corsica (information kindly given by Dr. G. Ravis-Giordani).

But what at least can be stated about Maria's family is the persistent use, in Gozo, of a family nickname derived from Pantaleone, Ta' Pantu, as well as its laudatory meaning. Maria says: "If somebody wanted to pay me a compliment for my hard work, guts or anything special, they would say: *'Dik* Pantua!" That is, "That [woman] belongs to the Pantu"; in other words, she has a tough character and is witty and clever, like her ancestors. Funnily enough, such features are the exact opposite of the characteristics of Pantaleone, the popular character of Italian comedy, whose name is supposed to be derived from San Pantaleone of Venice. But our Pantaleone, or Maltese Pantu, and the Venetian Pantaleone seem—as far as we know—to have nothing in common except their names.

4. Literally, "of Ġanton" (belonging to Ġanton). The phrase refers to lands which belonged to a certain Ġanton, whose renown was due—Maria says—to his herd of cows. Ta' Ġanton is still used to designate the area.

5. From the fifteenth century on, the inhabitants of Gozo lived under the threat of pirates coming from the sea: Arabs or, more precisely, Moslems from the Barbary states, used to come and pounce upon their victims within the Maltese islands and, vice versa, Christians of Malta would practice privateering along the Tunisian coasts. In the sixteenth century, Gozo was repeatedly raided and its inhabitants taken away as slaves: the great raid of 1551, led by Sinan Pasha, left the island almost empty; the Gozitan captives are said to have been taken to Tripolitania and have settled eventually in the locality of Tarhuna, "where their descendants have

kept distinctive customs although they switched over to Islam" (Wettinger 1990). After the fateful year of 1551, there were attacks on Gozo in 1560, 1563, 1572, 1574, 1582, 1598 and 1599. By the middle of the seventeenth century, the Maltese islands became more settled; a series of fortified lookout towers was built to strengthen the coastal defenses (Blouet 1987, 98–104).

6.   The pot of basil on the *ħarrieġa* indicates that there is a young girl of marriageable age in the house. The now-disused custom of placing a pot of basil on the windowsill is still referred to in the saying, "O my sister, pour water on the basil," to suggest that a girl goes out of her way to attract the attention of young men (*Maltese-English Dictionary*, s.v. *għazzi*). It is interesting to note that the association of basil with marriage and love is a Mediterranean traditional feature, as represented by a widespread cycle of folktales, usually known under the name of "The Basil Maiden" (Aarne and Thompson 1964, type 879; Eberhard and Boratav 1953, no. 192; Lo Nigro 1957; Couffon 1968, 91–94; Galley 1971, 163, 177, 178, 180; Cassar-Pullicino 1986–88, 155). The story is about a girl who is seen watering her basil plant on the terrace (or balcony) of her house by a young man, most frequently a prince, who is passing by; he then challenges her, usually in rhyme, as in this Maltese example (Bonelli 1897, 94):

Anġla Bella!
Issaqqi u tbaqqi,
Taf tghidli
Kemm il-werqa fih
Il-ħabaq għazzi?

(Lovely Angela!
Watering profusely,
Could you tell me
How many leaves there are
In the basil plant?)

From that very moment, there begins a relationship of an antagonistic nature (a verbal contest, in particular), leading eventually to marriage, and hopefully to procreation, since according to folk beliefs, a promise of fertility is contained in the numerous seeds of the plant, as well as in its rapid growth (e.g., Papamichael 1975). However, the relationship between the two lovers may turn into a tragic story as in one of Boccaccio's tales, "The Pot of Basil" (1948, 277–80). The brothers of the young lady murder her lover; she then places the victim's head in a pot of basil which her tears keep wet. In this case, the character of basil appears to be dual, both erotic and sinister (Gubernatis 1882, 2:35–36).

The basil plant is also referred to by folksongs in connection with marriage. In a game played for love divination by women and unmarried girls of Algerian cities (*buqâla*), the relationship of the married couple is symbolically foreseen: "The little bird has flown; it has flown and alighted on the basil in singing" (Boucherit 1984, 206); in Berber wedding songs, the bride is identified with a bunch of basil, which the bridegroom is recommended to tend, or literally "weed," carefully (Lacoste-Dujardin 1981, 113, vs. 147–48); in Arabic folk poems of the concise *ḥawfi* genre (western Algeria), a young man addresses his beloved in this manner: "You are the basil, and I, the dew to water it" (Marçais 1902, 230); in a Sicilian song, a married woman is supposed to warn her suitor that she is not available: "Young Nicholas, you are mistaken about that pot of basil, because that pot of basil belongs to my husband who brings me a cucumber every night" (unpublished personal collection). Basil is then clearly symbolic of the female sex, as also illustrated in the *One Thousand and One Nights* (933rd night). Similarly, in modern literature, basil recurs among the imagery relating to femininity, its fascinating power (Vassilikos 1968), and its savor (Meddeb 1986, 17).

In everyday life, it is primarily for its fragrance, according to folk interpretation, that the basil plant has been and still is appreciated in the Mediterranean area. This is why, it is said in the Maghreb, one has a pot of basil in practically all traditional as well as modern houses. In the Koran, the "aromatic plant" is mentioned among the marvels of creation on the earth (55. 10–11). In Morocco, *ḥabaq* (basil) is associated with the Prophet in the following recurrent formula at the beginning of folktales: "[Once upon a time] there was basil and there was lily in the Prophet's lap . . ." (El Fasi and Dermenghem 1926, 19). No wonder the idea, although found in recent cookbooks, of using basil as a culinary herb for seasoning either soup or fish, pizza or couscous, is still felt in some areas to be almost blasphemous.

7. Sliema is one of the seaside towns of Malta, a place where English residents tended to live. Perhaps the harmonious style of its architecture, in particular along the seafront, was the happy result of a fusion between British and Mediterranean features. It is regrettable that in recent years, many-storied modern buildings have sprung up, ruining the unity. See also note 86.

8. At that time, furniture was practically absent from a peasant's house. Obviously it was a mark of prestige to possess a wardrobe bought in Sliema (see note 7), a chest of drawers and, later, a clock. The second piece mentioned, the chest of drawers brought by Maria's mother as her dowry, replaces the traditional chest (*senduq*, an Arabic word) in which the bride's

trousseau was normally carried from her father's to her husband's house, in Malta (Cassar-Pullicino 1966, 51) as well as the Maghreb.

9. In rural Gozo at that time, "work was as scarce as hens' teeth," says Mr. Joe Gatt, an Australian citizen of Maltese origin, whose father was one of the Gozitans who left for Australia with Maria's father in 1916. In a letter sent to Maria (see Appendix A), Mr. Gatt relates what he gathered from his father's stories about the circumstances in which the emigrants embarked on a French Caledonian ship, *Gange*, lived aboard during a three months' voyage, were refused a landing in Sydney, and were finally off-loaded in New Caledonia until they eventually got permission to disembark in Australia and be employed in the construction of railway lines or in farming. At that period of the First World War, when conscription was being adopted in Australia, there was a need to import cheap labor to replace the local workers who were being sent to the battlefields in Europe (Dugan 1988, 70–2). Yet for political and social reasons, the authorities threw out the Maltese laborers (214 altogether) when they first arrived on the *Gange*, the argument being that they had come of their own initiative and therefore were "against the law of contract labour" (Dugan, 72). Later Maltese sympathizers, in particular Sir Gerald Strickland, who was Maltese born and had become governor of Tasmania, succeeded in promoting the Maltese as "suitable immigrants" (Dugan, 72). In 1920, the quota for a year was 260; in 1923, it reached 1200. Non-British emigrants (including Maltese) were no longer treated as "colored" people, as was the case at the beginning. In 1926, assistance was offered to encourage young Maltese women to emigrate with their husbands: that was undoubtedly a determining factor favoring durable settlement; priests also started to go and settle among the Maltese communities. In 1929, a Maltese commissioner to Australia was appointed. As a consequence, the attitudes toward emigration changed gradually.

In that respect, the personal experience of Maria's relatives gives an idea of what happened in general. Maria's father, Salvu, and his brothers, Ġużepp, Girgor and Carmelo, emigrated to Australia, stayed a few years, and returned home, whereas later generations have shown an increasing tendency toward settling on a more permanent basis in distant countries: Australia, as well as the United States, Canada and Britain.

Emigrating so far away was a new trend. The pattern of emigration had been very different before the First World War, a time when Maltese emigrants did not go beyond the Mediterranean area. As a matter of fact, a great number of Gozitans had to leave their home island from the beginning of the nineteenth century on, in search of either more favorable economic opportunities or the very means of survival (see Blouet 1987, 148–50 on the state of rural areas). The majority of them went to Tunisia or eastern Algeria (Donato 1985), as did Maria's maternal family. Some of the first settlers arrived before the French conquest (1830) and their descendants lived on Algerian soil, generation after generation, until the end of the colonial period (1962), marked by a disastrous war of seven years. They then left for France, where they have been living since then, a country which still, to a certain extent, appears to them as a land of exile.

10. In fact, the contract stipulates that the house is being sold to Maria's mother. Dated 1912, it was executed in the presence of Maria's mother, then a young unmarried woman, who was staying for a certain period of time with her uncle, Carmel, and aunt, Marguerite, at Bordj Bou-Arréridj in Algeria. Unlike his brother Antonio, who had twelve children, Carmel did not have a child. He certainly helped, by various means, his nephews and nieces from Gozo.

11. The house mentioned is the place where Karmni Grima was born, lived and died in the village of Għarb; it is maintained today as a museum. The popularity of Karmni (Carmela), a peasant girl, derives from the supernatural events attached to her: in 1883, she is said to have heard the voice of the Virgin as she was passing by a small chapel dedicated to her. Similar phenomena happened repeatedly in the following years, while miraculous healings were reported, and the renown of the shrine increased steadily. Nowadays the former little chapel has been replaced by an imposing, richly decorated church (Ta' Pinu), which is the most popular place of worship on Gozo, attracting islanders as well as emigrants from Australia and America. Ex-voto items can be seen in an exhibition room.

12. As had been the case in the past (Cassar-Pullicino 1989, 59–60), bread was still during the first decades of the twentieth century the staple element of food in rural homes. Interestingly enough, seventeenth century documents show the preference of the Maltese peasants at that time for bread and macaroni over meat: ". . . nel 1637 la gente del nostro contado . . . gustava molto i maccheroni, e la carne non le piaceva" (Cassar-Pullicino, 60). The Jesuit, A. Kircher, noted in the same year, while he was visiting Malta, that the people were "content with bread and cheese, garlic, herbs and onions" and that they sold their hens and cattle (Cassar-Pullicino, 60). Food habits have changed nowadays, but sometimes on unceremonious informal occasions, the peasants' traditional and delicious *ħobż biż-żejt u l-kunserva*, bread with (olive) oil and tomato paste (or slices of fresh tomatoes), is served with local wine for a snack.

13. There was none in Maria's house, but her Nanna (grandmother) on her maternal side had a loom.

14. At that time, cotton spinning and weaving were practiced at home for private purposes, but there was a period when the local cotton industry was prosperous in the Maltese islands. The process is described by Blouet:

"cotton was grown by small farmers and spun by their wives and offspring. A middleman then purchassed the spun cotton and exported it . . . or placed it with a different family which specialized in weaving" (1987, 112). In the eighteenth century, the value of cotton exports was "esteemed at half a million pounds sterling annually" (Blouet, 113). With the nineteenth century, the decline started and the country districts suffered from the breaking down of cotton exports (Blouet, 148–49 ; Cassar 1964, 357).

15. As a rule, bells ring six times a day to call the faithful to prayers: the early pealing, or Paternoster at 4:00 A.M.; the 8:00 A.M. Angelus, or *it-Tmienja*; the midday Angelus, *nofs in-nhar*; the Ave Maria at sunset; the prayer before going to bed, *t'orazzjoni*, and the prayer for the dead, *ta' l-imwiet*.

16. The little chapel dedicated to St. Dimitri, originally dating from the fifteenth century, is standing by itself on a wide extent of rocky land within sight of the sea in the territory of the village of Għarb. According to the legend, a young boy was taken away by the Turks. His mother made a vow to St. Dimitri, who liberated him, and since then an oil lamp has been burning in the chapel in conformity with the mother's vow (see Appendix B, Maria's version of the popular folk song about St. Dimitri).

17. Flannels, Maria says, were sold by Ġużepp tal-Għasri, Joseph of (the village of) Għasri, in Gozo; they came from British army or navy surplus stores in Malta.

18. Outside the village of Qala, a small church overlooks the sea, the island of Comino, and farther, Malta; its crypt contains the remnants of the vener-ated San Kerrew, i.e., St. Corrado (tenth to eleventh centuries). He is said to have settled in Malta, near Mosta, on his return from the Holy Land and lived the life of a hermit and "man of God" (*raġel t'*Alla). Because of persecution, he crossed over to Gozo, using his mantle as a sail (Buttiġieġ 1986, 9). He is venerated for the graces obtained through his intercession, mostly for the protection of young children. Traditionally the sick child was taken down by his mother to the crypt and for a while, "buried," so to speak, in the burial place of the benefactor; the child's clothes were left there, as if to remove magically the disease he/she was suffering from.

The same practice was common in other rural chapels and seaside shrines. At St. Julian's (Malta), the mother used to address the saint in this manner: "This is not my son. You have changed him. You must cure him. Or I'll leave him" (Cassar-Pullicino 1992, 78). Such beliefs in the supernat-ural substitution of sick children for healthy ones were common in the Maghreb. In Morocco, for instance, "a child is often thought to have been changed by evil spirits . . . . There is no other remedy than to give it back to the jinns and to demand the human child. To effect this exchange, the mother goes to a cemetery. She looks for a demolished tomb, puts the changeling into it, and an offering for the jinns. She withdraws for a

moment . . . . As soon as the child cries she comes back for it . . . ."
(Légey 1935, 155). Both in Morocco and Malta, the sick child is designated
as a "changeling": *mbeddel* in Moroccan Arabic dialect, *mibdul* in Maltese
(common Semitic root: *BDL*, which means "to change").

19.   On the history of Maltese costume, see Cassar-Pullicino 1966, 149–216;
an interesting section is devoted to laws and regulations dealing with dress
(165–77); another to the linguistic aspect of words designating male and
female costume (177–82). For a historical parallel between the Maltese
faldetta and the Sicilian *manto*, see Naselli (1966, 217–25). One of the
nicest descriptions of Maltese young women wearing what was, at that
time, elegant silken *faldettas* was written by Lamartine in his *Voyage en
Orient* (1959, 232):

> . . . par-dessus les épaules et la tête un demi-manteau de soie noire
> semblable à la robe, couvrant la moitié de la figure, une des épaules
> et un des bras qui retient le manteau; ce manteau, d'étoffe légère
> enflée par la brise, se dessine dans la forme d'une voile gonflée sur un
> esquif, et, dans ses plis capricieux, tantôt dérobe, tantôt dévoile la
> figure mystérieuse qu'il enveloppe, et qui semble lui échapper à
> plaisir.

> (Over the shoulders and over the head, half a mantle made of black
> silk like the dress itself, covering one side of the face, one shoulder
> and the arm which holds the mantle; this mantle, with its light stuff
> puffed by the breeze, takes the shape of a sail swelling out above a
> skiff and in its capricious pleats, in turns veils and unveils the
> mysterious face thus envelopped which seems to take great delight
> in escaping.)

20.   The phrase means: "for the souls (of the departed)"; this is a way of saying
thank you for the assistance received. Generally speaking, *għall-erwieħ* is an
expression of gratitude for a favor which has been granted to you. Maria
makes great use of it, whether to express relief after some period of tension, or enjoyment as, for example, when entering the seawater for a swim
at Għar Qawqla, a small inlet near Marsalforn.

21.   Indeed the rate of infant mortality was very high in the twenties when
Maria's three sisters died as infants, one after the other. At the end of the
following decade, it was still "one of the highest in the world at 224 per
thousand births in 1938" (Cassar 1964, 360). As a rule, the young victims
of fatal diseases—mostly from bowel disorders, as Maria says, and due to
lack of care by the parents—were under five years of age (Cassar, 360). No
wonder then that a young mother who might have lost several infants

beforehand would seek supernatural protection for her newborn child, maybe through the intervention of a saint such as San Kerrew (see note 18), as well as by imploring the Virgin Mother herself and making vows to her (Galley 1991), and even resorting to some superstitious practices (Bezzina 1985, 133). In any case, it is interesting for our purposes to observe ex-voto paintings related to the protection sought by parents after the birth of a child: an interior scene appears recurrently with a young mother holding her baby toward the Virgin, while several corpses of infants lie on the bed, as if to signify, in a very realistic almost-constraining address to the Protector, that tribute has been paid to death already (see photograph, p. 157).

22.   Young children are said to go straight into heaven when they die (provided they have been baptized). This is why, Maria says, the ringing of the bell is not sad; on the contrary, it sounds cheerful, as suggested by the word *frajħa* (from *feraħ*, "to rejoice").

23.   Professor Ġuże (Joseph) Aquilina was born in 1911 in the village of Munxar (Gozo). A student at the university of Malta, he found himself committed entirely, body and soul, to the defense of the Maltese language (a question of great issue which is discussed later in this book). Although he had become a lawyer, he chose to study in the School for Oriental and Asiatic Studies at London University and prepare a Ph.D. thesis (1939–40) on the *Structure of Maltese* (1959). His important scientific work has thrown light not only on the Maltese language and its history, but also on the social background of the Maltese people. Since he retired from his position at the University of Malta as head of the Department of Maltese and Semitic Languages, he has been devoting his time to research and has recently published his *Maltese-English Dictionary* in two volumes, a new contribution of great import. Apart from his scholarly publications, Professor Aquilina has written poetry, plays, a historical novel and literary essays. Yet never has he withdrawn into an ivory tower: he lives in his time and, through the medium of the press (sometimes of the radio), regularly expresses his personal views and feelings on subjects of a social, cultural and ethical nature.

24.   Victoria is the chief town of the Island of Gozo; it owes its official name to the commemoration of Queen Victoria's Diamond Jubilee (1897), but the local name, Rabat, is still used. Its old citadel, built on a small hill, overlooks the surrounding countryside; inside there are important buildings (now being restored) and an impressive baroque cathedral with, in particular, a richly decorated marble pavement (tombstones). The beautiful texture and color of the local stone with which everything—fortified walls, palaces, church and houses—was built during the sixteenth and seventeenth centuries has conferred a great unity on the ensemble, while the passing of time,

good years and bad ones, seems to have imparted an atmosphere of serenity to the place.

25. Judging from her recurrent remarks, Maria was much impressed by the "very chic" French-fashioned clothes which her mother received from her relatives in Algeria.

26. Maria is referring to the twenties, since her father came back from Australia in 1921.

27. See the letter by his son, Joe Gatt (Appendix A).

28. A name is usually given to a house built by emigrants, for example "Australia" or "Melbourne," and occasionally an additional symbol, such as a kangaroo, is carved or painted on the front wall, apparently as an expression of gratitude to the country of settlement, as well as the personal mark of the owner. In any case, house naming among emigrants provides information on the destination country, and each village has its own prevailing motifs which can be observed today: in the village of Nadur, for instance, the relatively recently built houses, on each side of one of the mainstreets, are called "Maple Leaf House," "Ontario Palace," "America the Beautiful," "Stars and Stripes," and so on, thus showing that the network of support and solidarity between relatives and neighbors reaches out toward Canada and the United States, in this case.

29. See note 9.

30. In Gozo, there is, among traditionally minded people, a great propensity to name things after personal characteristics in the same way as nicknames are used for people. As illustrated in this book, a field is called either by the name of its owners, like Ta' Pinu, or "(that) of Pinu" (in this case, the name also designates the church built on the spot), or after a land measure, such as "half a siegħ," or after the weeds that grow there, and so on. A bedcover (used on the bed of her parents for special occasions, such as the birth of a baby) is still remembered by Maria as *tal-għasafar*, "(the one) of the birds," because of its decorative motives. Even some lotto figures seem to have been designated by metaphor (a former code?): "the old (woman)" (*ix-xiħa*), associated with the number 90, may have derived from the connection with age, whereas "the sisters," substituted for number 22, is perhaps based on the similarity between the two figures. It would be, undoubtedly, interesting to go deeper into the subject.

31. Lace-making was spread throughout the whole of Gozo, representing a valuable contribution by the women to the budget of their families. For example, when Maria's father left for Australia, her mother relied on her lace as a means of livelihood: a middlewoman would collect the lace from the village and sell it in Malta, mostly to the British army, Maria says; then the price would rise or fall depending on whether lace was in great demand or not. To get an idea of the versatility of the design repertoire,

one should consult a small, accurate introduction to Gozitan crafts (Claridge 1972, 30–5). It is said that Queen Victoria was presented with a very fine silk collar worked by the best lace workers of the time (Claridge, 33). Still today, lady guests of the Maltese authorities may be lucky enough to be welcomed with a lace shawl of fine silk. The craft is thriving mostly in tourist areas.

32. Some of the noble families who were granted wide tracts of land for honorable service came with the Normans (eleventh century), and settled in Malta. On Maltese nobility, see Gauci (1986).

33. The word *qorq* (plural: *qrieq*) designates sandals which are no longer worn except by peasants. It can be given a pejorative sense, as in the following exclamation by a member of a *sinjuri* family, whose daughter wanted to marry beneath her. "*Se ndaħħlu il-qrieq id-dar!*" (We are going to introduce the sandals into the house!).

34. The *T'* is the shortened form of *Tagħ* or *Ta'*, which means "of" (see note 3) and is used before words beginning with a vowel: T'Ettru, "of Ettru," designates the offspring of Ettru, originally Ettore in Italian. The prestige of the family is made clear by an ironical proverbial phrase: "*Int qisek T'Ettru!*" which literally means "Your measure is that of the Ettore family!" Maria translates this as "Do you think that you are a king?"

35. "Italian was the business and professional language of dominant groups in the social hierarchy. It was a language utilized by the lawyers and the courts, the priests and the curia, and it was the language of the nobility. Italian was not the language of the majority of the population who spoke Maltese at home and in everyday transactions" (Blouet 1987, 187). The pro-Italian Dr. Enrico Mizzi led the Partito Nazionalista Democratico, organized in 1921, and became more and more influential among the Nationalists.

36. Salvatore Busuttil (1798–1854) belonged to a family of artists. He settled in Italy; he was in Rome when he executed an altarpiece for the parish church of Kerċem, where St. Gregory is venerated for having delivered Gozo from the plague in 1519. Busuttil's painting was meant to commemorate the votive procession which started after a new plague epidemic in 1813 (for more information, see Buhagiar 1990, 110).

37. Priests used to be sent on pastoral work among the Maltese communities. One of them, Father Manwel Magri, already mentioned in note 2, died during his mission in Sfax (Tunisia) in 1907. He had studied at home (Jesuits' College) and in several European countries. He knew various languages, including Semitic ones. He also had a passion for the Maltese cultural heritage: archaeology, as well as oral folklore. His contribution to the safeguarding of folktales, which he personally collected, is the work of a pioneer.

38.   Maria may have heard her brother, Anton—he was a great reader—speak
about *Madame Bovary* by Gustave Flaubert. Apart from the association she
likes to make between Emma Bovary and the interviewer (perhaps just
because they are both French), she obviously enjoys pronouncing the name
aloud. This is a recurrent feature with Maria, who is sensitive to the sound
of words; in this case, she even unconsciously inserts the particle *de*
between Madame and Bovary, as if to make the family name sound more
prestigious.

39.   The meaning of *Tork* (plural: *Torok*) is not limited to "Turk": it "is used
vaguely in the sense of unbaptized" (*Maltese-English Dictionary*, s.v. *Tork*).
In other words, all Moslems can be designated by this word. The phrase *it-
Torok ta' Barbarija* refers to the corsairs who came from the Barbary states
during the previous centuries (see notes 5 and 16). The phrase is still used,
with a note of impatience, in particular by parents to warn their children
that unless they are good, the "Turks" will come and take them away.
Therefore, in the mind of Maria, still a child at that time, the image of the
"Turkish" (or Tunisian, in this case) peddler was not reassuring.

40.   We have already mentioned Lord Strickland's Anglo-Maltese origin, as well
as his action on behalf of the Maltese emigrants in Australia while he was
governor there (see note 9). When he retired from the Colonial Service, he
returned to politics in Malta: he led the Anglo-Maltese party (1921), later
the Constitutional party, the objective being "to promote the individuality
of Malta, while at the same time strengthen the British connection . . ."
(Blouet 1987, 184). He was prime minister from 1927 to 1932 (Koster and
Smith 1984). Needless to say, Strickland and Mizzi (see note 35), as well
as the parties (Constitutional and Nationalist) they embodied, had diamet-
rically opposite views on the English/Italian so-called language question:
the pro-British—together with the high officials in London—became increasingly concerned at the time (the thirties) of Mussolini's claim to Malta
with the Nationalists' attempts at Italianizing the younger generation
through the system of education (as illustrated here by Maria's testimony);
whereas for the Nationalists, preserving Italian culture and language was
"a matter of loyalty to the Church in Rome" (Blouet 1987, 187).

Interestingly enough, the linguistic controversy created favorable
conditions for the Maltese to become conscious of what would be called
today their own identity. And this played a remarkably dynamic role in
lifting Maltese, a former dialect, to the status of a written language, which
was to become the official language of Malta, as well as the medium of its
young, very promising literature (see note 23). In a recent essay, Francis
Ebejer, a Maltese novelist and playwright, throws light on the process; he
does it in his colorful, talented way:

Strange but true—and perfectly feasible—as the Maltese language came to fall under the hegemony of two super-languages, so it came to seem to us that there was something specific in it, a certain unique quality of civilisation which was worth preserving. This awakening was supported and helped along by the pro-British Party and London which brought itself round to the idea that in our formidable grass-roots arsenal lay an important weapon against Italian fascist infiltration. Result: Much put-upon, and beautifully clichéd Cinderella was given a fresh set of clothes and, finally, let out of the kitchen! Starting off as a political pawn, she was soon to assert her presence as an independent adult (1989, 12).

41. Maltese was made the language of the courts in 1934 (Blouet 1987, 187).

42. For an accurate account of the research conducted by Surgeon Major (later Sir) David Bruce and Dr. (later Sir) Themistocles Zammit, from the end of the nineteenth century on, see Cassar 1964 ("Brucellosis," 240–47). It was found that the microbe was ingested in raw milk from infected goats. Therefore measures of prevention were taken (as shown by Maria), but were not very successful; it was only with the pasteurization of milk (1938) that the incidence of the disease fell (Cassar, 240–47).

43. "Ton" or "Tony" are diminutives of Anton (Anthony). Maria is referring to her brother.

44. On the subject of tuberculosis in the Maltese islands, see Cassar 1964, 218–23.

45. See note 1.

46. See note 5.

47. The water trough was the size of a tub, just big enough for a child to have a dip. But, with the passing of time, in Maria's imagination it assumed a much bigger size, proportionate with the happy memories attached to it. This is why Maria experienced almost a shock when she revisited the place in 1989 in the company of the interviewer. On the following day, while we were both in her house, Maria suddenly stood up under the impulse of her feelings: she stood straight with her face tightened with concentration and sang, in a loud voice, this impromptu quatrain:

Il-bieraħ Ta' Ġanton ħadtni.
Rajtu inbidel sew:
Dak il-ħawt kemm hu ċkejken;
Qabel għalija kien Musulew! [Laughter.]

(Yesterday you took me to Ta' Ġanton.
I have seen it totally changed:

That water trough, how tiny I've found it;
For me it had the size of a mausoleum!)

This type of haikulike song (usually four lines of eight syllabes, rhyming *abcb*) lends itself to emotion tempered by humor; it is still alive and very popular in the Maltese islands. Maria explains that she could not sing about satellites, nor the moon, but must focus on real, everyday topics, and that she likes to use singing, in the privacy of her home, as an outlet for her emotions, or simply for the pleasure of versifying (*taqbil*). Her comment on life may be sad, but it always reflects a great deal of wisdom and tenderness, as illustrated by the following two songs I heard her sing once. The first is about a dog whose master, nicknamed "the Pilot," has just died:

Il-kelba tal-Pilot tingħi
Għax ma tafx x'ġara u x'ġej.
Pilot tar l-aħħar titjira,
Għal ġenna hdejn l-Mulej.

(The dog of the Pilot is whining
Because he does not know what has happened and will happen.
The Pilot has flown his last flight,
To paradise, near the Lord.)

The second is a more personal reflection:

Kemm hi sabiħa l-ħajja
Meta jkollok kumpanija!
Min jgħid kelma, min jgħid oħra,
U l-ġurnata itir bħal siegħa.

(How beautiful life is
When you have company!
One says a word, the other says another,
And the whole day flies like a single hour.)

48. In the Maltese islands, nicknames have been and still are a popular unofficial form of personal identification, existing side by side but independently of surnames (Wettinger 1971, 34–46). A nickname (*laqam*, "graft," from the Arabic *laqab*) is generally composed of the definite article *il*, followed by the word or phrase chosen to characterize the holder. He is then referred to by both first name and nickname, like, for instance, Żeppu s-Sultan,

"Joseph the king." Later the nickname usually passes down to the next generation, becoming a family nickname with the addition of the possessive *Ta'* (of, belonging to), as in the present Tal-Batuta. Properly speaking, *batut(a)* means "poor," "miserable"; yet it is attributed here by an antiphrasis to an apparently prosperous and ostentatious family: the man of the house is remembered, as he was sitting outside his house on the pavement, as wearing silk, having a meal on a white-clothed table, and occasionally shouting at his wife who was serving him: "Katarin, *ġibli l-melħ*!" (Catherine, bring me the salt!).

Since nicknames are inherited patrilineally, a young woman is designated by her father's nickname, as are all the members of the same household. But when she gets married, she normally receives the nickname of her husband. However, there are women (very few) who are given personal nicknames. In Gozo in the twenties, one woman used to collect lace from the villages and make money by selling it to the British sailors or soldiers in Malta. Perhaps because she was leading a life comparable to a man's (public) life, she was nicknamed after a word (coined from English) which related to her trade: ix-Xilina (literally, "the one with shillings"); and according to tradition, the term was eventually "grafted" onto her offspring, who therefore were designated as Tax-Xilina.

It goes without saying that the use of nicknames is not strictly Maltese in this Mediterranean area: it rather appears as a rural feature, the main reason being that surnames are scarce and extensively shared. Consequently nicknames have become a convenient means of personal identification (Pitt-Rivers 1961, 162; Brandes 1975, 141). Another social function has been that of recreation: the (anonymous) process of nicknaming requires a sense of poetic invention which is not uncommon among Mediterraneans (see notes 47, 62, 81, and 105). The trick is to designate an individual in the most concise (in one word, rarely two) and striking (often funny) manner, so that the nickname will be unanimously adopted. The result can be either laudatory, neutral or pejorative. In Muslim countries, laudatory nicknames are frequent when associated with religion, as in the following phrases: "the one learned (in Islamic law)," "the one attracted (to Islam)," etc. (Antoun 1968, 163). In the northern Mediterranean, there is nothing comparable, yet complimentary nicknames are not completely absent (see note 3 about the positive connotations of Ta' Pantu). Interestingly enough, there is a specific group of people in Malta whose nicknames are always either idealized or expressive of praise: folksingers and guitar players, called, for instance, "Paul the falcon," "Xavier the man," "the Moon," etc. At least, this is observable nowadays, and a similar phenomenon has been noted in Spain with Gypsies and toreros (Pitt-Rivers 1983, 143).

However, the majority of nicknames are more or less of a mocking nature, either humorous and harmless, or derisive and derogatory. From one social group to another, preferences may vary: in Sicily, as suggested by the word "nickname" itself, the genre is apparently expected to be disparaging (Boissevain 1969, 43), whereas on a Greek island, nicknames are reported to be "more humorous than obnoxious" (Russell 1968–69, 65–74).In Gozo, there seems to be a tendency to use baby vocabulary (e.g., referring to food, names of domestic animals), thus alluding to some kind of infantile behavior by the adult in question. On a more general scale throughout the Mediterranean, what is felt to be particularly offensive is the mention of either illegitimacy (e.g., the Arabic *ibn ḥarām*, "Unlawful Son" or "Bastard"), or physical defects and, above all, of sexual impotence (e.g., "the Capon," "the Eunuch"). In the first case (a supposedly illegitimate child), the honor of a family (through two generations) is involved; in the second case, the person concerned is symbolically emasculated and deprived of his own identity.

Efforts seem to have been directed in the past against the practice of defamatory nicknames in Christian and Muslim countries alike around the Mediterranean: "Neither defame one another, nor insult one another by nicknames!" the Koran recommends (49. 11–12). Nicknaming is sinful and must be punished, a Maltese traditional proverb says: "He who invents a nickname shall spend seven years in purgatory" (*Min jaqla' laqam, għandu seba' snin il-purgatorju*). Nowadays the use of nicknames has not disappeared from rural communities even though people say they abhor the offensive ones. Yet among themselves, they resort to them, savor the humorous element (if any) and enjoy the meaning. Several anthropologists of the Mediterranean have analyzed the phenomenon, coming to the conclusion that like gossip, carnival, satirical versification and other "institutions of public derision" (Pitt-Rivers 1983, 101), nicknaming ensures social cohesion, whether it is seen as part of a friendship network which strengthens social ties (Brandes 1975, 143), as an element "propagating egalitarianism" (Antoun 1968, 163), or as a form of aggression which, once it is channeled into nonviolent inventive expression, contributes to social stability and cultural continuity (Gilmore 1987).

49. Ġanna Roża, Jane-Rose, Maria's mother.

50. In Maria's opinion, her mother was exactly the "Pantu type" (see note 3, and photograph). In other words, "she had a mind of her own and was not easily manipulated," as her daughter puts it.

51. The partner of Maria's father was not originally nicknamed Ta' Żerrek (the Seducer), but Maria chose the phrase and substituted it for the actual nickname which "was not nice," and therefore might be seen as an insult by the family (see Boissevain 1969, 43–44). The project Maria is alluding

to was a small theatre that both men—her father and Ta' Żerrek—wanted to run during their leisure time. "They had been friends while they were in Australia maybe," Maria says. Anyway they put up a stage and had actors, and one very good-looking actress who came from Malta. The entrance fee was very low (a penny), and the children could even peep from the outside through a hole in the wall and occasionally watch the actress getting dressed. But the undertaking was against the wishes of Maria's mother, and it was given up after some time.

52. The events Maria is now relating are probably what impressed her most when she was a child; she has already told this story in Chapter 2.

53. The play, *The King and I*, was on in London during one of Maria's stays in England. She still remembers the song about young Eliza, who had to run away from her persecutors.

54. Preference was given traditionally to village endogamy, or at least, as is the case here, to marriage between partners from neighboring villages (Cassar-Pullicino and Galley 1981, 82). But what people disliked, as noted by Maria, was the choice of residence in the husband's village; the tendency was for the couple to live in the wife's village, because of the strong ties between a married girl and her family (Boissevain 1965, 36).

55. Ġamri is Maria's cousin, the son of her aunt Lucia on her mother's side. The name Ġamri is made from John plus Mary (*Maltese-English Dictionary*, s.v. Ġamri).

56. This is a repetition of a story Maria has already told in Chapter 2 (see page 31).

57. Salvu, Maria's father, was the eldest child.

58. Later they also resented the marriage of another son, who had remained a bachelor until he was thirty or forty, Maria says. And like Maria's father, he had supported his younger brothers and sister. It was mainly his sister, a spinster, who grumbled. When she found herself among gossipers, she even declared, as if to take her revenge against him: "*Dak mhux huna . . . dak huna mill-leġittima.*"—"That one is not our brother (i.e., he is not of our blood) . . . that one is our brother [only] from legitimacy (i.e., he is like a bastard)." Like most unmarried women at that time, she must have felt particularly insecure. In the Mediterranean, a spinster was considered to be left over, or, as a Maltese proverb says, to "remain on the shelf." The alternatives for a woman were, according to a Tunisian saying, to either get married or die, literally: "To an aging girl, a male or a grave!" (Cassar-Pullicino and Galley 1981, 81).

59. The lease was based on emphyteusis, a term of law which involves a perpetual right in a piece of another's land.

60. When she was just learning to read, Maria discovered in a small room of her parents' house these letters, which were stored in a traveling case (see original reference in Chapter 1).

61. Time was traditionally calculated by the ringing of the bells throughout the day (see note 15).

62. After hearing one of the Maghribian tales about the Mediterranean trickster known in Arabic as Johâ (Maltese: Ġaħan, see Galley 1988, 91–4), Maria immediately adopted the proverbial phrase derived from the tale, *mismâr* Johâ, "the nail of Joha," which became *il-musmar ta'* Ġaħan in Maltese. She also called a hat peg in the entrance hall of her flat in Marsalforn "Ġaħan's nail," and one day she started singing a humorous stanza, because there was an unusual item hanging from the peg:

> Il-musmar ta' Ġaħan, x'waħda ġralu?
> Għandu malja ħadra blu.
> U min jidħol hawn minn barra
> X'waħda din dana x'inhu? [Laughter.]

> (The nail of Ġaħan, what happened to it?
> It has a bathing costume, green and blue.
> Whoever enters from the outside
> [Would say] what on earth is this?)

On Maria as a singing enthusiast, see note 47.

63. According to tradition, relatives are invited for a meal on the occasion of the yearly *festa*. Thus, apart from its religious and social aspects, a *festa* also has a role in reinforcing, once a year, the bonds of kinship between relatives: " . . . each family opens its doors to its relations, especially to those who live in other villages. Grown sons and daughters return to their paternal home, married brothers and sisters meet, nephews and nieces call on uncles and aunts. Younger children learn to recognize more distant relatives whom they might not see at any other time of the year. In this way they become aware of the network of kin relations that stretches out from their home . . . ." (Boissevain 1969, 69).

64. Quoted by Margaret Wolfe Hungerford (1878) and Lew Wallace (1893) as "Beauty is in the eye of the beholder."

65. Maria's father died in 1948.

66. Quoted from Paul's Epistle to the Colossians (3. 9–10): "Lie not one to another, seeing that ye have put off the old man with his deeds; and have put on the new *man*, which is renewed in knowledge after the image of him that created him."

67. Balzan is one of the three contiguous villages—the others being Attard and Lija—which form a residential area nowadays: the central older part, with its narrow meandering streets, its plain and magnificent-looking houses side by side, its gardens and palaces, is surrounded by a building area in which a considerable number of villas are being constructed, most frequently by newly married couples.

68. Maria's brother, Anton, was the founder of the Gozo Handicapped Fund, later called the Helping Hand Society. Apparently it was after meeting Sue Ryder, an English lady known for her action in favor of handicapped or seriously ill people, that he "felt," according to Maria, "he must do something for the many handicapped children and adults kept hidden in Gozitan homes." At that time, it was taboo to bring these unfortunate beings out in the open: Anton's efforts were aimed at persuading the families to seek help through his association, so that the handicapped might somehow be integrated into society.

69. Maria is referring to the statue inside the church of Xewkija with Christ on the cross and the Virgin at his feet (see Maria's and Anton's visit to Xewkija on Sorrow Friday).

70. On Maundy Thursday, it was traditional to go and pay seven visits to the Holy Sepulchre, which was decorated with flower arrangements and candles in the churches. Nowadays the faithful either go in and out seven times if they stay in their village, or go to seven different villages: in this case, they go in their private car, or join a group that hires a bus.

71. Ċirkewwa is now being used instead of Marfa (which means "harbor"), both sheltered places being situated in the western part of Malta, the side which is the closest to Gozo. It takes only about twenty minutes to cross over to Mġarr, the small port of Gozo.

72. Obviously Maria likes the sound of the surname "Shamiya," and pronounces it for her own pleasure. In Arabic, the ending -*i*, -*ija* in the feminine, used to form adjectives, denotes descent or origin: the surname (*al-*)Shamy refers to a person coming from shâm, i.e., Damascus and its area.

73. Short for Auberge de Castille et de Léon. It is an elegant building dating from the time when the knights, who originated from various European countries, used to be grouped according to their "langue" in their own "auberge" (see Mahoney 1988, 125–50). The Auberge de Castille has been beautifully restored; it now serves as the official residence of the prime minister.

74. Manwel Dimech (1860–1921) was a man of "ideas too advanced for his time who died in exile" (*Maltese-English Dictionary*, s.v. Dimech). His writings defended socialist and anti-imperial views (see Frendo 1972).

75. Frenċ ta' l-Għarb was a Gozitan farmer who lived in the first half of this century. His popularity as a faith healer was not limited to Gozo: even

people from Malta used to seek his advice for an illness, as well as for problems in families, marriages, and so on. He would see his visitors after his farmer's work was over, and heal them with simple herbs; he would massage them (especially, Maria says, "when it concerned the ligaments being a bit twisted"), or advise them what herbs to use, where to find them in the wild countryside, and how to boil them or prepare some ointment with them. He never took money for himself, but accepted gifts to adorn the neighboring church, dedicated to the Virgin (Ta' Pinu; see note 11), with very expensive mosaics brought from Italy. Nowadays people go on pilgrimage to his grave in the small cemetery of Taż-Żejt in his village, Għarb. People implore his intercession, and he is associated with the Virgin on the ex-votos in the church of Ta' Pinu.

As far as traditional herbal medicine is concerned, Maria believes in its beneficent effect, in particular that of a concoction known as *duwa tas-suffejra*, or "remedy for shocks" (literally, "for jaundice," the root of *suffejra* denoting the yellow, *isfar*, color). She sounds positive about it: "I sometimes suffer from even slight shocks when I hear very bad news: inside me, I feel something go . . . and my face goes pale . . . I know that I have a shock. So I make my own *duwa tas-suffejra*, and—believe it or not—when I take just one mug of it, all my whole physique turns right, the color in my eyes gets bright, the color in my face . . . my whole physique goes all right . . . ."

To make her *duwa*, Maria grows the elements needed, the only ingredient she orders from a chemist in Sussex being a special kind of rhubarb powder; she proceeds as follows:

> In the garden, I have a lovely lemon tree. So: lemons. Then a herb called *marrubija* (horehound) which I grow—it's decorative, but for me it's functional; then some *erba bianca* (wormwood), which also grows in my garden, and I dry it up like you do clover. I let this boil slowly, slowly, slowly, and when it's over, I sieve it. Then I get some rhubarb powder—I think they bring it from roots of trees in China—so I get some rhubarb powder in a bowl with cold water, and I mix it as when you do starch; then I mix it all together; I let it boil well. Then the morning after, I drink a mugful of that, and believe me, it's the best, the best medicine whatever for me!

76. On the island of Malta, the "Grand Harbor" extends from the historical Fort of Saint Elmo (see Braudel 1949, 846, 848–9, 852) down to the port of Marsa. It is a wide expanse of water, calm and beautifully framed by military architecture: on one side, the three cities: Birgu (named Vittoriosa for her valiant resistance during the Great Siege of 1565), Bormla (now

Cospicua) and l-Isla (now Senglea); on the other side, the city of Valletta, which was built by Grand Master Jean de la Valette in such a way as to render it impregnable and make it the seat of the Knights of Malta.

77. In stormy weather, a similar tragedy involving a boat employed in the passenger- and cargo-carrying trade between Valletta and Mġarr in Gozo had happened before (in 1933, for instance), as illustrated by ex-voto paintings (Prins 1989, 16–22). Judging from the number of ex-voto items exhibited in Ta' Pinu church, shipwrecks come, in order of importance, just after infant mortality. Generally there is a descriptive text in the inferior part of the painting. In the present case, it runs as follows: "In thanksgiving to the Most Holy Great Virgin Mary of Ta' Pinu, for the reason that through her intercession, I, Pawlu Zammit from the village of Xagħra, escaped drowning in the tragedy of Gozo which happened on the 30th October 1948 near Taċ-Ċawl rock: twenty-four souls got drowned; I, who had strong faith in the miraculous Virgin of Ta' Pinu, was saved after eight hours of suffering. Be glorified forever, the Most Holy Virgin of Ta' Pinu" (translated from Maltese).

78. Maria stayed a fortnight in Paris (Summer 1987).

79. See note 10.

80. For a long time, country folk were very much opposed to burials outside their churches. It was thanks to the clergy that the civil authorities succeeded gradually in doing away with church burials in rural districts (Cassar 1964, 339–44).

81. The word *fatt* (from Italian *fatto*) means true fact or event; it also describes the narrating of the event; it has the nature of an exemplum in a religious sermon as in the present context, or that of a traditional folk song: the *għana tal-fatt* (literally, "song of a fact") designates a very popular genre of folk poetry, represented by long, elaborate narratives in verse, either on a well-known sensational or tragic event (ballad type), or on a recent humorous topic inspired by everyday life.

    Among the favorite themes of the ballad type in the Mediterranean area is that of the lovers who are doomed to a tragic end, whether the two families are bitter enemies (see *Romeo and Juliet* in Italy, *Layla and Qays* in the Arab world), or the girl's father keeps his daughter sequestered, because he is totally opposed to her choice, as in the Maltese *Judith's Song* (Cassar-Pullicino and Galley 1981, 124–27). But perhaps the most popular song in Malta, judging from the number of versions in both oral and written tradition, is based on events which happened in the sixteenth century (probably in 1526), when a young lady from the village of Mosta was taken away on the day of her wedding by corsairs from the Barbary states. The same subject is treated in several neighboring countries, in particular, Sicily, where the Christian captive invariably appears as if she would rather die than yield to the entreaties of her Muslim abductors. Here is an excerpt:

> "Young bride," they said, "do not let your heart darken:
> We'll make you Sultana of Djerba."
> "What use being Sultana," she said,
> "Since I fell into the hands of Barbarians . . . ?"
> (Cassar-Pullicino and Galley, 111)

Interestingly enough, a comparable story is treated in a completely opposite manner by a Moroccan song, in which the young female captives from Malta are shown enjoying their new luxurious life in the company of their kidnappers (Brunot 1920, 323–28).

82. Reverend Professor Karm Sant is a biblical scholar. In 1966, he undertook, within the Maltese Biblical Society, the translation (from Hebrew and Greek into Maltese) of the Holy Scriptures, which has been published since then in installments.

83. See note 22.

84. In the Mediterranean area since ancient times, amulets have been worn as charms against all evil, disease, poverty—all that was traditionally attributed to "the evil eye" (Cassar-Pullicino and Galley 1981, 57–73). To fight against, and counteract, the effects of the evil eye, all possible means have been used, provided that they were felt to possess religious and/or magical power.

In spite of the efforts of the clergy, there is evidence in the archives of the Inquisition (Mdina Museum) that Maltese women resorted to various practices, including talismans written in Arabic script by Muslim captives (sixteenth and seventeenth centuries). In the previous century, inquisitors had also prosecuted a Jew of Malta, Rafaeli Ketib, who, in spite of his conversion to Christianity, was found carrying a charm written in Hebrew and accused of magic (Wettinger 1985, 89). Nowadays young mothers may still put around the neck of their young children both pious medals and amulets of various kinds in the shape of horns, of hands (in the position of the Sicilian *jettatura*), and of red peppers.

In the present case, getting hold of a piece of cloth which has been in contact with a saintly person is regarded, at least by its holder, like a relic and a source of protection. Such beliefs and practices have survived here and there, as everywhere in the world, although they are laughed at and greatly disapproved of by religious-minded people like Maria.

85. See note 80.

86. See note 7. By choosing the city of Sliema, as opposed to a village in Gozo, in his comedy *L-Inkwiet tas-Sur Martin* ("Mr. Martin's Ordeal," 1971,

48–93), Joseph Aquilina emphasizes the gap between city life and old village customs. The writer treats in a very humorous way the conflict in attitudes to life between a Gozitan villager and his daughters, who work as maids in Sliema. The two girls are pictured as mimicking their English-speaking employers and adopting their manners and language: they say "Daddy" to their father, insist upon being called "Mary" and "Tessy" instead of Maria and Tereża, and want to have "boyfriends" even though they are engaged in Gozo. However fictional the story is, it reflects reality to a certain extent, Sliema appearing, mostly from the Second World War on, as a crucible and a symbol. Among the reasons accountable for such a state of things were, according to Salvino Busuttil, the individual relations between the English and Maltese during the war: " . . . The War necessitated a joint effort by both English and Maltese; the brotherhood of the battlefield, where English and Maltese blood mingled on the altar of defence, nurtured a growing understanding between the two nations. A mutual respect was fostered; alongside it, there developed a desire for emulation of English standards on the part of the Maltese" (Busuttil 1965, 335). And the writer goes on to develop his argument:

> Though the average Maltese loved his island home intensly, yet he viewed Britain and her way of life with pardonable envy. This attitude was in evidence in the cosmopolitan Sliema area, where Englishmen tended to settle. Here the craving for all things English grew deep roots. The English language became the medium of conversation at the Maltese Sliema-ite home, English food became their food and English customs were largely adopted. The denomination *"ta' Tas-Sliema"* (from Sliema) came to describe that breed of Maltese "emancipated" to the English way of life. (Busuttil, 335).

87. Literally "of Ċenċ," i.e., belonging to Ċenċ, or rather Cenci, an Italian family surname (*Maltese-English Dictionary*, s.v. Ċenċ). Ta' Ċenċ is currently a place name designating the area formerly owned by Cenci, now converted into a luxurious hotel.

88. See note 36.

89. Lunzjata (which means "annunciation") is a place name at the limits of the village of Kerċem. Maria remembers the time when a fountain gushing out of a cave (Għar Gerduf) provided delicious drinking water. In Roman times, another fountain supplied neighboring baths with heated water, hence its name: *l-għan tal-ħammimiet*. Later Lunzjata was one of the favorite game reserves of the Grand Masters; it is still a well-irrigated green valley which inspired a lyrical description by Sir Harry Luke: "Whether this glade is seen in the spring, when it is a mass of blossom . . . or in the summer,

when its tangled mass of vegetation forms an almost solid screen of verdure from the blazing sun, it would seem a fitting lair for the daughter of Atlas if it did not rather conjure up, with its figs, its vines, its calamus and its pomegranates, a vision of the Song of Songs" (1949, 240).

90. See notes 9, 10, and 25.

91. See note 78.

92. All the parishes of Gozo used to take part according to the order of precedence (actually an inverted order): the youngest parish was at the front of the procession, whereas the clergy of the cathedral, including the bishop, came last.

93. Maria gives her comments on the birth of the Gozo Party:

> . . . Whether left, right or center, if a party was coming from Malta, the candidates would all be a little out of touch with Gozo affairs, because somehow we have our own problems, not always in conformity with those in Malta. Now in 1947, some prominent Gozitans decided that it would be much better for Gozo to have a political party of its own, independent from any other in Malta. The Partit Għawdxi (Gozo party) came into being with its own newspaper, *Leħen Għawdex* (The Voice of Gozo), edited by my brother, who was a young lawyer and *avukat*, newly fledged from university.

Three members of the Party, including Maria's brother, were elected in 1947 as representatives of Gozo in the Assemblea Leġislattiva (Calleja 1982, 145–49).

94. See note 9.

95. Naming a child after his grandfather was common in traditional families.

96. It is a graceful baroque building on the central square of Victoria, Piazza it-Tokk. Formerly the office of the jurors of Gozo, it is now used as an information office (see Gauci 1969, 36).

97. In the 1947 election, out of the forty seats, twenty-four went to the Malta Labour party, led by Dr. Boffa. He was prime minister from 1947 to 1950 (Blouet 1987, 214–26). Paul (later Sir Paul) Boffa was a widely respected figure.

98. This is a phrase Maria heard from her French friend Monique, Dr. Grech's wife.

99. In the Maltese islands, where all houses were, and still are, built in the local stone, wallpaper was unknown. Through both examples (wallpaper and railways), Maria shows that utilizing lessons grounded in a different environment (they were initially written for British pupils) would have been nonsense.

100. Ta' l-Iljun ("of the lion") and Ta' l-Istilla ("of the star") are the two "band clubs," or parish associations of Victoria; the former is linked to the cathedral, and the latter to St. George's Basilica. Each club has charge of the outdoor celebration (procession) connected with its parish feast, including street decorations, statues, illuminations, firework displays, and brass music.

101. The lady died in 1990. I met her once and was struck by her high sense of education.

102. The Ta' l-Iljun band club is entrusted by the cathedral with the external celebration of Santa Maria Festa, whereas Ta' l-Istilla is in charge of St. George's Feast. It is, in particular, over the celebration of their respective *festas* that they compete with each other. Rivalry may assume a passionate shape among the members—including the children, as shown here—of two opposed clubs of the same town or village. For an analysis of conflicts and factions in Maltese festive and political life, see Boissevain (1965 and 1974). Interestingly enough, while providing "an institutional basis for the rivalry" (Boissevain 1965, 75), the band clubs play a predominant role as centers of social life. They own premises with concert halls or theatres (see note 104), bars, and reading, television and billiard rooms. Their production of plays and operas—for example *Aida* and *Carmen*, respectively produced by Ta' l-Istilla and Ta' l-Iljun in 1988—is, at all levels, of remarkable quality.

103. The main square in Victoria, with its daily open-air market.

104. The Astra Theatre is run by the Ta' l-Istilla band club, the Aurora Theatre by Ta' l-Iljun.

105. *L-għana* (song) is the general term for folk poetry in sung form. It covers various genres from long elaborate memorized narratives in verse (see note 81) to short extemporized stanzas (see note 47). Improvising a song (usually a quatrain) may assume a playful character or be the expression of personal emotions, as we have seen before (notes 47 and 62); it may also serve as a deliberately harmful, although indirect, weapon aimed at somebody within hearing distance. Maria says that she has never forgotten how cruel her neighbor's song sounded to her ears: "Injuries made by words," she adds, "are inside you and can never be cured." Had she responded, a verbal confrontation would have started in the form of a song duel, each singer hitting back stanza for stanza. Nowadays, as Maria states, the exchange of insults through *l-għana* is forbidden. Regulations imposing decency between singers are applied in particular during the poetic competition which takes place every year (June 28–29) in Buskett (Malta) during the festival of Mnarja (Cassar-Pullicino 1983, 65; Galley 1983).

106. In Mediterranean traditional societies, to be childless for a young married woman after a few years of married life was synonymous with insecurity.

In Muslim countries, the husband was entitled to divorce her unless the solution of cohabitation with a new wife could be arranged. In Christian countries like the Maltese islands, although the childless wife kept her monogamous status, her situation was uncomfortable, inside and outside her family.

This is one of the reasons why in Malta, as well as in neighboring European countries, several saints and, above all, the mother par excellence, the Virgin Mary, have been implored to facilitate pregnancy, childbearing, and breast feeding, and to keep the infant in their protection. A great many small silver items (anatomical representations of the female body, figurines of babies in swaddling bands, sacred hearts, etc.), as well as beautifully embroidered clothes worn by the new born child on the day of its baptism, have been offered in thanksgiving in certain places of worship. Some of these chapels and shrines dedicated to the Virgin are called after the function she is asked to perform, such as the "Madonna of Delivery" (in the village of Qormi) and the "One of Slippery" (in the village of Gĥargĥur).

107. The conversation reproduced here was recorded at the interviewer's place during Maria's stay in France in the summer of 1987.

108. See notes 100, 102.

109. The two rival band clubs of Victoria (see notes 100, 102).

110. The Xewkija monumental Rotunda, with its high dome and rich interior decoration, was built over a period of twenty years (1951–1971), thanks to the efforts shared by a whole community: besides regular fund-raising organized by the parish priests among the families (seven hundred), volunteer workers helped the local masons on feast days, women offered some of their gold and jewels, farmers and fishermen gave a share of their produce, and emigrants sent donations. The Xewkija experience is not exceptional in Gozo, where a church is still nowadays not only a place of worship, but a place of beauty and riches, which is felt by everybody within the parish to be his or her own.

111. Maria was not even aware of the exact (obscene) meaning of the phrase. She heard it from villagers and used it as if she wanted to emphasize her irritation: ". . . in cases of highly emotional language, the Sound/Sense process very often disintegrates completely in such a manner that while the words we use literally mean one thing, emotionally they are no more than emphatic expressions set loose from their literal meaning" (Aquilina 1975, 32).

112. In a secret place, a "false drawer," Maria says.

113. Maria's father came back from Australia after a five years' stay: he very likely returned in the early months of 1921.

114. See note 21.

115. They could communicate for the simple reason that they were speaking languages which were akin to each other. As linguists' analyses have established, Maltese is basically Semitic with a Romance superstructure (Aquilina 1959). The historical background of Malta accounts for her linguistic situation: with the end of the Arabs' influence on the Maltese islands from the thirteenth century on, Maltese has been developing apart from other Arabic dialects, borrowing and integrating Romance elements.

116. Dr. Grech was present at the deathbed of Maria's mother (see Chapter 6). He and his wife, Monique, were friends of Anton and Maria (see note 98).

117. On the celebration of carnival in Malta, see Cassar-Pullicino 1976, 21–26; Busuttil 1964, 14–18.

118. On transactions between the two groups of relatives about the bride's dowry (property, cattle, etc.), see Boissevain 1969, 26–30.

119. About three thousand Maltese are estimated to have taken refuge in Gozo. In fact, Malta was raided by the Italians from the first day when they entered war (June 11, 1940), and it was mostly throughout the early months of 1942 that the air attacks were intense: in April alone, 6,700 tons of bombs were dropped on Malta and 11,450 buildings were destroyed or damaged (Blouet 1987, 203, 207). But bombing was only part of Malta's ordeal; the acute problem was lack of food. Since the archipelago could not support itself with its own agriculture, it depended on imports brought by sea, which were exposed to German and Italian aircraft and submarines. Privation and its consequences were extreme: deficiency of vitamins and diseases (Cassar 1964, 564). Malta was awarded the George Cross by King George VI on April 15, 1942, "to bear witness to a heroism and devotion that will long be famous in history."

120. At that time, Maria was getting a teacher's salary.

121. St. Paul is considered to be the patron saint of the Maltese islands (see Cassar-Pullicino 1944).

122. See notes 78 and 107.

123. As explained before (note 115), the Maltese language has two components: Semitic (the main one) and Romance. As far as surnames are concerned, the number of Semitic ones is not more than fifty in Malta and Gozo, "yet each of these fifty surnames is borne by a large number of families," whereas the more modern Romance surnames are borne by just a few families (Aquilina 1987–90, 2:191).

124. It is a graceful eighteenth century theatre in Valletta (see Mahoney 1988, 290–92).

125. As Maria explains later on, the play pleads for solidarity toward the developing countries of Africa. Anton, Maria's brother, wrote the prologue. We have already noted Anton's brotherly love for human beings (see his work for the handicapped in note 68). From the following anecdote told by

Maria, we gather that he showed sympathy to the victims of apartheid:
"One summer afternoon, after a swim in Ramla Bay, as we were walking
back to the car—it's very hard to walk on the shifting sand—Toni started
walking briskly towards a reed shed serving as a bar. I noticed that two
black men who were sitting drinking had left their seat and were running
toward my brother! I caught up with Toni, of course panting heavily, and
saw those blacks embracing my brother! One of them said: This is the sort
of man we want to meet! That must have been the time when apartheid
trouble was starting in South Africa and Anton wanted to show his
solitarity."

126.   Anton is remembered by Maria as he was standing, with his arms wide
open, on a rock which overlooks the sea and occasionally singing an improvised praise to his God. He would also enjoy reciting and acting a scene
from Shakespeare with a friend, a retired actor, "just for fun," Maria says.
He would even venture into limericks of this type:

> There was an old man of Għarb;
> He played his big harp,
> As he sat on a keg,
> But he shot the first fly
> That came to his leg.

127.   Anton was a great admirer of T. S. Eliot, whose *Four Quartets* were his
favorite poetry. The epitaph was inspired by "Little Gidding": Maria
assembled two separate lines (lines 215 and 238) and adapted them in
order to strengthen the Christian message left by her brother.

128.   See note 16.

129.   See note 82.

130.   See note 23.

A Glimpse at the Historical Background of the Maltese Islands

"The beginnings of human occupation in the Maltese Islands belong to the later part of the 5 M B.C. Not until this relatively late date did a few boatloads of people carrying with them their simple possessions, together with some seed corn and domestic animals, venture to cross the sixty odd miles of sea which separate the group from Sicily . . . Thus in an unspectacular way, Maltese history began . . ." (Evans 1968, 9). However, the early inhabitants and the following generations evolved some remarkable cultures of their own, as shown by the megalithic temple complexes, among which is the massive appropriately named Temple of Ġgantija, "the Giantess," near Xagħra in Gozo (see Bonanno 1990, 22-25); in Malta, a visitor should not miss the greater constructions of, for example, Tarxien (with its typical curvilinear designs), Ħaġar Qim, or "the Standing Stones" (which possesses a peculiar design characterized by clusters of rooms in semicircular or horseshoe shape), as well as the Hypogeum of Ħal Saflieni, an agglomeration of underground chambers cut out of soft globigerina limestone. Pottery statuettes and ornaments which have come from the various sites (e.g., Zammit and Singer 1924) are exhibited at the National Museums of Valletta (Malta) and Victoria (Gozo).

Later on Phoenician navigators came; their settlements, according to archaeologists, date back to 800 B.C. An interesting feature of Phoenician sites, brought to light by relatively recent excavations (in particular at Tas-Silġ), was their utilization of the preexisting sacred areas and structures; continuity also marked the deities worshipped: the Phoenician-Punic Astarte was simply superimposed on the former Neolithic Mother Goddess (Moscati 1973). It is worth mentioning that the discovery on Maltese soil in the seventeenth century of a bilingual Phoenician-Greek cippus, now in the Louvre, has contributed to the deciphering of Phoenician.

As a result of the Second Punic War, the Maltese islands became part of the Roman province of Sicily. At that time, Malta seems to have enjoyed great prosperity, as reflected by Cicero's *Verrines* (1787, 311-2): by denouncing for his depredations Verres, then propraetor (73-71 B.C.) of the province of Sicily (including the Maltese islands), Cicero gives an idea of the richness of the local fine cloth, as well as of the treasures kept in the temples of Proserpine, Apollo and Juno.

But undoubtedly, a more significant event during the Roman period for the Maltese, whose Christian faith is still so deep today, was St. Paul's three-month stay in Malta after his shipwreck (ca. 60 A.D.), as described in the Acts of the Apostles (Chapter 27-28 in the Bible). A Pauline tradition has been built around the story of the shipwreck over the centuries (Cassar-Pullicino 1944).

A great controversy developed in the press for several months after September 1989 on the question of whether the Christian religion was maintained while the Maltese islands were under Muslim control from the ninth through the twelfth centuries (Wettinger 1989). In fact, from the time the (Aghlabid) Arabs took possession of the Maltese islands (ca. 870), the Muslims exercised their influence, and continued to do so even after the expeditions of 1048 and 1091, and the conquest of 1127, made the Normans the new rulers (Luttrell 1975, 27-32). There seems to have been "little Christian penetration before about 1200" (Luttrell 1976, 19), whereas the practice of Islam is attested to (during the twelfth century) by the epitaphs on Muslim tombstones: several of them can be seen in the Museum of the Roman Villa (Rabat, Malta). Another Arabic tomb, known as Il-Ħaġra ta' Majmuna: (Maimuna's Stone), which was found in Gozo (Ta' Ċenċ), is kept in the Museum of the Citadel in Victoria: it is a fine sample of reused Roman marble, beautifully carved with Cufic script and dated 569 Hijrah (1191 A.D.) (Rossi 1929-30).

However, the Norman conquest marked a change in the Mediterranean balance of power, and Malta passed definitely into the Latin sphere of influence. The result is that today "almost every manifestation of Maltese cultural life other than the language places it clearly in the stream of European, more specifically Italian, civilization" (Cachia 1964, 226-27). But the language belongs to the Arabic-speaking world: now the official language of Malta, Maltese results "from the interaction and fusion of North African Arabic, but with its own dialect features outside the North African group, and Siculo-Italian, covering two different cultural strata. The Arabic element in Maltese historically very often corresponds to the Anglo-Saxon in English, while the Romance loans correspond to the Norman-French element" (Aquilina 1959, v).

In medieval times, Malta passed under German (Swabian), French (Angevin), then Spanish (Aragonese and Castilian) control until it became, in 1530, the seat of the Hospitaller Order of St. John of Jerusalem, after the knights were driven away from Rhodes by Suleiman the Magnificent in 1522 (see Braudel 1949). From that time on, Malta served as a shield protecting southern Europe against Islam. The knights and the Maltese population resisted serious attacks by the Turks, culminating in the "Great Siege" of 1565. Soon after, the Turkish defeat at Lepanto (1571) was decisive, at least in this part of the Mediterranean. Yet the Maltese islands—more particularly, Gozo (Wettinger 1990, 64-66)—did not cease to be the victims of raids by the Barbary corsairs. However, Malta seems to have entered a golden era of architecture and art: since the knights came from the richest families in Europe, they were in a position to bring over engineers and artists. The city of "La Valette," named after the French grand master of the time, with its magnificent palaces; its harmonious, richly decorated cathedral; and its artistic treasures deserved the compliment paid to her by Sir Walter Scott: "a city built by gentlemen for gentlemen."

Later, when Bonaparte stopped at Malta (June 1798) on his way to Egypt, the Order of St. John was in its decline. But French rule was short lived: in September 1798, the Maltese rose up in arms, and after a blockade lasting two years, they sought the protection of the British throne. Malta became a Crown Colony.

After the first decade of the nineteenth century, Malta began to thrive on commerce. The Grand Harbor of Valletta was turned into an entrepôt center for British Mediterranean trade (of coal and grain, in particular). Great docks were built, and the opening of the Suez canal (1869) increased the importance of Malta as a naval base on the route to India. The presence of British military forces, maintained because of the strategic position of the Maltese islands in the center of the Mediterranean, also contributed to prosperity, at least on the main island.

In rural Gozo, the situation was different. Cotton growers were particularly affected by the gradual deterioration of the cotton industry at the international level. In Gozo, they used to grow cotton (including the "red" species), and spin and weave it in their homes both for their own use and for exportation. The Gozitan farmers rarely owned the land. The majority were, if not laborers, tenants on long-term leases, who found it more and more difficult to pay their rent on account of the general decline of prices in agriculture (Blouet 1987, 168). Some of them emigrated to neighboring Mediterranean countries, mostly to Algeria, Tunisia, or Egypt, one of the reasons being that Maltese was akin to the language (Arabic) spoken there. By the end of the century, fifty thousand Maltese are reported to have been living around the shores of the Mediterranean (Blouet, 171). Two men from the village of Nadur in Gozo had even ventured to go as far as North America.

On the main island, another factor fostering emigration from the towns was overpopulation due to the fabulous demographic growth (100 percent in a hundred years). However, mortality was severe at the time of the great epidemics (the plague in 1813, cholera in 1837 and 1887).

During the 1880s, the so-called Language Question started, which was to become a momentous political issue for several decades, actually until after the Second World War. Among the elected members of government, there were two strongly opposed groups on the choice of the language on which to base education. On the one hand, there were those who wanted to adopt English and strengthen the British connection. On the other, there was the antireform group, traditionally attached to Italian, the language of culture and religion, and determined to remain close to Rome. At that time, Maltese, the spoken language of the ordinary people, was not taken into consideration at all. Yet important contributions to its study had been undertaken one century earlier by Maltese scholars such as Agius de Soldanis, the first librarian of what is now the National Library, who wrote a grammar.

At the beginning of the twentieth century, the economic boom was still, to a certain extent, a reality. There was employment in the dockyards (Attard 1983, 1). However, a period of economic uncertainty had started. As usual, the situation was worse in rural areas. The cost of living rose rapidly in 1914, although the war meant greater naval activity and, in consequence, more employment around the harbors.

The Maltese islands did not find themselves directly involved in the fighting during the First World War. However, the people made a considerable contribution by volunteering for foreign action (more than one thousand Maltese took part in the Gallipoli campaign against the Turks) and by transforming the island into a war hospital: eighty thousand British, Canadian and Australian wounded soldiers and sailors were looked after on Maltese soil. For this reason, Malta was affectionately named "Nurse of the Mediterranean."

Meanwhile, in 1916, emigrants, including Gozitans, left for Australia aboard the "ill-fated" *Gange* (see note 9). They were, in fact, the pioneers of emigration to far-away countries; their experience took on epic proportions (York 1986, 54-65; Dugan 1988; Attard 1989, 81). For internal political reasons, the Australians tried to keep these emigrants out, although they were themselves British subjects: an education test was imposed on the newcomers (in majority illiterate) in one European language, which, in 1916, happened to be Dutch (York 1986). As a result, people became conscious of the danger of unplanned emigration. Mastering some English appeared to be a prerequisite for those intending to emigrate. Among the Maltese authorities, the linguistic question was raised again. Passionate debates took place within the Legislative Assembly (as shown by the official reports of 1921-22) on whether evening classes of English should be organized for prospective emigrants. The Italianites tried to fight against the growing influence of English, but all were compelled to consider emigration as inevitable.

Interestingly enough, Maltese emigration, which was now increasingly oriented toward distant English-speaking countries—Australia, then Canada, the United States and Britain—constituted a stimulus to education (Attard 1989, 16). Gradually practical information on work conditions was diffused by the Department of Labor. Advice was given to those who were going to Australia in order to help them avoid discrimination among a somehow prejudiced population. The motto was: "Try not to be different" by refraining, for example, from haggling in shops, praying aloud at church, wearing the traditional sash, and so on (Attard, 14). Little by little, attempts at organized emigration facilitated what was to be called "the Great Exodus" (Attard, 18). Yet nothing could alleviate for those who went the pain of being separated from their homeland. They sometimes expressed their homesickness in a song, such as the following, "Tears of a Maltese Far from Malta," by Felic Buhagiar (Attard 1992, 17):

Helua Malta, ghalchemm bghid minnec,
Jien ma nista' katt ninsic;
Omm ghaziza, omm helua tieghi,
Minn kiegh kalbi, is-sliem natic . . . .

(Sweet Malta, how far I am from you!
Never shall I be able to forget you.
Beloved mother, my sweetest mother,
From the depth of my heart, I send you
my greetings . . . .)

Political unrest led to deadly riots in 1919. In 1921, a new constitution granted responsible government, a legislative assembly and senate,
with defense and foreign affairs reserved to the imperial government. The
Nationalist party (in favor of Italian culture), led by Enrico Mizzi, and
the Anglo-Maltese or Constitutional party, led by Sir Gerald Strickland,
won the elections in turn. When Strickland became prime minister
(1927-32), he decided, in spite of the hostility of the church, that
Maltese and English should be the official languages of Malta. The
Nationalists, in contrast, had in mind the Italianization of youth through
an appropriate system of education; they came to power again in 1932,
and the following year was marked by the withdrawal of the 1921
constitution and a return to Crown Colony government. A new constitution (1936) provided for nominated members to the Governor's Executive
Council; it was followed by the "MacDonald Constitution" (1939) which,
in its turn, was suspended. Malta was then on the eve of the Second
World War.

On the fall of France in 1940, Mussolini joined the Axis forces with
Hitler. On the very day following his declaration of war, Italian bombers
attacked Malta. From that moment, Malta found herself in the front line;
her Calvary began. Immediately measures were taken to keep watch over
those Maltese whose pro-Italian sympathies were well-known; in 1942,
about forty of them were transported to Uganda until the end of the war
(Mercieca 1947).

In 1941, the Italian Air Force was joined by the Luftwaffe. The sea
was ruled by the Italian navy. Malta's position appeared hopeless. The
cruelest month was April 1942. In addition to suffering from air raids,
Malta (the main island) was in a state of semistarvation. Relief came from
two sources: First, from her sister island, Gozo, where grain was collected
from farmers, door to door, through the initiative of Monsignor Michael
Gonzi, later archbishop of Malta (Wettinger 1990, 81). And second, from
a large convoy of Allied ships which, in spite of appalling losses in the
Mediterranean on the way, managed to reach Malta with food supplies.
One of them was the American tanker Ohio, whose valor was honored by

the award of the George Cross. During the same summer (1942), the Axis forces had planned to invade Malta, starting from Libya, then an Italian colony. But it seemed that at last the tide of battle had turned: in October, the famous marshall of the Afrika Korps, Rommell, was defeated at El-Alamein and Malta was saved.

By the end of the war (1944), serious damage had been inflicted on the main island. Gozo had not been spared by air raids, either, but, unlike Malta, it did not represent for the Axis forces a great strategic interest. In fact, the small island served as a refuge for Maltese families. Like her colleagues, Maria Calleja gave a helping hand: "We teachers," she says, "used to work in shifts: in the morning as teachers, in the afternoon as cooks, sometimes as 'magistrates' when some sort of litigation rose in the camp . . . ." It was during the same period—with war in the background—and on Gozitan soil, that Ġuże Cassar-Pullicino felt an urge to contribute to the preservation of Maltese culture, as he himself explained: "The war brought with it a new sense of spiritual and national values and it was not long before this feeling found expression in a fresh appreciation of the traditional native elements in Maltese culture, side by side with the raising of the Maltese language to a position of dignity in the Administration and at the University" (Cassar-Pullicino 1963, 144). From then on, he devoted his life to folklore and history.

After the war, the elections brought alternatively to power the Labor party (1947-50, 1955-58, 1971-87) and the Nationalists (1950-55, 1962-71, from 1987 to the present). In 1947-48, a new constitution provided responsible government under a unicameral diarchy: the Maltese government would be responsible to the wholly elected Legislative Assembly under the prime minister, and the imperial government under the governor would take care of matters of safety and defense. In 1955, a proposal was initiated to integrate Malta with the United Kingdom, but difficulties soon arose, and when a referendum was held, the result was negative. In 1958, the Maltese government resigned and the constitution was suspended. In 1959, a new constitution was enacted and the restoration of self-government was planned for 1961. Talks on independence started in 1963, and in September 1964, the Maltese islands became an independent state within the Commonwealth. In 1974, the Republic of Malta was proclaimed; two years later, the British troops left. Malta chose to have a status of neutrality among the nonaligned countries (1987) and to welcome Mr. Bush and Mr. Gorbachev (1989). With the visit of Pope John Paul II (1990), Malta reaffirmed its Christian identity within Europe, and, in the same year, Malta's application to join the European community was presented.

While engaged after the war in trying to achieve independence, Malta needed at the same time to become self-sufficient economically. Efforts were made to build new industrial structures. Dockyards were adapted to the servicing of the oil industry. Roads were built, and tourism developed considerably during the next few years. On the other hand, emigration continued to increase and bring money back to the islands.

The island of Gozo, by its position, was always slightly apart, having no regular connection with the main island until 1949, when a Gozo-Malta service was created. In 1968, the crossing by car ferry started—"a source of a regular revenue" (Wettinger 1990, 78). However, Gozo's essential resource came from emigration with a higher percentage of emigrants in the fifties and sixties. Today the population (about twenty-three thousand) is less than the number of Gozitans abroad. Statistics recently published by the Malta Emigrants Commission* (Attard 1992, 20) indicate there are 119,504 emigrants in Australia, Maltese and Gozitans together.

In the political sphere, Gozo has asserted its individuality, as well as its will to look for local solutions: a Gozo party was created in the forties and fifties, and a ministry for Gozo was created in 1987. Tourism has been developing with the building of several large hotels and holiday flats. A service by helicopter between the international airport of Luqa on the main island and Xewkija in Gozo is now working. Poverty belongs to the past on the island of Gozo.

---

*It came into being in 1950. The offices of the Commission at "the House of Emigrants" in Valletta are open to those who need help or advice on matters relevant to migration.

Ġgantija Temple, near Xagħra in Gozo.

Majmuna's Tombstone.

A war memorial at the entrance to the Grand Harbor in Valletta.

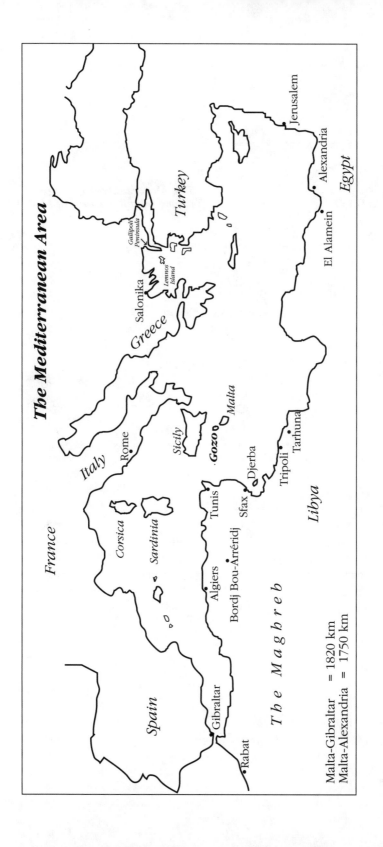

The Mediterranean Area

France

Spain

Gibraltar
Rabat

The Maghreb

Algiers
Bordj Bou-Arréridj

Corsica

Sardinia

Italy
Rome

Tunis
Sfax

Sicily

Gozo
Malta

Djerba

Tripoli
Tarhuna

Libya

Salonika

Greece

Gallipoli
Peninsula

Lemnos
Island

Turkey

Jerusalem

Alexandria
El Alamein

Egypt

Malta-Gibraltar = 1820 km
Malta-Alexandria = 1750 km

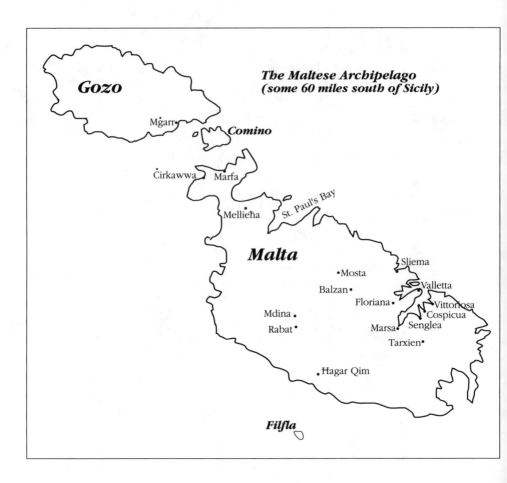

Gozo

Mġarr

Comino

Ċirkawwa   Marfa

Mellieħa   St. Paul's Bay

Malta

Sliema

•Mosta

Balzan•   Valletta

Floriana•   Vittoriosa

Mdina•   Cospicua

Rabat•   Senglea

Marsa•

Tarxien•

•Ħagar Qim

Filfla

The Maltese Archipelago
(some 60 miles south of Sicily)

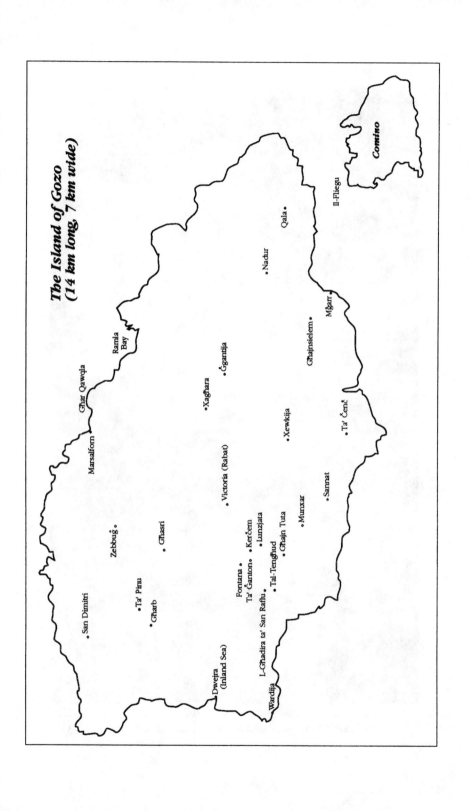

The Island of Gozo
(14 km long, 7 km wide)

Comino

Il-Fliegu

Qala

Nadur

Marsalforn

Għar Qawqla

Ramla
Bay

Xagħra

Ġgantija

Għajnsielem

Mġarr

Xewkija

Ta' Ċenċ

Victoria (Rabat)

Zebbuġ

Għasri

Ta' Pinu

Għarb

San Dimitri

Sannat

Munxar

Fontana

Ta' Ġanton

Kerċem

Lunzjata

Għajn Tuta

Tal-Tengħud

L-Għadira ta' San Raflu

Dwejra
(Inland Sea)

Wardija

Joe Gatt and his wife with their granddaughter in Australia. Gatt's father accompanied Maria's father to Australia in the 1920s and never returned to Gozo to live.

Appendices

A: A Letter by Joe Gatt from Australia*

Hi My name is Joe Gatt I was born in Gozo more than 70 years ago. My wife Frances is an old school mate of Miss Maria Callaja. As we were talking one day I happen to mention some of the hardship and suffering our fathers had when they went to Australia for work. Miss Calleja asked me to put down on tape some of the things I was told by my late father, Augustus Gatt.

In August 1914 the grate War I broke out in Europe Malta was the Med main naval station so that mean there was some works for the Maltese, but for the Gozitan the war brought no work, but more mizery and high cost in food and clothes. Few of the men of Gozo joint the Army for a few pences a day.

In April 1915 the Australian, New Zealand's and some English soldgers attack Turky gallipeli† what has come known as Anzac‡ Cove. And these armys needed help, food, and amonation [ammunition]. The Maltese Govnment called for a labour Battelion of 2000 men. My father, and 2 of Marias uncles on her mother side were one of them. they were send on the Ilsland of Lemona§ near the Dardinels, its Captail Mudress [its capital

---

*The letter is not dated, but it was written in 1982, at a time when Joe Gatt, now almost blind, could still write, although with difficulty. The letter has been duplicated as written.

†Gallipoli Peninsula is situated at the entrance of the Dardanelles Strait: it was the scene of disastrous land and sea battles for the Allied forces in 1915.

‡A.N.Z.A.C. is a word coined from the initials of Australian New Zealander Army Corps. In Malta, a memorial has been erected in Floriana near Valletta, and Anzac Day (April 25) is commemorated every year.

§This is probably Lemnos Island.

Moudhros] on the other way round.* The Anzacs pulled out and went in France, and my father came home, but he didn't stay in Gozo for long. At that time the wages in Malta was 2/- [2 shillings] a day for labor and 3/- [3 shillings] for trade men, and in Gozo works was as scars as hens teeths. Good news was coming from Aust[tralia.] there labours were earning up to 12/- [12 shillings] a day, so like so many others my father decided to go to Australia and this was in 1916. The Gozotin are like the film maker of Hollywood. if a company make a film and its a Hit. Other film makers make dozens more like it. Now back to our taile. My father know the English language well, so when he decides to emigrate to Aust most of his friends and relatives wanted to go to. There were 12 from St Lucia and 18 from Kercem, and Salvo Callaja, Maria father was one of them, Salvu Callaja was a good Carpenter by trade[.] some one must have told him, that he will earn good money in Aust. When the shipping agents found that he have some 2 or 250 passagers on hand, and each one want to get out of Malta as quick as can be done, he cable his Company in France, to make some rough accomodation for 250 passagers on the first steme boat that leaves France for Aust and call at Malta. Now this old cargo boat happens to be the "Gangeis" It had some 1 class Cabins for only 30 passagers, who use to dine with the Captain and his Officers. My father use to tell us that some of the Anamels [animals] they had on board were better accomoaded then the men. It was a living hell. but we ask for it. He use to say This remind me of the Convicts sailing ship that left England for Aust some 120 years before. Now the sad day arrived. The boat was in Malta takin Coal and water and very early one morning my mum waked us up and my father kissed us 3 boys and a baby some 6 months old. It was they only time I saw my Dad kissing Mum.

I suppose many more such sad farewells were takin place on that fatefull morning. many of them were never to see their native Gozo again. My Dad is one of them, I am sure that most of there young men who were not married, had a sweet heart, you and I don't know how many promises were made on the night before. I am told that half of Gozo were at Imgar to see them off. They were the biggest lots that left Gozo at onetime. They left Malta on that same day in the afternoon. Beside her father Maria had 2 uncles in this lot, one name Paul and the other Denuil, Poor Denuil was sea sick for 4 or 5 days. and he though[t] he was going to die. My Dad had

---

*After 9 months and some 30,000 deaths. (Joe Gatt's footnote in his original letter).

some Inchovis [anchovies] and Olives and they fed D on it, and years after he told some one that it was my Dad Olives that saved his live.

The food and beding was bad. some wanted to go for the Captain and trouw him over board. but some how they were calmed down, then they decided to pick 8 men one from each town, and some who can speak English and my Dad was one of them. Maria father was very intellingent, he use to say to my Dad, Wistin dont worry this will not be for ever: they seen the Capt and he promise to improve their food when they arrived in Port Said. When they got in Port Said they loaded some tons of Macaroni and cheese. after they left P. Said it was boiled more and cheese nearly everyday. they had some Orange This boat had no freezing sistem. So for meat they use to carry alive anamils such as Cows Bulls, sheep and goats. also few Rabbit and hens. Once in a while they use to kill a bull, and the Butcher was a man from Rabat who happen a friend of most of Kercem and St Lucia men. So everytime there was going to be a killing they use try to help him, and they get the tongue and some of the Levers [livers] and steaks and cook it on a Coal shovels, where the ship firemen works This happen everytime there was a killing, and the Engine Crew didnt like it. because it interfare with their work. Danuil was about 6 FT high, and he told the French man, if he open his mouth he will make a roast beef out of him, and there was no trouble after that. The Kitchen was in the lower deck, The stewards had to carry the food for the first Class passenger had to go up 2 Stairs, Carring food in a tray on their shoulders, Danuel used to stop the steward about and when he see something good coming up he use to grab a whole tray, saying I like this, you can go and get some more. My father spent half his time writing to Mum or For some one who couldnt write, because in them days only 7 to 10% went to school. A good few use to go by themself in some quite place in the quite of the night to say the Rosiry. Some others had a small hand accorden, and they use to seranade their wifes and sweetheart and they were already thousand of miles away.

Live on board wasnt always sad and lonely[.] they use to form some entertainment among them, such as telling jokes and storeis or some tales from Gozo past. One day Salvo Callaja Maria father, he put a coat on, and went up the 1 Class near the Capt Bridge, he seen a big Laoung [lounge] and some well dressed men playing Cards, some drinking wine or whiskey, and a big notice board and a big Chart or Map with the 'Rout' [route] of the Ship (Boat) on it I think some French man mistook him for a first Class pass Anyway he found out that some of the Officers shiif [shifted] a little button towards Aust every day and it usualy done at midday, he told my father, that he knew how many miles the boat is doing every 24 hours; and some of the men they "hoh hoh" him, and they, they told him, the next thing we will hear is that you are dining at the Capt table and the very next day my father put on his Coat on, and they went up the first Class part. and my Dad and Salvo met an officer who knew some English and he show them thic Chart. and explane how he work it, Salvo Callaja told my father to keep it quite, because the boys will "hoh hoh" him to. My father use to say that if Callaja went to school, he would end up some one high in the Church or at Law. After that they were good friends and some years later they met again in North Queensland They say, absent makes the heart grow fondest (Oh how I know it) These people were already missing their loved ones, Its in the evening when these toughs [thoughts] come to one mind.

After 9 or 10 weeks they arrived in Fremantle, Western Australia In them days there was no Maltese in West Aust, so they didnt see anyone, and after putting some cargo down, and took some new cargo aboard, they saild out and West Aust behind, and were saying to each other it wont be long now. Just as well they didnt know what was in store for them. The next call was Adelade, but most of the Maltese in South Aust were at Brocker Hills next was Melbourne, Victoria I dont know what happen there, but some ran a way, they were cought and brought back on board. At last they arrived in Sydney. and what a welcome they had, Some who had brothers or relative come to see them, but no one was allewed to get off the ship My father brother whos name was Salvo like Mr Callaja happen to be in Tasmania. They were taken along side of an old burned out ship in the middel of Sydney harbour some 1/2 a miles a way from the shore, and transfared on it[.] their food use to come from the shore At that time, William Morris Hughs was Prim Minister. and Gelard Strickland, afterward (Lord Strickland) was Govener of one of the Australia States, this man have always loved the Maltese people.

My Dad was a good swimmer[.] while in Sydney harbour he jump off this old boat into the water and he had his suit and shose or boots in a tin and somehow he swam to the land with this tin and it was more then 1/2 a mile away and it was near Christman time, that is hot days when Sydney harbour is full of Sharks but he didnt know till he was told; he went up the City and found a Maltese bordoriang [boarding] house and he was picked up before 24 hrs and taking back to the old ship by the water police[.] only a few managed to get away and good few Maltese [a fair number of Maltese] were back to Malta and while they were in Sydney the papers call them Billy Hughs mob. because he wanted them to stay in Aust.

The Australian were about let them land, but they just were unlucky. Some newspaper man come on side to interview some body and it just happen he met a very nasty man, who though[t] he was smart, It went something like this, Newspaper Reporter. Do you think its right that we let you down to work, while our boys are sailing out every day for the war front. and you get their jobs? Mr Smartie, Not only we will get their Jobs, but we look after their Wives and Daughters as well. and you can be sure of this. The next day the Sydneys newspapers were full of Stories against the maltese, some big head lines: "Send them back to War." The Australian didnt know that some of the maltese had already done their part in the War. My Dad was one of them. as I told you in the beganing, When the Ganges unloaded his Cargo they had for Sydney and was ready to sail for new Caladoia [New Caledonia.] the Captal city is Noumeia, is a small Iland belong to France, and some 1500 miles to the north East of Sydney in Paracific Ocinon, and they speak Franch. These poor emagrant found themself back on the old boat, to this Island mention about

When they arrived they taken to an old Warehouse and some in tents, they had the freedom of the town, and few went to Mass every morning. Some manage to find some light work for pocket money It was getting near Christmas It is a custom for most Maltese that at Christmas day they make a Confession and recieved holy Communion. very few could talk English or Franch, so the Parish priest got a Dispension from his Bishop to confesse these people like they do in War time and in emergency and on that day 90% of they received the holy Communion. I dont know how long they stayed in New Caladonia but at last they were taking back to Sydney, and the Government let come down few at the time. My father got away again and found his way up to the North Coast, his first job was on a big Cattle farm chopping down young trees, wages £2-10 [2 pounds 10 shillings] a week and the old farmer supply the food, when that finish he got another job on a Cane farm for 4 months looking after 12 horses wages £3 [3 pounds] a week and keeps, then there was an Ads in the papers for labours on the new railway line and there he met Salvo Callaja again Salvo was working on a Train in Paramatta with some of his friend This railway line was Miles away from Civelation living in old leaking tents and no bread or Meat but the "Pay" was good. A man was leaving this "hell hole" and my Dad bought his gun, and one Sunday he went out hunting some miles away from the Camp and he nearly got lost. the sun was going down when he come on a River and some Wollebys came for drink and he shot one of them[.] he carryed it on his back and found his way home when he climed on a hill and saw the Camp fire some miles away to the West, when he got home some of his friend were getting worryed about him. and Salvo Callaja said thanks God you are home, dont go too far out next time, sit down and I will skin it for you and we try to preserved this skin, it might comes handy. That night all my father friends ad Wolleabys stake for Supper, and for the next few days, One day an Australian show Dad how to make bread cooked in hot ashs, He and Callaja use to make some bread every second day. Salvo, he had a good job driving a Drag a sort of tipping box Cart, he use to earn a few shillings more then my Dad, and he didnt work so hard, but he had to clean his horse and feed it They use to have a long tolks together about Gozo and when that job finish they parted and never met again. Mr Callaja went down to Sydney and after 4 years went back to Gozo. My Dad went futher noth for the Cane season[.] he cut it once only In the Med 20s he came down to New castle, We arrived in Newcastle few weeks before Christmas of 1920, After 18 years in 1939 I came back to Gozo. The first time I met Dr Callaja* was when he was in his early 20s. We met after Church[.] he was very quite young man, and very well dressed

Some months later I join the RAF and we use to meet on the Gozo Ferry going to Malta In them days Dr Callaja became an M.P. Dr Callaja was always carrying a book of some sort under his arm, that how I remember him Then in July 1974 on the Kercem Feasta day, I was in front of the Church, just by myself, when someone tap me on my shoulder and said have you been to Sardinia lately? I turned round and looked at him and told him, how do you know that I was in Sardinia? You are not a Maltese nor an English man, Who are you? When he told me I was very supprise, And we shook hands and talked for the next hour, and that was the last time I spock to the late Dr Callaja because we went back to Australia

Joe Gatt
77 Floraville Rd.,
Belmont North,
2280 N.S.W.
Australia

---

*Maria's brother, Anton.

B: "San Dimitri," a Folk Poem

SAN DIMITRI

Dik Żgugina mara Għawdxija
Kienet toqgħod 'l Għarb 'il ġew,
U fid-dinja kulma kellha
Tifel biss jismu Mattew.

Darba waħda ġew it-Torok
U 'l Mattew mal-lejl serquh,
U ġarrewh lejn it-Turkija,
U ġo Għawdex ma sabuhx.

U l-imsejkna ta' Żgugina
Tibki u tixher lejl u nhar,
Dejjem titlob lil San Mitri
Biex jerġa' jġibulha d-dar.

O San Mitri, ġibli 'l ibni;
U nixgħellek qasba żejt;
Nixgħelhielek minn filgħodu,
U ddum taqbad sa bil-lejl.

U San Mitri ġibilha 'l binha
Wara l-wegħda ftit sigħat,
Ġibulha fuq żiemel abjad,
Halla difru ġewwa l-blat.

SAINT DIMITRI

That Żgugina was a Gozitan woman
Who was living on the outskirts of Għarb,[*]
And all that she had in her life
Was a son, only a son named Matthew.

But once came the Turks
And Matthew they stole at nightfall,
Took him away toward Turkey,
And in Gozo one found him not.

And the poor soul of Żgugina
Wept and cried all night and day,
Always praying Saint Dimitri
So that to her he bring him back.

"O Saint Mitri, my son bring me;
I will light a measure of oil[†] for Thee;
For thee from morn I'll light it up,
And till night it'll be alight."

And Saint Mitri brought back her son
A few hours after the vow;
He brought him back on his white horse,
Which left its hoofs printed on rocks.

---

[*] Għarb is an old village situated in the western part of the island.

[†] Literally, "a spatula of oil" (*qasba żejt*); *qasba* means both the tool itself and its contents or measure, like "spoon" and "spoonful." It was used, in particular, as a measure of oil (*Maltese-English Dictionary*, s.v. *qasba*; Barbera 1939-40, s.v. *qasba*).

Bibliographical References

Aarne, A., and S. Thompson. *The Types of the Folktale*. A classification and bibliography translated and enlarged by Stith Thompson. 2nd rev. F.F. Communications 75, no. 184. Helsinki: Academia Scientiarum Fennica, 1964.

Antoun, R. "On the Significance of Names in an Arab Village." *Ethnology* 7 (1968): 158–170.

Aquilina, J. *The Structure of Maltese*. Malta: The Royal University of Malta, 1959.

—— "L-Inkwiet tas-Sur Martin." Translated by F. William ("Mr. Martin's Ordeal"). *Journal of Maltese Studies* 6 (1971): 48–93.

—— *Comparative Dictionary of Maltese Proverbs*. Malta: The Royal University of Malta, 1972.

—— "A Study in Violent Language." *Journal of Maltese Studies* 10 (1975): 29–54.

—— *Maltese-English Dictionary*. 2 vols. Malta: Midsea Books, 1987–90.

Attard, L. *Early Maltese Emigration (1900–1914)*. Malta: Gulf Publishing, 1983.

—— *The Great Exodus (1918–1939)*. Malta: P.E.G., 1989.

—— *Lil-Hutna* (To Our Brothers). Edited by L. Attard. Malta: Malta Emigrants Commission, May 1992.

Barbera, G. *Dizionario Maltese-Arabo-Italiano*. 4 vols. Beirut: Imprimerie Catholique, 1939–40.

Bertaux, D., and I. Bertaux-Wiame. "Le patrimoine et sa lignée: transmissions et mobilité sociale sur cinq générations." *Life Stories* 4 (1988): 8–25.

Bezzina, J. *Religion and Politics in a Crown Colony, the Gozo-Malta Story 1798–1864*. Malta: Bugelli Publications, 1985.

Blouet, B. *The Story of Malta*. 3d ed., rev. Malta: Progress Press, 1987.

Boccaccio, G. *Il Decamerone*. Milan: Ulrico Hoepli, 1948.

Boissevain, J. *Saints and Fireworks*. London: The Athlone Press, University of London, 1965.

—— *Hal-Farrug: A Village in Malta.* New York: Holt, Rinehart and Winston, 1969.

—— *Friends of Friends.* Oxford, England: B. Blackwell, 1974.

Bonanno, A. "The Archaeology of Gozo: from Prehistoric to Arab times." In *Gozo, The Roots of an Island,* edited by C. Cini, 11–45. Malta: Said International, 1990.

Bonnelli, L. "Il Dialetto Maltese." In *Supplementi periodici all' 'Archivio Glottologico Italiano' ordinato da G.I. Ascoli.* Dispense 4, 6–8. Turin: Loescher, 1897.

Boucherit, A. "Des Buqalat." In *Mas-Gellas,* edited by A. Roth, 197–217. Paris: Geuthner, 1984.

Bourdieu, P. "L'illusion biographique." *Actes de la recherche en sciences sociales,* nos. 62/63 (1986): 69–72.

Bradley, E. *The Great Siege: Malta 1565.* Harmondsworth, England: Penguin Books, 1971.

Brandes, S. *Migration, Kinship and Community. Tradition and Transition in a Spanish Village.* London: Academic Press, 1975.

Braudel, F. *La Méditerranée et le monde méditerranéen à l'époque de Philippe II.* Paris: A. Colin, 1949.

Brunot, L. *La mer dans les traditions et les industries indigènes à Rabat et Salé.* Paris: Leroux, 1920.

Buhagiar, F. "Bichi ta Malti bgħid minn Malta" (Tears of a Maltese Far from Malta). *Lil-Hutna* (To Our Brothers), edited by L. Attard, 17. Malta: Malta Emigrants Commission, May 1992.

Buhagier, M. "Paintings in Gozo: A Concise Analytical History." In *Gozo, The Roots of an Island,* edited by C. Cini, 83–119. Malta: Said International, 1990.

Burgos, M. "Life Stories, Narrativity, and the Search for the Self." *Life Stories* 5 (1989): 29–37.

Busuttil, E. D. *Holiday Customs in Malta.* Malta: Empire Press, 1964.

Busuttil, S. "The Maltese Economy During World War II." In *Malta Year Book,* edited by Bro. Hilary, 333–41. Malta: St. Michael's College Publications, 1965.

Buttiġieġ, A. *Ir-Raħeb tal-Qala.* Qala, Gozo: Santwarju Nazzjonali tal-Qala, 1986.

Cachia, P. "Cultural Cross-Currents in Maltese Idioms." *Journal of Maltese Studies* 2 (1964): 226–37.

Calleja, A. *Frak mill-Ħajja* ("Fragments of Life"). Edited by Maria Calleja. Gozo, Malta: Gozo Press, 1982.

Cassar, P. *Medical History of Malta.* London: Wellcome Historical Medical Library, 1964.

Cassar-Pullicino, J. "Pauline Traditions in Malta." *Scientia* 10, no. 1 (1944): 19–31.

—— "G. A. Vassallo. Il-Poeta Tas-Safar." *Leħen Is-Sawwa*, January 26 (p. 6) and 29 (pp. 6–7), 1955.

—— "Folk-Narrative Research in Malta Since the War." *Maltese Folklore Review* 1, no. 2 (1963): 144–6.

—— "Notes for a History of Maltese Costume." In *Maltese Folklore Review* 1, no. 3 (1966): 149–216.

—— "Documentary Material Relating to *l-Imnarja.*" *Littérature orale arabo-berbère* 14 (1983): 5–97.

—— "Some Parallels Berween Maltese and Arabic Folklore." *Acta Ethnographica* 34, nos. 1–4 (1986–88): 143–75.

—— *Studi di Tradizioni Popolari Maltesi.* University of Malta, 1989.

—— *Studies in Maltese Folklore.* 2d ed. Malta: University of Malta, 1992.

Cassar-Pullicino, J., and M. Galley. *Femmes de Malte.* Paris: Editions du C.N.R.S., 1981.

Cicero, M. T. *The Orations of Marcus Tullius Cicero against Caius Cornelius Verres.* Translated by James White. London: T. Cadell, 1787.

Claridge, M. *The Gozo Story. A Background to Crafts.* Malta: Progress Press, 1972.

Couffon, C. *Histoires et Légendes de l'Espagne mystérieuse.* Paris: Tchou, 1968.

Degh, L. "Beauty, Wealth and Power: Career Choices for Women in Folktales, Fairytales and Modern Media." *Fabula* 30, nos. 1–2 (1989): 43–62.

Donato, M. *L'émigration des Maltais en Algérie au XIXème siècle.* Montpellier: Africa Nostra Collection, 1985.

Dugan, M. *The Maltese Connection, Australia and Malta—A Bond of People.* Melbourne: Macmillan Company of Australia, 1988.

Ebejer, F. *The Bilingual Writer (Mediterranean-Maltese and English) as Janus.* Malta: F.I.S., 1989.

Eberhard, W., and P. Borotav. *Typen Türkisher Volksmärchen.* Wiesbaden: F. Steiner, 1953.

El Fasi, M., and E. Dermenghem. *Contes fasis.* Paris: Rieder and Co., 1926.

Evans, J. D. "Malta in Antiquity." In *Malta Blue Guide*, edited by Stuart Rossiter, 9–28. London: Ernest Benn Ltd., 1968.

Frendo, H. *Birth Pangs of a Nation: Manwel Dimech's Malta 1860–1921.* Malta: Mediterranean Publishing, 1972.

—— *Party Politics in a Fortress Colony: The Maltese Experience.* Malta: Midsea Books, 1979.

Galley, M., "L'île aux trésors existe-t-elle?" *Cahiers de Littérature Orale* 23 (1988), 77–108.

—— "Voto Fatto, Grazzia Ricevuta. Ex-voto d'hier et d'aujourd'hui à Malte." *Schweizerisches Archiv für Volkskunde*, edited by Ueli Gyr, 67–75. Basel: Swiss Society of Folk Tradition, 1991.

—— *Badr as-Zîn et six contes algériens.* 2nd ed. Paris: Classiques Africains, 1993. Distributed by Editions des Belles-Letters, Paris.

—— "A Glimpse of Maria Calleja's Life History." *International Folklore Review* 9 (1993): 94–102.

Galley, M., and M. R. Gatt. *L'Imnarja, Fête des Lumières à Malte* (Imnarja, a Festival of Lights in Malta), 16 mm, 52 min., color. 1983. Distributed by C.N.R.S.-Audiovisuel, Paris.

Gauci, A. *Gozo, A Historical and Touristic Guide to the Island.* 2nd ed. rev. Malta: St. Joseph's Press, 1969.

Gauci, C. A. *A Guide to Maltese Nobility.* Malta: Publishers Enterprises Group (PEG) Ltd., 1986.

Gilmore, D. *Aggression and Community. Paradoxes of Andalusian Culture.* New Haven, Conn: Yale University Press, 1987.

Gonseth, M. O., and N. Maillard. "L'approche biographique en ethnologie: points de vue critiques." In *Histoires de vie. Approche pluridisciplinaire, recherches et travaux* 7, edited by Institute of Ethnology in Neufchâtel, Switzerland: 5–46. Neufchâtel: Editions de l'Institut d'Ethnologie et Paris: Maison des Sciences de l'Homme, 1987.

Gubernatis, A. de, *La mythologie des plantes.* 2 vols. Paris: Reinwald, 1878–82.

Jelmini, J. P. "Les histoires de vie: le point de vue d'un historien." In *Histoires de vie. Approche pluridisciplinaire, recherches et travaux* 7: 67–112. See Gonseth 1987.

Kininmouth C. The Brass Dolphins. London: Secker and Warburg, 1957.

Koster, A., and H. Smith. *Lord Strickland Servant of the Crown.* Malta: Progress Press, 1984.

Lacoste-Dujardin, C. "Chant de louange kabyle." *Littérature orale arabo-berbère* 12 (1981): 103–24.

Lamartine, A. de. *Voyage en Orient.* Edited by Lotfy Fam. Paris: Nizeé, 1959.

Langness, L. *The Life History in Anthropological Science.* New York: Holt, Rinehart and Winston, 1965.

Légey, F. *The Folklore of Morocco.* Translated by Lucy Hotz. London: Allen and Unwin, 1935.

Lévi-Strauss, C. "Sun Chief, The Autobiography of a Hopi Indian by Leo W. Simmons." *Année Sociologique*, 3d. ser., vol. 1 (1949): 329–30.

Lo Nigro, S. *Racconti Popolari Siciliani.* Florence: L. S. Olschki, 1957.

Luke, H. *Malta, An Account and an Appreciation.* London: George Harrap, 1949.

Luttrell, A. T. *Approaches to Medieval Malta.* London: The British School at Rome, 1975.

—— *Hal Millieri: A Maltese Casale, its Churches and Paintings.* Edited by A. T. Luttrell. Malta: Midsea Books, 1976.

Mahoney, L. *A History of Maltese Architecture from Ancient Times up to 1800.* Malta: Veritas Press Zabbar, 1988.

Maltese-English Dictionary. See Aquilina, J.

Marçais, W. *Le dialecte arabe parlé à Tlemcen*, Paris: Leroux 1902.

Meddeb, A. *Phantasia*. Paris: Sindbad. 1986.

Mercieca, A. *Le Mie Vicende*. Malta: Tipografia Casa S. Giuseppe, 1947.

Moscati, S. "Cultural Interactions in Ancient Mediterranean History." In *Proceedings of the First Congress on Mediterranean Studies of Arabo-Berber Influence*, edited by M. Galley and D. Marshall, 7–19. Algiers: S.N.E.D., 1973.

Naselli, C. "Manto siciliano e 'faldetta' maltese." *Maltese Folklore Review* 1, no. 3 (1966): 217–25.

Papamichael, A. *Birth and Plant Symbolism*. Athens: 1975.

Perret-Clermont, A. N., and P. Rovero. "Processus psychologiques et histoires de vie." *Histoires de vie. Approche pluridisciplinaire, recherches et travaux*, 113–29. See Gonseth 1987.

Pitt-Rivers, J. *The People of the Sierra*. Chicago: University of Chicago Press, 1961.

—— *Anthropologie de l'honneur. La mésaventure de Sichem*. Paris: Sycomore, 1983.

Pollack, M. "La gestion de l'indicible." *Actes de la recherche en sciences sociales* (1986): 30–53.

Prins, A. H. J. *In Peril of the Sea. Marine Votive Paintings in the Maltese Islands*. Malta: Said International, 1989.

Rossi, E. "Le Lapidi Sepolcrali arabo-musulmane di Malta." *Rivista degli Studi Orientali* 12 (1929): 428–44.

Russell, B. "Paratsoukli." *Ethnologia Europaea* 2–3 (1968–1969): 65–74.

Vassallo, A. *All About Gozo*. Malta: Gulf Publishing Ltd, 1981.

Vassilikos, V. "La Plante." *Trilogie* 12–106. Paris: Gallimard, 1968.

Wettinger, G. "Late Medieval Maltese Nicknames." *Journal of Maltese Studies* 6 (1971): 34–46.

—— *The Jews of Malta in the Late Middle Ages*. Malta: Midsea Books, 1985.

—— "Did Christianity Survive in Muslim Malta? Further Thoughts." *The Sunday Times* (Malta), November 19 1989.

—— "The History of Gozo from the Early Middle Ages to Modern Times." In *Gozo, the Roots of an Island*, edited by C. Cini, 47–82. Malta: Said International, 1990.

York, B. *The Maltese in Australia*. Edited by M. Cigler. Melbourne: A. E. Press, 1986.

—— "The Maltese and the Dictation Test: How do Historians know?" *The Times* (Malta), July 16, 1992: 12.

Zammit, T., and C. Singer. "Neolithic Representations of the Human Form from the Islands of Malta and Gozo." *Journal of the Royal Anthropological Institute of Great Britain and Ireland* 54 (1924): 67–100

Indexes

Index of Names & Places

General Index

Acting. *See* Plays

Adoption, 141, 148

Agriculture, decline in prices of, 210; economic development and decline of, 29; exhibitions, 151, 156; minister of, 122; not sustained during war, 205n. 119; products donated to priests, 53

Algiers, Algeria, emigration to, 13, 75, 184n. 9; Maltese in, 2, 18, 33, 64, 115, 163, 179n. 3, 188n. 25, 210

Almonds, 32, 33, 55, 110

Amulets, priestly vestments as, 112; as charms, 200n. 84

Anger, expression of, 36, 61; Maria's response of, 160; of uncle, 42

Animal fodder, cutting of, 24; emigrant boats carry, 35; implement for cutting, 22; left for women to feed animals, 25; sacks used as barricade, 42, 68; storage for, 17, 64

Animals, as dowry, 80; buying of, 54; carried on emigrant boats, 35; children had experience with, 126; cows, 24, 67, 123, 124, 156, 180n. 4; dogs, 16, 25, 39, 92, 104, 161, 192n. 47; donkeys, 16, 22, 24, 25, 54, 77, 83, 132, 170; ewe, 79; feeding of, 24, 25; goats, 16, 24, 48, 50, 54, 58, 59, 71, 77–79, 121, 146, 191n. 42; horses, 16, 22, 26, 31, 52, 54, 97, 109, 118, 156, 163; houses shared with, 13, 16, 21, 64; in antiquity, 207; lambs, viii, 19, 54; metaphorical use of name of, 194n. 48; mules, 16, 22, 25, 26, 31; pigs, 31, 156; poultry, 27, 48, 54; rabbits, 20, 54, 132, 156, 168; rent could be paid with, 48; sheep, 16, 18, 24, 48, 50, 54, 76–81, 146; shown at exhibitions, 156; turkeys, 5, 33, 70; used for threshing, 22

Arabs, and the development of Maltese language, 205n. 115; ballads of, 199n. 81; father told Maria about, 76; living among the, 164; pirates threatened Gozo, 180n. 5; sitting on floors like, 43; took posession of Maltese islands, 208; worked for Buhagiar family in Algiers, 66

Architecture, "Grand Harbor" of Malta framed by military, 198n. 76; harmonious style in Sliema, 182n. 7; Malta's golden era of, 209; Maria's school sketched by students of, 137; modern hodgepodge of, 152

Australia, emigration to, vii, 13, 35, 64, 75, 119, 179n. 3, 183n. 9, 211; Maltese in, 7, 11, 36, 67, 76, 190n. 40, 214; Maltese return from, 43, 64, 71, 169, 184n. 11; Maria's father's experiences in, 9, 38, 56, 57, 72, 74, 77, 165, 183n. 9; Maria's father's reasons for going to, 18, 29; Maria's father returns from, 34, 73, 83, 166, 167, 204n. 113

Avukat. See Lawyers

Bands (*see* ta' l-Iljun and ta' l-Istilla), from Valletta, La Valette and King's Own, attend *festa*, 154; healthy competition among, 150; parade in *festa*, 115, 117; serenade Anton after difficult exams, 170; serenade Maria, 57

Baptism, celebration of, 21, 109; clothing worn at, 49, 204n. 106; infants first seen at, 19; performed soon after birth, 40; starched linen to celebrate, 17

Barter system, 20, 48

Basil, 12, 16, 181n. 6, 182n. 6

Bath, 65, 66; bathroom, few people have, 133; tiles covering sidewalks, 152

Bells, at Anton's procession, 97; call out time of day, 196; punctuated days, 13, 24; ring a *frajħa*, 32, 112, 187n. 22; ring during *agunija* (agony) of dying, 101; ringing each day, 185n. 15,

237